Santa Fe
Tales

Politics, Crime, and Culture

ALEX MICHAELS

Continental
RIGHTS LLC

Library of Congress Control Number: 2025908974

ISBN
978-1-967804-03-0 (Paperback)
978-1-967804-04-7 (eBook)

The more I know, the more I know how much I do not know.

1

He was known as Father Midnight, but there was nothing dark or sinister about his tending to the weak and dying, for it was his duty. Monsignor John Carrol Serrano often received pleading calls to administer the Last Rites, and often the calls came in the late night or early morning hours. The odd hour requests did not bother him. His obligation was to comfort any soul in its hour of need, not only as a priest but also as a man born in the Catholic diocese and in the city where he lived for most of his sixty years.

"Satan does not care about the time of day when he is determined to add to his evil dominion. As God's representative, I cannot put off until morning a matter that needs his immediate attention," the feisty priest was known to tell his colleagues. "If a soul is in trouble, I will give it my help at the time of need... not at my convenience."

In reality, the two other priests who served the parish, as do all priests in general, shared the same credo. So neither Father Orlando Gomez, nor the younger Father Jason Cavanaugh, gave any concern when Father Midnight accepted the eleven o'clock call.

"Just be careful out there," Reverend Gomez told him. "It's been misting for awhile now, and the snowstorm is expected to be moving in soon. There may be some black ice out there, so don't go gunning the accelerator or hitting the brakes."

"I know, I know, Orlando. I've been driving in Santa Fe long before you received your first communion."

It was a good-natured banter that the two priests frequently exchanged. This time it was Reverend Gomez who got in the last word. "I'm sure you have. It's just that I've ridden with you too many times to suspect otherwise."

Taking his purple sacramental stole and anointing oil from his desk drawer, the monsignor quickly crossed to the rack where his overcoat hung. He always kept a prayer missal in his car, so being satisfied that he had all he needed for God's calling he departed. Since he had a long way to drive in the threatening weather to meet a dying man's request, Monsignor Serrano regarded each second to be precious.

An icy mist met him at the door of the rectory, and as he hastily walked to his old Plymouth Breeze the priest skidded on the ice that had begun to harden in the rectory parking lot. Agile for his years, he caught himself before completely hitting the ground. With his right leg stretched forward, he rose from his left knee back into a standing position, and after assuring himself there were no pains or strains, he continued quickly, but cautiously, to his car. Never looking back, he did not see the stole that fell out of his pocket. It landed in an unfrozen puddle where it would soak up the moisture from the light rain that was making its transition into snow.

Pulling his car out of the parking lot onto Agua Fria Street, Monsignor Serrano let his mind drift back to the phone call he received just minutes earlier. An uneasy strangeness loomed in the conversation, and as he listened to the scene being described to him, the voice on the other end seemed too calm. He could tell by the hollowness and occasional static that the caller was using a cell phone.

"This is Officer Vagas with the New Mexico State Police. I'm here at Waldo, just off of the southbound exit, about four miles past La Cienega. Do you know where it is?"

"Yes. Yes, I do."

"There's been an accident," Officer Vagas said. "A Mexican national overturned his pick-up. He was not wearing a seat belt, and he's pinned under the cab. He's still alive, and he begged that I call a priest for him. From what I can determine, your services are urgently needed."

"I understand," Monsignor Serrano replied as a chilling darkness invaded his thoughts. For more than thirty years he made himself present before death could make its repetitious claim, and the effects it had on him never changed. As an afterthought, he asked, "Is rescue there yet?"

"They're on their way," the officer said. "I trust we'll see you soon." An abrupt disconnect immediately followed.

The casualness of the officer's tone and the abruptness of the hang-up bothered him. *I guess one hardens after seeing so many accidents,* Monsignor Serrano thought, reasoning on behalf of the officer's overly calm demeanor. *It just seems unusual to get a call directly from an officer on the scene,* he continued with the puzzle. Allowing for policy changes, and the fact that the officer had a cell phone, he thanked God for the expediency of the call. It may very well have given him the extra time needed to arrive and hear the poor victim's last confession.

It's been a long time since someone referred to it as 'Waldo', his thoughts continued. In the past, exit 267 off of I-25 was referred to as the Waldo Exit. It lies at the peak of the steep La Bajada Hill, and no town or village exists there, it's just a turnaround exit used by the New Mexico Department of Public Safety for inspecting the safety conditions of trucks and semis. A narrow paved road extends to the southeast, seemingly leading to nowhere. The two dirt roads that streak away from the exit do not lead to anywhere, only to dead ends. Over time it had lost its identity, and for a two decade long period the highway department had removed any signs identifying the location as being Waldo. It was just within recent months had the sign been suspended again over the highway, giving back an identity to the lonely location.

Driving west on Agua Fria, he took a right onto Airport Road, leading to Rt.599 two miles down. Four miles south and the monsignor was connected to I-25, leaving him still another eight miles from his destination.

The mist now turned into a moderate snow, and the temperature drifted downwards into the shallow freezing twenties. Freezing temperatures quickly turned the road moisture into a slick layer of treacherous ice that could not be seen…black ice. Concerns for the road replaced the uneasiness he had about the phone call.

Reaching the apex of the hill rising up from La Cienega, the monsignor eased his speed down to fifty miles per hour. Exit 267 would be to the immediate right as the curve of the highway gave way to a straight road.

Coasting down the ramp at a steady, but safe, twenty miles per hour he kept his eyes peeled in search of his ultimate stop. A fine white blanket of snow already covered the road and the southwestern earth. He could not see any emergency vehicles. In fact, no other signs of life existed, not even the expected flashing lights of a state patrol car.

Monsignor John Serrano had no uncertainty that he was at the right place. The instructions were clear: Waldo, Exit 267, four miles past La Cienega. Besides, he was a native to this area of New Mexico. Surely he would know it if any other location existed that could cause confusion. No! There was no doubt as to where he should be.

The priest did concede that he might have misunderstood Officer Vagas as to which side of the highway the accident occurred. It could very well have been northbound, and not southbound as he thought he had heard. Parking the Plymouth Breeze under the highway overpass, he peered through the thickening white downfall in search of his objective. There was nothing, just the wall of falling snow that limited his visibility to maybe a hundred feet or so. Abandoning his dry, secure spot, the monsignor ventured out into the wetness for a better view of the highway exit ramp. Again, nothing. He retraced his steps and explored other areas. The large turnout lot, used by the DPS to inspect the large commercial trucks, was vacant. Turning his eyes eastward he finally located a vehicle a third of the way up the highway entrance ramp, but it was not the expected patrol car.

The intensity of the snow worsened with each step he took toward the vehicle. He could not make out the model of the car, but he could see the parking lights dimly glowing through a fine layer of crystal snow, and the exhaust escaping and spreading out from the tailpipe. Approaching it he felt a little awkward as to how to explain his purpose for being out there, in the middle of nowhere and in a snowstorm. It did not matter, for when his knock upon the window went unanswered he rubbed away the snow and peeked inside, only to find an empty interior.

Further perplexed, he asked himself who would abandon a car with its engine running. Stepping back and away from the vehicle, he once again gazed into the open fields. This time his eyes searched for a human who might be wandering about aimlessly. There was no one, not even human footprints in the fresh white snow.

He waited, and as he waited he tried to determine his next course of action. He considered searching the fields, but he did not know into which direction to begin. Even if he did go out there, chances were he would come back empty, especially because the layer of snow thickened and grew higher as it covered the ground. If someone were in serious trouble, valuable time could be lost. Being old fashioned and not up to date with modern electronics, he did not have a cell-phone, but a public rest area was a little more than a mile away. From there he could call the state police.

Retreating to his own car, barely able to make out his own steps he had already imprinted on the ground, he grumbled at the circumstances he found himself in. He reasoned that it was someone's idea of a prank. Though not a person to anger easily, the monsignor became mildly riled that someone would use the excuse of a dying man to lure him into the desolated location.

But, what about the empty car – with its engine running? After a moment he audibly said, "I don't know. I just don't know."

With his keys in hand, he found his car door locked. He did not remember locking it, but then after the way things developed since leaving the rectory, he conceded that he could have done so. As he fumbled for the correct key he felt another presence penetrating his own aura. It was soundless, but it was there. He turned and became startled by the figure wielding something long and hard downward toward him. The object crushed down upon his collarbone causing him to scream in agony. Like a terrified shout echoing in a canyon, his scream resonated against the walls of the underpass, bouncing from wall to wall, over and over again. But, aside from him and his assailant, no one else could hear his pain. Whatever sounds escaping the scene would die as it spread into the waste of empty desert space.

On the ground, writhing in pain, he curled his body into a ball to ward off other blows. *My God! What is happening to me?* His mind shouted. Another blow crashed into the back of his rib cage, followed by a kick into the groin region of his body.

"Please, God! Make it stop!" he audibly cried. But, God did not intervene as another blow came down upon his back, followed by more kicks into his torso. "Help! Stop! Please stop!" The words pleading from his lips could barely be heard. Looking toward his attacker, he again begged, "Stop! Please!"

This time his plea would be fatally answered as the object came smashing down across the front of his skull.

The monsignor could no longer feel pain as his brain mercifully blocked all connections to other parts of his body. He could see nothing but what the blankness had to offer. His final thoughts were, *Please, God! Take me into thy kingdom.*

This time God did listen, and Monsignor John Carrol Serrano lay dead upon the cold wet ground.

In the distance a coyote howled. A long silence followed. The rumble of a heavy-duty tractor on the highway above interrupted the silence. After that, nothing more broke the deadly stillness of night.

2

A deep layer of fresh snow blanketed an older one hardened by a week of sub-zero temperatures. It was an early and unusually cold winter in Northern New Mexico. Cold air, brought on by severe arctic fronts forging southeastward into the lower Rockies, gave way to warmer fronts circling in from the Gulf of Mexico and over most of Texas. For decades Santa Fe County, and most of Rio Arriba County, was spared with light to moderate winters producing moderate amounts of snow. Ironically, not too long ago the region was hit with a drought. This year, especially in Rio Arriba, both counties anxiously waited for the thaws of spring before assessing the damages done to apple orchards, and to the abundance of other fruit trees that lavishly bloom in season within the valley. February was but two weeks away, and with it usually came the first tease of spring. At that time an assessment could then begin.

Sam Dawes made his own assessments as he studied the fine sparkling flakes dancing downwards, adding inches of new snow to an accumulation already piled up over a foot. His concerns were multiple and complex, and they were not for the outside weather.

Twenty years earlier, fresh out of New York's Columbia Law School, Sam Dawes arrived in Santa Fe for what was to be a brief vacation. Like so many tourists that come and go, he was charmed by the city that seemed quaint and restive. He lingered on, and months later he was practicing criminal law with one of Santa Fe's more prestigious firms.

By the end of his second year, Sam accepted the fact that his adopted city of residence would become his permanent home. During the years that followed he earned a reputation of not only being a fine defense attorney, but one also bound to fairness and honesty.

Over time he tired of working for the defense. Some of his clients were wrongly accused, and for this he took strong pride of winning the deserved acquittals. Most of the others were from the dregs of society, from drug dealers to child and spouse beaters to murderers. Many were repeat offenders who held society responsible for their actions, and it was further exacerbated by the lenient sentences administered by the courts, a common practice in the northern part of New Mexico. It contrasted sharply with the extremely harsher penalties administered in the southern part of the state.

Committed to his vocation, and to the community, Dawes had no time for a wife. Even though he could be considered a tall and handsome man, his involvements never really came close to the state of marriage. His work was his mistress, and at the age of forty-five he decided to run for the District Attorney's job.

As the newly elected DA, there were unsolved murders to contend with. Ranging over several years, there were several female victims, mostly tourists. The cases were linked together by fragmented bits of evidence, but because they were committed over a large span of time, tying them conclusively together became difficult.

Although solved, there was also the recent assassination of the city's mayor, Philipe Chavez. Chavez was deeply revered by those who felt that Santa Fe was being sold out by growth, and in the process their cultural heritage was being destroyed. He was known for his attempts to force newcomers to either leave or to acquiesce to the dictates of the older indigenous culture. Chavez was also hated. The feeling stemmed primarily for his known dealings with the criminal element, and in particular, for his association with drug dealers. Almost all of his detractors also abhorred the admitted racism that he exhibited toward Anglos and even to other Hispanics whose orgins were from places like Puerto Rico, Cuba, or South America. Regardless of Sam's personal feeling for the man, murder was murder, and it was his duty to prosecute Chavez's assassin.

Dawes also had to contend with the spread of juvenile and gang related crimes. Santa Fe is a small provincial city, and the city of Espanola some thirty miles north in Rio Arriba County is even smaller, but their combined crime rate per capita exceeded that of a city like Los Angles. Drug crimes were the dominating concern for Espanoloa. Only Los Alamos, with its large number of brilliant cone-heads who worked at the science labs, represented a much less violent part of his prosecuting territory. In all, his jurisdiction covered nearly one-fifth of the state, and about two hundred thousand people.

Then there was the brutal murder of Monsignor John Carrol Serrano; a clergyman, loved and respected for his compassion. He was brutally beaten and bludgeoned with a heavy metal object, and his body was left in a field to be covered by a late November snow. Three weeks after his disappearance his body was found by highway engineers, some twelve miles south of Santa Fe.

The unsolved deaths were only a portion of Sam Dawes's concern. There was also his dealing with the political elite who controlled the counties. He had disdain for the patriarchs and their political machinery, but he knew he had to deal with them in order to accomplish the chores that lay before him.

Sam was a registered Democrat. Running as a political independent, easily trouncing his Republican rival while barely edging out the hand picked Democrat, Sam realized that the politics before him would have to encompass the art of give and take, and he had to find a working ground with his political bosses. Out of political respect he would try to play ball with them, but not to the point where compromising his responsibility to the people came into play. He hoped the bosses would render him the same token of respect, but he doubted that would ever be the case.

Giving the bosses respect would not be an easy task either, particularly giving it to the political honcho, Ruben Gonzales. Dawes despised Gonzales mostly for the patronistic grip the man held on his constituents, the people who elected him to serve in the state senate over the past four decades. Gonzales controlled the machinery throughout Rio Arriba County, extending his hand into neighboring counties, all the while wielding his influence into the senate. He headed committees for highway transportation, human development services, and farm subsidies, but little of his legislation actually served to benefit the people in his county.

Dawes compared Ruben Gonzales and his clan to the mafia. The only exception was that as a politician Gonzales groomed an aura of legal sanctioning for all of his activities. Of course they did not exist, but the appearance did. Much speculation abounded that no illicit deal succeeded without first receiving the Don's, or in this case, the Patron's blessing. However, without solid evidence, a willing inside informer, or someone willing to risk his life by becoming a witness, there was no way to prove it.

In some ways Sam considered the situation to be worse than the mafia. In most clans of organized families the leaders encouraged education, and even supported the children of those who wanted their offspring to escape the entrapment of organized crime. Here it was different. The basic philosophy was to keep the children only moderately educated.

There was logic behind this thinking: if the young are educated they will eventually seek to move elsewhere; if they did move the political machinery would loose its political base. The solution is basic: keep the constituents suppressed and they cannot go anywhere.

In fairness though, Dawes realized that the population in most New Mexico counties was small, and family clans had a reluctance to separate. A commonalty of names has even been prevalent. Newspaper stories often exemplified it:

> "Espanola police today arrested one Jamie Trujillo for the shooting death of store owner Robert Trujillo (unrelated). Police Detective Dominic Trujillo (not related to the victim or the suspect) claims that the gun used…."

The story may have been written by Marcia Trujillo who, in turn, was not related to anyone mentioned in the article.

At one time they may have been related, but generations, dating back almost five hundred years, have spread different seeds and eventually different identities. Most may be Hispanic, but many with the same names are Native Americans. Marriages between different families with the same surname but with different bloodlines, formed new family lineages. New Mexico could easily find a fugitive with the surname of Trujillo, but be totally unrelated to his victim, to the arresting officer, to the reporter covering the case, or to the judge handing down the sentence.

Switching his attention back to the more immediate problems, Sam refocused it back to the weather. He and his staff had five trials scheduled for the coming day, but if the snows continued the courts might decide to postpone them. It did not matter for he knew that all five cases were in the bag. Despite having such confidence, Sam hoped that no weather delays could keep his office from enjoying the fruits of their hard fought victories. A short time later, his secretary advised him that the top judge was reserving his decision to close the court until the very last minute.

As he thumbed the files of the cases pertaining to the unsolved crimes he told himself that it did not matter. Even if the cases did not go to trial that day there was still a ton of other work to do. The delay would also give him a chance to touch base with the state police, and get an update and education as to the status of the unsolved deaths.

Captain Eduardo 'Cap' Guiterrez of the New Mexico State Police was in charge of the criminal affairs division covering all of Northern New Mexico. He carried the nickname 'Cap' ever since his days as a rookie, some fifteen years ago. Impressed with his attention to detail, his insight and reasoning, and a psychic ability called intuition, Cap's training officer labeled him with the nickname.

"Someday, Cap," senior officer, Sergeant Stottle, would say, "you're gonna make captain. Yes-siree. You keep up this kinda work and they'll pin double-bars on you."

Twelve years later, years during which he astutely performed his responsibilities and crammed studies to earn a Masters in Criminology, and two months after passing the exam on the first try, at age thirty-six Guiterrez reached the rank of captain. Being given the opportunity of filling a vacant slot in Raton or of heading the criminal affairs division in Santa Fe, he chose the intrigue of criminal affairs. His and his wife's roots were in Santa Fe, and over the years Cap was stationed in all four corners of the geographically large state. At long last, he could seize upon the opportunity of having never to face another assignment outside of Santa Fe. There always would be short spells of spending some days away from Margarette and his daughters, Teresa and Charlene, but that was something he could learn to deal with.

Leaning off to one side, Captain Guiterrez presented an interesting image of a man, five foot eleven inches and a lean but firmly muscled body, studying the falling snow from his second floor window at the state police headquarters. His jet-black hair, gray eyes, and an olive complexion on a cleanly shaven face seemed to stand out against the stark white background outside.

With a little strain, peering through barren trees, he could make out the artery leading in and out of the city. Cerrillos Road was already blinding white. A few large trucks, hauling loads of white substance atop of the roofs, slowly challenged the hazardous force that nature provided. Most frequently, the tractor-trailers crawled eastward, and in most likelihood they were heading to one of the nearby motels to wait out the storm.

He pitied his men, who along with the county sheriff's department, had to handle the smaled traffic along I-25 and state roadway. The city police were more fortunate since they had only the small city's traffic to deal with. To aggravate matters, the county's highway department probably would have but a couple of trucks out plowing and sanding roads. Because of budget restrictions, most of the snow removal equipment would remain immobile until signs of the storm's passing came. When asked why the machinery would remain idle for so long, the answer would inevitably be the ubiquitous 'we've always done it that way'. It is a term used for generations by those resistant to change, even if change was for the good.

We sure as hell have an odd way of handling problems by never being prepared for the unexpected emergencies. As an afterthought, he added another ubiquitous term used to shrug away unwanted questions, *'That's Santa Fe for you.'*

"Umph! That's The City Different for you," he serenely murmured to himself as his eyes continued to absorb the rare sight. The City Different was the nickname given to Santa Fe, and nobody was sure who gave it to the city. It could have been a native Santa Fean, or maybe someone who simply spent some time there, experienced its ancient uniqueness, and then moved on.

The handling of problems was not limited to snow storms. Like Dawes, he had crimes to contend with, all too many of them that could have been handled by local enforcement. Cap could understand the Monsignor Serrano case that occurred on state property, but some fell within city or county jurisdiction, both of whom did not have the manpower or the capability to handle many of them.

Cap's department had an added responsibility of educating the new district attorney on the progress of each case.

He met Sam Dawes several times over the last several months, and he was impressed, impressed enough to give him his vote on Election Day. He knew Dawes was a bachelor, but who would want to marry someone who already tied the knot to his career? Then again, Cap himself was a non-tiring worker and he managed to have a wonderful family. Perhaps he was just better than Sam Dawes at splitting up responsibilities.

"Beautiful weather we got out there, eh, Cap?" The voice belonged to Lieutenant Mike Shannon, the captain's second in command.

"Ah, good morning, Mike. Just taking all that white stuff in," Cap returned the greeting. As an afterthought, he added, "Being a Brooklyn boy, you should be used to this."

"Nah!" Mike answered. "It's been a long time. Besides, we've seldom had anything this bad in the big city. Most of it was upstate."

Mike left Brooklyn to attend college in New Mexico and, except for occasional visits, he never returned. After graduating from the College of Santa Fe, he joined the Santa Fe Police Department. Seven years later he transferred to the state police. Outgoing and affable, his five foot ten inch frame held the rounded features of a jolly man. His cleanly shaven bald head added to it. Mike took to change with the same welcoming grace as he did new friends. Six years senior in age to Captain Guiterrez, Mike had the world of respect for his young commander. "The man earned his bars," he would tell his colleagues and friends. "It's too bad we don't have an entire force like him."

"Well, what kind of a day do we have in store for us?" Cap asked, starting down to business.

"A basic review," Mike replied as he settled comfortably into his favorite chair in the captain's office. "First, our boys in Espanola made a small drug bust inside Chimayo. The same usual story…they pull a car over with a couple of locals in it, only this time the driver was going too slow and impeding traffic. It turns out the occupants had a pound of pot. Records check shows they have one prior each." Continuing on to the next report, "One of our boys was on hand for a weapons assault arrest – this one's being handled by the Espanola Police. Here in the Santa Fe area, nothing. I guess the bad weather's keeping the bad boys indoors."

"That's a bit of a break. On the other hand, if they stay indoors too long they might start beating upon each other."

"Probably, but at least they won't be taking it out into the public," Mike replied.

Cap looked at Mike with a half-smile before asking, "Anything new on the priest's case?"

"Nothing," Mike answered with a little disgust. Since the case was one that had countywide implications, it was one that he took on with his own personal attention. "This one is gonna be a real toughie. All we know for sure is, one: he was drawn out there, so that makes it premeditated. Two: he was struck with a heavy object, most likely a pipe. Beyond that, the first snow screwed everything up, and today's snow's gonna make it worse. We found no tracks of any kind, and we can't really do a thorough search until the snows are gone."

"And, we don't have a motive," Cap added.

"Right!" Mike agreed. "What can I tell ya'; we know he was a straight arrow all the way. No scandals involving sex, being a pedophile, or anything like that. So that eliminates one class of motives."

"Plus, we know robbery was ruled out. So the motive door is still wide open." It was a statement by Cap that took the form of a question.

"Yep…" Mike said. He then uttered a sigh reflecting a deeper thought. "Here we have anything from an anti-religious nut to a thrill kill, to someone who might not have liked the penance given out at confession. The city boys are helping out as much as they can by questioning parishioners, and hopefully picking up bits on the streets."

"Good. Any help we can get we'll take." Cap then added, "Do me a favor. Make extra copies of whatever comes up so I can give them to the DA."

"No problem," Mike agreed. "In fact, I see Sam every Wednesday at Ray's Pub. We play darts together with a bunch of other guys. That's about the only night of the week that he takes off."

Cap was at first surprised, until he realized that there was probably no one in Santa Fe who Mike did not know. "How well do you know Dawes?"

"Well enough to know that he can't play darts worth a crap," Mike said with a little humor. "I've known him for years, and he's the kind of guy you like working on your side. Dedicated, almost to a fault. It seems that Wednesday is his favorite night. After darts a few of us sit around and b.s., solving the world's problems. It ranges everywhere from just ragging each other to talking philosophy. Sam seems to enjoy that."

"I see," Cap said approvingly.

After Mike left, Cap thought about the conversation and Sam Dawes. *Seems like he's a workaholic who takes one night off a week. It's nice to have someone so dedicated, providing he doesn't burn himself out. He won't be any good to us or to the community if he wears himself out.*

3

Compared to the previous week's frigid temperatures, this night's thirty degrees seemed balmy. Over the past couple of days, the warm mid-day sun began the melting of the snow that accumulated in most parts of Santa Fe County. The neighboring Espanola Valley was spared with only a few inches, but no matter where, the snows that melted during the day turned to ice at night. Most New Mexicans are generally not accustomed to adverse winter weather conditions, and to Joseph 'JoJo' Aragon's chagrin, they became painfully poor drivers when confronting it. Growing up in one of New Mexico's northernmost towns, nestled in the higher altitude and mountainous terrain, JoJo saw more snow and had much more experience driving in it. Tonight he had an important meeting, and he did not want bad road conditions or bad drivers getting in the way.

Joseph Aragon is a man driven with the desire to lead, a desire that burned in him while still a teenager, developing during the radical movements of the seventies. Most groups were decimated by then, but in the late seventies and early eighties elements still remained as a thorn in America's everyday structure. Inspired initially by the writings of Che Guevera, JoJo, now in his sixties, he had a dream of someday leading his people out of capitalistic bondage, and of someday building a cultural wall reinforced with socialist values around his New Mexican brethren. If he could not do it for the entire state he would then succeed in doing it for those of Northern New Mexico. To him, the land and its people were bastions of his culture and of his beliefs. In his wildest desires he would, if he could, separate himself and his people from the rest of the country. He would, if he could, declare New Mexico independent. It would secede from the union.

He would, if he could, but reality forced him to concede that he could not. In practical terms he had to come to grips with a nation that would never permit it, not even under the flow of blood. But, oh, wouldn't it be a glorious war, a kind of war that Castro or Che would lead. He even envied a takeover like the one Venezuela's now dead Hugo Chavez employed.

To be effective it would take aid and assistance from countries like Cuba, Russia and China, something he conceded was not practical. Help from any of them would extract too much a price, a price enslaving his people no different than the exploitation they suffered under now. To be practical, he would still have to fight the Anglos that claimed New Mexico as their home. To be practical, he would still have to confront the Native Americans who were handed down stories of the atrocities committed by his early ancestors some four hundred years ago. To be practical, he would also have to do battle with many of his own people, people who have become traitors by adopting much of the Anglo and capitalistic ways.

He considered being practical his best virtue. It was not something he was born with, but rather something he had to learn to adapt to if he were to succeed. The learning was slow, and there were occasional relapses, but he did learn.

Less than three years after graduating from college, he ran for a seat on the city council and won. The path was set. All he needed to do was to show patience and within a few years he could run for mayor. After that he just might snowball his way all the way into the state legislature. Since Santa Fe is already the state capital, the capitol, better known as the Round House, is but a few short blocks from city hall. Until then, he would slowly cultivate his influence with those he considered 'his people'.

Over the years he founded four small companies, all in the construction industry. His employees were all pirated from his competition, and they all shared his ethnic and cultural background. His clients were mostly affluent Texans and Californians building second homes. Many others were steadily relocating into Santa Fe and the surrounding areas. Combined, they shared one common thread in that they were all the same people he condemned for their negative influences upon his city and his people.

JoJo was elected five times to the city council, stirring up antagonistic controversy against outsiders, those who were not Santa Fean by birth or did not subscribe to his social and political views.

JoJo Aragon wanted to run for mayor sooner, but Ruben Gonzales who favored Philipe Chavez discouraged him. True, Ruben Gonzales came from the poorer and less influential Rio Arriba County, but Gonzales controlled the political machinery in that part of the state.

"Don't worry, JoJo. You will get your opportunity. You are too bright not to climb the ladder," Gonzales told him, placating the wanting Aragon.

Philipe Chavez based his campaign openly against growth and the intrusion of people from other states. Quietly and secretly he pushed his anti-Anglo sentiment with loyal followers, and they carried out the resentment. Dissention came about from various ranks railing against Chavez, but as is the nature of Santa Fe's politics, instead of uniting behind just one or two opponents, seven candidates joined in on the fray to become mayor of Santa Fe. The votes were split among them allowing Chavez, with his constituency united behind him, to become mayor with just thirty-five percent of the vote.

Aragon had to admire the now dead mayor's tactics, but he himself would be subtler in employing them when running for the now open mayor's seat. While he would attack the outsiders as the destructors of his city and his culture, he would not openly criticize growth for fear of loosing support from some of his people. He would instead preach unity among his own, and let his small army go out and covertly preach the criticism for him.

He still had several weeks before the special election to choose a new mayor. That gave him plenty of time to play both sides of the fence. And, again, there were seven other candidates who had registered to run for the office, something that would heavily favor him. Though confident of winning, he took nothing for granted. He wanted the help Ruben Gonzales could offer through his guidance.

Driving northward towards Espanola, he marveled at the way the snow covered roads gradually cleared as he approached the Espanola Valley. The valley was seldom buried the way the capital city often was. Thirty miles separated them, and temperatures often differed by ten degrees. Also, the snow clouds usually clung around the immediate low mountain range that walls Santa Fe in on the east. The valley had its fair share of white deposited upon it, but the warmer temperatures aided in its melting, running its water into nearby arroyos. Much of that water would be absorbed into the soil to nurture the crops and orchards waiting to be farmed in the coming spring.

A straight line of sweet smelling smoke spiraled upwards from the idle panatela grasped gently, but firmly, between the thumb and two fingers of Ruben Gonzales' aged hand. As it reached towards the ceiling it plumed out, mixing with the aggregated clouding of sweet cigar smoke and the repugnant fumes emitted from the cigarette of Ruben's special assistant, Tommy Trujillo. A non-smoker, Joseph Aragon suppressed all signs of his discomfit. He was a guest in the home of a man who would help deliver him the election. He could afford to inhale the poisonous air for the next hour, or for that matter the next week if he had to.

"You seem to have a comfortable edge," Ruben Gonzales said, toying with Aragon as he studied the composure of the candidate from his neighboring city. "As you know, I still have to rally my people who are running for county and city council seats here in Espanola in April. Yet, you think I can help you in Santa Fe."

"Yes, sir, I do." JoJo said as he tried to relax the grip that he felt tightening around his nerves. He fought hard to appear calm as he addressed the senior political figure facing him. "You are a respected and influential man, and I believe that you, in some way, can assist me in the race."

Ruben Gonzales appreciated the mild flattery as he eased deeper into his leather easy-chair, drawing in a deep breath of smoke from his cigar. He smoked them for nearly forty-five years beginning with his own first election win of a Rio Arriba County seat, at a ripe young age of twenty-seven. If the cigars did not kill him by now, he was certain that indulging himself with an occasional deep inhale would not do him in.

"Tell me, in what way do you think I can help you?"

JoJo wanted to remind Gonzales of when, at Ruben's request, he stepped aside for Philipe Chavez. He wanted to remind him of when Gonzales told him that his day would come, suggesting a promise that Gonzales would help when the time came. JoJo's time arrived, but he knew better than to lower himself by reminding the Patron of intimated pledges most likely forgotten.

"Well, sir. Mr. Gon…."

"You may call me Ruben. You have addressed me that way in the past, so there is no need to change now."

"Thank you," JoJo said. He could feel his nerves begin to relax. "Ruben, you are a well known and respected man. Many of your people are now living in Santa Fe, and many others have jobs there. I see a chance where we can once again make our culture strong, and in so doing teach many of the Anglo outsiders who this land really belongs to. We have been here for centuries, and it is ours. If you attend a rally I'm sure we can be very persuasive."

"That is very idealistic of you, Joseph. In general, I tend to agree. But the Indians were here before us, and they argue that the land really belongs to them."

"True, Ruben. But, we were the ones to first develop it…to turn it into something. Besides, as you know the Indian vote accounts for less that one percent in Santa Fe."

"Ah, yes, I agree. But the Anglo vote there is much, much stronger. They are fifty-one percent of the population. Unlike here in Rio Arriba where we can harness them into our party and make it tough for those outside of it, you have to contend with a much larger Anglo voting base. You have to be careful as to how you offend them."

"I truly don't believe it is that much of a problem," JoJo replied with confidence. "You see, unlike here, their vote is widely divided. Many are naturalists and conservationists. They also want to see the growth stopped. Most of them don't care which culture is dominant, just so long as ecological controls are imposed. To them, controlling growth is ecologically sound."

"And the others?" Ruben questioned.

"Many are newcomers who don't really care, so they won't vote. Still others believe that our culture must be preserved. Admittedly, the rest are backing other candidates who they feel can bring down our culture. When I become mayor I might be able to encourage them to go back to where they came from."

"I can easily share your sentiment," Ruben Gonzales said. He thought for a moment before posing his next question. "Once you have imposed the no-growth, what do you think will happen to our people? What about the jobs that will be lost?"

Joseph Aragon did not anticipate this particular question from his would-be supporter. His squat body squirmed, but his mind had to quickly respond.

"We don't project a significant job loss. There will still be many state openings that we can help to fill with our own people. Furthermore, with companies like mine, we can take on additional help. Plus, when we force the outsiders to leave our people will fill in the vacant spots."

Sure there will be a job loss, he admitted silently to himself. *With a no-growth philosophy we can expect that. It might even be worse when we start to reverse growth, but that is the price I'm willing to pay until this land is completely controlled by my people.*

Not allowing himself to ponder too deeply on his convictions, JoJo quickly jumped to the next obstacle in his race.

"As you know, Ruben, I'm running against six other candidates aside from Anthony Duran. Right now, each of them is taking more votes away from him. What I fear is that if a couple of them drop out, he'll pick up their support."

"Ah, there I can definitely be of assistance. Two of your opponents owe me huge favors, especially Montoya who is running third. Don't worry about them dropping out, because when they do they'll be throwing their full support behind you."

The words were like a Spanish symphony to JoJo's ears, causing his inspired thoughts to dance with joy. It prompted him to push a bit further.

"What can you do about Jack Bedell?"

"Ha-ha-ha," Ruben chuckled. He began to enjoy JoJo's enthusiasm. He took another deep inhale from his panatela before releasing it back into the room. "Let's not get too greedy, Joseph. Bedell's votes are not going to affect you or anyone else. He is an artist, and he'll attract the eccentric voter who wouldn't give you their vote anyway. Let him have them. It'll be more democratic. Besides, their votes would mostly go to Duran anyway, so let Bedell stay. You'll get Montoya's and Salazar's support when they bow out, and I will attend your rally. That should help you tremendously."

Fantastic! Joseph Aragon's mind jumped with additional joy. So much so that Ruben Gonzales' next surprising commitment nearly sent JoJo's brain into a stroke from excessive excitement.

"What is more," Gonzales continued, "I and a few of our colleagues are going to buy a full page ad in The New Mexican, fully endorsing your candidacy. We won't do that until the very last weekend, this way your opponents will not have an adequate chance to retaliate. That, my friend, should put you over the top."

As he readied for the drive back to Santa Fe, JoJo asked himself what more he could ask for. He received a whole lot more than what he expected.

"Just one little thing," Ruben said, interrupting JoJo's mental revelry. "I need a small favor from you."

"Sure, name it." Outwardly JoJo was enthusiastic, but inwardly he was apprehensive. He knew that whatever favors the political honcho asked for were never really small.

"William Johnson is applying for a permit to build a new art gallery on Canyon Road. The city council is evenly split. A couple don't want another gallery, and a couple because of his reputed background. I'd like for you to find a way to change your vote so that he's awarded the permit."

This is the game of payback Aragon understood. He did not like it, nor did he like Johnson, but Ruben Gonzales had favored him into a corner. Refusal could only destroy him.

"Fine, I'll do it. I'll come up with some good reasons for changing my mind so that my people can also accept it."

"Good. Very good. I must admire you for your quick learning of the art of compromise. It shows signs that you'll make a very good mayor."

With that Joseph Aragon paid his respectful farewell and departed.

Mostly joy imbued his emotions during his drive home. Still, there was the touch of disappointment.

Why the hell does he want me to help Johnson? He's nothing but a rich white guy who pushes drugs. Hell! I should know. I even bought grass from him.

Once again, like back at Ruben Gonzales' home, JoJo had to remind himself that it was part of a game of give and take. He had no choice, even if he did not like it.

I wonder what Johnson's tie is with Gonzales. I know that Ruben has sanctioned drug deals on his home ground, but I didn't think he reached out around the state. God! Who knows what else he may be involved in. With a guy like him you better not step out of line or there'll be consequences, the kind I wouldn't want to know about.

❧

Alone, just the two of them, Ruben Gonzales and Tommy Trujillo sat across from each other in the cigar and cigarette smoke filled room.

"You really went out on the limb for him with your commitments," Tommy Trujillo commented.

"Yes, I guess I did," Gonzales replied as he reveled at his coupe. "We'll find ways of using him when he becomes Santa Fe's mayor."

"Is he worth it?"

Ruben Gonzales looked up with a smile broadening on his face. "Oh, for an aging middle-aged man he is still somewhat naïve and idealistic. But that is fine; we need some idealistic values in politics if we want to make our people stronger. Yes, he will do the job…he's worth it."

"Somehow, I can't help suspecting you have more important motives for supporting him. May I ask what they are?"

"Of course, you may. That is why we have been friends for all these many years, Tommy. You are intuitive. That is what has made you so very valuable to me." Ruben watched Tommy light a cigarette. It prompted him to take one last drag before extinguishing his cigar. "Yes, you are right. As you are aware, my political powers are waning. Let's be honest, they are getting weaker. Within time, only my daughter, Maria, will be left to carry on my legacy. There are very strong possibilities that the new puppies in our party will grow to be strong coyotes, and within the next couple of years they will try to push me out. That's okay. After nearly fifty years, change is bound to come and my powers will shrink. However, I still have my other enterprises, and they will become my liability. Other coyotes will be targeting them, forcing me to open other markets for my enterprises. That is where Joseph Aragon may be very instrumental for me. He has debts now, and when the time comes, and believe me in time it will come, I am very confident he will be in no position to refuse payment."

"You're still a sly crafty bastard, aren't you, Ruben?" Tommy said with laughter in his voice as he nearly choked on the smoke of his cigarette.

"Oh, that I still am," Ruben Gonzales proudly agreed. With laughter of his own in his voice, he then said, "Now, if you will kindly put out that foul smelling cigarette, before you kill the both of us."

4

Georgina Becaud made her fateful decision when she chose to spend the night in Santa Fe. Approaching Cerrillos Road, the last major exit off of I-25 before continuing on south to Albuquerque, Georgina felt the strain of six hundred miles and ten hours of driving. The old light Honda Civic made the long drive more tiresome. She had hoped to go further, but an inner voice told her to take it easy. With still a day and a half of driving, Los Angeles and the job that awaited her would still be there.

A gifted young woman of twenty-three, Georgina spoke fluent French and a bit of Spanish. More importantly, she could dazzle anyone with her drawings, a talent that helped to land her the position as an illustrator with one of Southern California's leading advertising agencies.

Having been born, reared, and schooled in Casper, Wyoming a new challenge in the large sprawling city beckoned to her. Los Angeles would be her first experience of living far away from the quiescent ranch she knew as home. She visited Los Angeles two months earlier to show her work, and it resulted in the job offer. This trip, and her relocation, was the beginning of the next step of her life.

Heading northeast on Cerrillos Road, the illumination of motel lights could be seen as she approached the intersection where Rodeo Road became Airport Road as it crossed Cerrillos. For a two-mile stretch, she could choose from any of the thirty motels for her night's rest. Not wanting to spend more than necessary, while at the same time not wanting to settle into a fleabag, Georgina drove further towards the heart of the city. About a mile and a half up Georgina opted for a motel because of its name recognition, knowing that it should be comfortable at a reasonable price. Now, for just a bite to eat and a good night's sleep. This was all she needed before setting out on the second third of her long trip.

A local restaurant stood but a short driving distance from the motel. She last ate six or seven hours earlier, somewhere in the middle of Colorado. A light salad, and perhaps a hamburger, would appease her small appetite until the next morning.

Sitting, and waiting for the waitress to bring her salad, Georgina removed a small sketchpad from her shoulder bag. The hours of driving left her in a feeling of a continuous forward motion, and although tired, energy still remained. She wanted to quell it so that it would not keep her from falling into a fitful night's sleep. Sketching always helped to relax her.

What first started out as doodling eventually began to take a defining form. Turning over the page to a fresh sheet, she began to work on a design for a French perfume. Heart-shaped bottles, wavy fragrant airlines, and a delicate nose formed a visual message. In a circular pattern of lines she printed in French the words, "The Fragrance of Love." The design had no special meaning, except to help spend time waiting for her evening meal. It did, however, stir a response from another customer.

"Aaah…you know French. Your drawing is magnificent." The complimentary statement was in French, but it was spoken by someone who seemed more confident speaking English.

Georgina turned to acknowledge the smile greeting her from a nearby table. They exchanged pleasantries, and within a short time her booth hosted two people instead of one.

The guest and the conversation helped to pass what would otherwise have been an uninspiring dinner. Being able to converse a little in French ran her spirits high. Her mother was born in France, and her father was originally a native of the French Providence of Quebec before resettling in Casper. Theirs' was a unique mixture of speaking the same language but with two different accents. Because her father's horse breeding responsibilities kept him away from home for days at a time, Georgina came to adopt her mother's manner of speaking French.

Being aware of being in New Mexico, and not wanting to shun a third language she was familiar with, in Spanish she asked her table guest, "Su Habala Espanol?"

"Yes, but very little," was the reply in English.

The dismissive response was quick, almost too quick. There seemed to be no transition in thought, and the reply came without any effort. Taking into consideration that she was in New Mexico, she removed the thought from her mind. Spanish is the second most spoken language in the state, but a large number of people with Spanish surnames do not speak it. A non-speaker could therefore respond effortlessly, 'yes, but very little'. Therefore, the conversation switched entirely to English.

An hour passed by and Georgina felt the need for the comfort of the motel bed. Relaxed from sitting motionless for a while, she knew that her tightly wound nerves were now calm enough for her to sleep. Excusing herself, Georgina bid good-by to her table guest, paid her tab, and departed.

The fresh night air carried a mild mid-February breeze, and it felt good as it brushed her face. She drove back across the street to the motel and parked her car. Sidestepping pools of water from the melting snow, she took her final strides before reaching the staircase, all the while clasping the key card to her room tightly in her hand. Soon, it would feel good to bathe, and then to sleep.

After reaching her small suite she set out her clothing for the next day. That done she went to her suitcase for her toiletry kit, but it wasn't there. Thinking for a moment, she remembered stuffing it behind her seat in the car where she could have easy access to it. Since she had to go down to her car to get it, Georgina thought it best to empty the vehicle of the two other pieces of luggage. There was no sense in tempting fate, or thieves.

The Honda was parked directly below the balcony of her room. Not wanting the hassle of locking up and of having to fumble with keys and suitcases, she swung the room's door wide open. Since the staircase descended at the north end of the building, she guessed it would take about one or two minutes to empty the car and be back indoors again.

The hot bath water, soaking the aches from her tired muscles, felt wonderful. It relieved some of the tension brought on from being mostly in one position while driving, and she knew she would have little to no trouble falling asleep.

Stepping out of the tub, she dried her body and then used the towel as a wrap. The bath had achieved its purpose as a pleasing tiredness took over. Switching off the bathroom light she made straight toward the warmth of the bed where a welcomed sleep was waiting.

Snuggled comfortably under the covers, she closed her eyes. Minutes passed before semi-conscious dreams fluttered her eyes, and sleep had made its nightly call. A rustling of drapes, and a screeching of drape hooks dragged through the traveling rod stirred her, startling her into a sharp awakening. Fear pumped her adrenaline as she realized someone else's uninvited presence occupied the room.

"Who is it?" she demanded.

There was no answer.

Georgina twisted her petite body as she clicked on the bed lamp. Turning back around, she saw the intruder.

"How…how did you come in here?"

The adrenaline pumped harder, and her heart beat faster. Despite all of the fiery energy that flowed within her body, Georgina was mentally paralyzed. Fear immobilized her, freezing her mind. Her thoughts started to race. She wanted to rationalize, and she wanted to scream. She could do neither. Screaming might cause provocation. Rationalizing might delay the intruder's actions.

Do Something! Her mind shouted. *What!* It could not be decided.

Within swift seconds it did not matter. Two firm and powerful hands were at her throat. The intruder was atop of her. The urgency to scream prevailed. She could not. Tightly wrapped hands cut off her vocal sounds. Georgina struggled. She fought to loosen the grip, and to caste off the weight pressed upon her. But her body was small, and the grip and the weight were oppressive. She tried to twist…to turn her body. The hold and the pain were unbearable. She could see a blue and red light flashing through the sides of the drapes that covered the window. A police patrol car sat outside. Was it there to save her? If only she could scream, she knew she could be rescued. If only she could free herself, she could be saved…be protected. If…

The 'ifs' were gone. Her last oozing breath left her body limp.

❦

Other red and blue lights flashed. They came from four city police vehicles and one sheriff's car. Early afternoon daylight reduced the cautioning effects that were so prevalent at night. For Georgina Becaud caution would no longer matter, and the van to the morgue would be a slow and quiet ride.

Detective Sergeant Francesca Madrid arrived on the scene in an unmarked official's car, and her driver and her escort were not ordinary. It is not every day that the city's police chief would escort a cop, with the chauffer being his top aide.

To Francesca, this was not the way she wanted to begin her first day on the job. It would have been nicer to get to see her office, meet her new colleagues, review a few open files, and in short, get her feet on the ground. Having just joined the Santa Fe Police Department after leaving behind ten uneasy years with the Albuquerque Police, she would have appreciated a smoother transition with the new force.

Graduating from the University of New Mexico with a degree in business, Francesca immediately signed up with the APD. The image of challenges and excitement lured her to the force, but ten years of working with sexists drove her to transfer up north. The kindling of her discord varied, changing mostly with the attitude of the brass in charge for any given period. From some, there was an emphasis of cooperation between ethnic groups and sexes. It was during that period that she was able to earn her way to the rank of sergeant in the homicide division. A new mayor, a new police chief, and the retirement of a couple of deputy commanders changed it all. Expecting at least a status quo, she became quickly disillusioned as a new laxness set in, and with it a renewal of old bias. Giving herself a choice of riding it out until a stronger, more disciplined administration took over, or leaving for a more opportunistic position to open elsewhere. Francesca, unmarried and with no family responsibilities to tie her down, chose the latter. Waiting for change within the department, one that may or may not come, could only lead to wasting the better part of the years that lie before her.

The Santa Fe Police Department would not necessarily be a bed of roses, and she knew it. However, the current police chief, a retired state cop and a carryover from previous city administrations, had gone a long ways in improving the force and recognizing its people for their individual accomplishments. Despite an attempted ouster by Chavez, he had gained the respect of most of the city council and it resulted in their defeating the former mayor's new appointee. All this could possibly change after the special spring election, and Francesca knew it. But, the SFPD was only a third of the size of their Albuquerque counterpart, and the city council would not have any major changes for at least another two years. They could override any detracting changes should the new mayor try to impose them. By that time, with her abilities and perhaps a bit of luck, she might be able to make her positive marks impressionable within the department.

She was going through orientation in the office of her new top boss when the call came in. Preliminary reports were sketchy – young female – 23 – Caucasian – indication of strangulation – money and jewelry not taken…robbery does not seem to be a motive – apparently a tourist or a passer-through. The last bit of information in particular caught Police Chief Rudy Perez' attention.

"Keep as tight of a lid on this as you can," he instructed the detective on the other end of the phone. "Try to keep the reporters out of it. The incompetent bastards might wind up twisting the facts and scare off half the tourists."

His tone was sharp; his accent had the occasional lilting singsong pattern of a long time New Mexican. He hated the New Mexico press and how they took statements and facts out of context. For the most part, Perez relied upon his contacts with associates in other municipalities to get much of the state news, and on CNN, FOX Cable News, and the Internet for the rest. He took no solace in knowing that keeping the press out of his new case was slimmer than a sheet of paper passing through a reporter's printer.

"Well, detective, here's a chance for you to get your feet wet," he said to Francesca as he welcomed her aboard. "I'm sorry that you didn't have time to ease your way in, but at least this will give us an opportunity to see what you're capable of. I won't give you the particulars now, but you'll get them when we're at the scene."

Inside the motel room with the police chief at her side, she began her own observation while donning her surgical gloves. The drapes were drawn open, allowing the sun to light up the room. Except for the bed, the room was neat and orderly, with all of the victim's personal items carefully stacked atop a table or under the credenza. Fresh clean clothes were laid out on a guest chair set beside the bed. Without touching the body, she leaned forward to study the victim laying face up. Looking around the room she saw no marks on any of the furniture, the walls, the shut windows, or the doors.

"I guess this is our new sergeant, uh, chief?" The voice belonged to Captain Marco Tessa, head of the violent crimes division.

"Yes," Police Chief Perez replied. "Sergeant Madrid, I'd like you to meet your new boss, Captain Tessa."

"How do you do, sir? My pleasure," Francesca responded with a quiet confidence.

"How do you do? The pleasure may be mine…we've been expecting new blood for a while now." He gave himself a moment to visually evaluate the new detective who possessed deep red hair, a five foot six frame to support her approximate one hundred and twenty pounds, and a pretty round face that showed strength and a 'don't mess with me' look. He then asked, "Do you have any comments on what you see here?"

Knowing that she was being tested for her observational skills, Francesca confidentially replied. "The victim's purse, money, and necklace are on the credenza, so that seems to rule out robbery. There are no bruises or marks on the lower part of her body to indicate that sex was involved. There are no signs of forced entry into the room. That indicates that she either knew her killer, or that the killer was already in the room. Then again, someone with a passkey may have gained access. That means we should do a thorough check on the motel staff."

"Good. However, since the bed has a box spring, and there are no closets, it should rule out someone already being in the room. I think its either one of the staff or she knew her assailant," Tessa commented. He may have caught her overlooking an obvious factor.

"Yes, I see that," Francesca tended to agree. "Were the drapes open or closed when the body was found?"

"Closed," Captain Tessa answered. "The maid admits that she opened them before she noticed the body."

"You mean the body was covered?"

"Yes. The M.E. drew back the blanket so that he could do his work."

Crossing to the window she examined the large drapes that were twice the width of the window. She then asked, "May I?" indicating that she wanted to draw the drapes closed.

"Sure. Go right ahead," her new boss permitted.

Closing the drapes to their fullest, she then examined them. Finding the seam that separated the two halves, she stepped behind them. After a moment, she returned to the front and gave her analysis.

"From the way the drapes are hung away from the window, and considering their overall width, it is possible the intruder may have been in the room. There is enough room back there to hide a couple of people."

"Very good," the captain replied, welcoming an aspect he did not see. "That means that he could have been here all the while. Using that scenario, do you have any determination as to how he got in? Any ideas?"

"Nothing concrete," she answered. "If the victim did know her assailant, it's possible he was in the room beforehand. Or, it is possible that she stepped out for a moment, left the door unlocked, and her murderer entered during that interval. If that is the case, it suggests to me that the guy may have been observing her, and then seized upon the opportunity to enter the room."

The police chief and the captain smiled at her analysis.

"Good insight," the police chief complimented her.

"Good insight, indeed," the captain echoed. "As the ranking officer on the scene, you'll be the primary investigator. I'll introduce you to the people you'll work with later on."

"Thank you." But, Francesca was not finished. "There is something else, the marks around the victim's throat. The person who murdered her did not have very large hands."

"You mean that he might have been a small fellow?" Police Chief Perez queried.

"Possible. Then again, it could have been a big man with small hands, or…it's possible that it could have been a woman with larger than normal hands. Perhaps the M.E.'s office can enlighten us on that."

"We'll let them help us with that. Maybe they'll come up with some DNA samples, or something that will help even more."

"We now have to come up with a motive," Francesca concluded.

The two senior officers shared an agreeing glance between them. It was Captain Tessa who then spoke.

"To come up with that, I think you are going to have to study a couple of other files. You're going to find that some have similar M.O.'s, and I'm pretty sure this one is going to fit right in."

An hour later, after she had finished her own analysis of the scene, she rode back to the office with Captain Tessa. Her morning meeting with the police chief, and then the on- scene meeting and test with the captain, seemed promising. All indications were that they would accept her as a female cop based upon her abilities, and not for any other reasons. It was just too bad that the day, and her new job, had to begin so abruptly with the murder of an innocent young woman.

5

Step two feet into Ray's Pub some weekday afternoon and you might be tempted to turn around and step back out. A dank bar laced with acrid cigarette smoke, and an aroma of stale beer greets you. Sounds of Mexican Mariachi music soothes the ears of the three or four customers sitting by themselves at different sections of the bar. An aging barmaid wipes away the bar stains, remnants of spilled drinks from the night before. She then packages the garbage of crumbled cans left over by the previous night's crew.

That is the usual scene by day. By early evening a slow influx of people moves in, some to sit at the bar to chat with friends, and others who gravitate to the back room where they will entertain themselves with the game of darts. The music becomes mixed with old rock, country and western, some R & B, some Sinatra, and still the usual mix of Mexican sounds. It is an eclectic mix, as eclectic as the mix of people who drink and play there. With little exception, there is a quiet and mutual respect that one has for the other.

"Heck! All I needed to do was to hit one stinking bull to win," you can hear Alex Dombrowski lament like a competitor who has just been beaten. "One bull...but I blew it."

"Hey! What can I tell ya? You choked," Mike Shannon, with a grin on his face, razzed back at his friend. "You should'a been like Sam here. He needs two bulls, so he does it by hitting a double with one dart."

The bull Mike referred to not only won the game, but it also won that night's blind draw tournament. Carried by Mike throughout the night, Sam did manage to save face by throwing the dart to win it all.

"Well, congratulations. You guys deserved it," Alex conceded. "Now I think it's your turn to buy my partner and me a couple of beers."

"Cripe! Buy a beer for a guy who chokes with the game on the line? Get outa here." Mike playfully rubbed the salt into a wound called loosing.

"All, right! Don't buy it, you prick," Alex said. He then called the bartender, "Ray, do me a favor. Give us a round of beers on me. Just don't give the cheap bastard one."

"Get the hell outa here! I'm buying this. And just to show you I'm a nice guy…hey, Ray! Cancel his order. This one's on me. Give Alex one, too, before he goes home cryin'."

"Come on, be consistent and stop being incongruous about buying me the beer."

"Yeah, you're right. I'm about as congruous as a vegan owning a butcher shop. So drink up, and be quiet."

There was some mild laughter at the ragging exchanged between the two. People knew they were both from Brooklyn, a place where one learns the art of zinging his buddies, and within time they learned by being a victim of Mike's quick and sometimes stinging wit. Minutes later Mike would be talking individually to them, inquiring about their families or of personal concerns. This time it was concern for Gregg Pardon, a Navajo whose family lived in Shiprock located in the northwestern Four Corners area of the Southwest.

"So, Gregg, how's your brother? It's not the bad bug, is it?"

"Nah, thank God," Dennis said with a smile of relief. "That's what the Gallup hospital was worried about at first. It's just a bad flu, but it's not 'the virus'."

The 'virus' referred to was the feared Hantavirus that was first discovered in the Four Corners area in the mid 1980's. Over the next several years, eighty-five of the ninety nationwide recorded deaths were attributed to the Sin Nombre subspecies of the virus. It was this subspecies that still terrified parts of New Mexico many years later.

"Did the New Mexico Environmental Health get involved?" Alex Dombrowski asked with a likewise concern and curiosity.

"Yeah. Matter of fact, they did. They gave my folk's place a clean bill of health. They said we have a good foundation – whatever the heck that means."

"It means that you don't have the Hantavirus which plagued the Four Corners Area a couple of decades back."

As an owner of a small pest control company that treated against the known vector, deer mice, Alex had to learn quickly about the Hantavirus. "Guessing, your folks probably have a newer home and everything's probably sealed tight around the doors, windows, and plumbing."

"Yeah," Gregg answered. "The house is less than two years old. How does that help?"

Alex went on to explain that the best line of defense agains mice is exclusion. The Navajos had a heavy deer mouse population, which was the known vector, and that most of the old housing had crawl spaces with porous floors. He further explained how the virus emanated from the mice dropping and rose up through the floor boards.

"Wow!" Gregg said. "So what's our chances of it coming back?"

"To ease your mind, only three or four non-fatal cases have been reported over the past few years. The thing is, don't become paranoid. Concerned – yes! Paranoid – no! Just follow the CDC recommendations and you should be okay."

"How come it's named 'No-Name?" Gregg asked.

Alex gave him a cynical grin with his answer, telling him that a newly discovered virus is usually named after the region or area where it was found

"The CDC first wanted to call it the Muertes Virus for the Muertes Mountains nearby. But in Spanish Muertes means death. So 'Death Virus' was discarded. Nobody in the Four Corners area or here wanted to be associated with it, so it became a virus without a name. Hence – Sin Nombre – the No Name Virus."

"God! I'm sure as hell glad it's something I have to deal with," Sam commented.

Again, Alex produced a cynical smile and gave a wink to Mike. It gave him a chance to plot a conspiracy scenario. "Oh? Don't be so sure."

"Bullcrap!" Mike said with a bit of evasiveness. "How?"

"Hey! I ain't the expert," Alex replied, "but the scary thing is that almost any numbnuts, with a little education off of the Internet and with the proper equipment, can manufacture a bio-weapon. After 9/11, Iraq had some brilliant doctors who worked with the stuff, so it became a major concern to our National Security people. Nukes and conventional weapons aren't the only things. There're also bio-weapons….."

"How dangerous is it compared to other weapons?" Sam asked.

"….As it is now, a couple of subspecies in the Ebola and pox virus each have about a 50 to 80% kill rate. As a reconstruct – a reengineered virus – any of these can potentially kill at 100%. Australian microbiologists already achieved this with the mouse-pox virus back in 1999. So? Who's to say that someone can't concoct any other deadly virus into a pure kill and release it on the public?"

"I don't think Santa Fe would be a target," Dawes said, giving his opinion.

"Maybe not Santa Fe," Alex agreed. "But Los Alamos, where some of the greatest scientific minds are, could be a big target. And, that's where you and Mike come in. Fortunately, I won't have anything to do with it."

"That's what you think," Mike said, not letting Alex off of the hook. "I'll find some way to drag your sorry ass into it."

"Gee, thanks, you prick," Alex said, picking up on the ragging. "Now I'm ready for another beer."

"Geez, you tightwad. Hey, Ray! When you're ready, let's have another round."

A half-hour later Alex departed his company from Mike, Sam and Gregg. They were all part of the group who gathered for the after-darts yak sessions.

"Alex take off?" Gregg asked as he returned from the a brief trip to the game room.

"Just left. Why? You miss him?" Mike found someone new to kid with.

"Get outa here," Gregg said with a boyish laugh. "But, he is an odd ball."

"You're just finding that out? Christ! Where have you been? That's why we call him 'professor'. He's got an opinion on every oddball thing."

"You know what that guy did to me last week?" Gregg asked. "He kissed me!"

Upon hearing what Gregg said, Mike's eyes bulged wide open as Sam roared with laughter. It gave Mike his opening.

"I didn't know. I always thought you two were different, but I never knew you had a thing going."

"No way!" Gregg's face turned red. "It was nothing like that."

"Oh, sure. Like we can believe that," Mike said, not wanting to let go. "I bet your wife doesn't even know. Come on, tell us about the little romance you two got going on."

"Stop it, huh!" Gregg's machismo was being tested, and his face was lighting up the room. "It wasn't that kind of kiss."

"Oh? Tell me, what kind of kiss was it? Any tongue involved?"

"Damn! No way! Blah!" Gregg said as he turned away and wiped his mouth from an imaginary kiss.

"You got us curious. Tell us about it."

"Well, you remember when we were tellin' all those Polish jokes?"

"Yeah, yeah. What's that got to do with your new love life?"

"It's got nothin' to do with it. I mean…give me a break, huh, Mike."

"All right! Don't get flustered. Go on…tell us your story."

"We were tellin' all those Polish jokes, and I looked over at Alex and noticed that he wasn't involved like he usually is. I thought maybe the jokes offended him. So I asked him because, you know some people are like that. And, if they don't like it, I don't want to insult them."

"And that's when he laid one on ya."

"Yes…I mean, no! He looks at me, thanks me, and says something like, 'you're the type of people I love knowing'. He then puckers his lips and gives me a quick peck on the cheek."

"Hell! There I figured you're gonna tell us a nice hot juicy tale."

"That figures," Sam said, joining in on the levity. "That's something he would do."

"Oh? He tried to plant one on you?" Mike said.

"No way," Sam said, shrugging off Mike's attempt to refocus the banter into his direction. "He's not my type. It's just that he doesn't like prejudices. If you ever notice, he'll take them, but he never dishes out those kinds of jokes. Yet, he appreciated Gregg's sincerity by asking if he was offended."

The rest of the evening modulated up and down with jokes and serious conversation. Some time later, after Gregg left, Mike and Sam's conversation turned to business and to politics.

"Decide how you'll vote for mayor?" Mike asked.

"Most likely your friend, Anthony Duran. He's quiet, a good listener, and he's got no personal agenda. It's easier to decide who I'm not voting for."

"You mean that idiot, JoJo?"

Sam nodded his agreement.

"You're right about that," Mike continued. "He gets elected and you and I both will get busy rather quickly. With those thugs he's got to support him, you can bet your ass he'll appoint his Patron brother-in-law as city police chief."

"If he feels he can get him past the city council, he will. You don't like him much, do you?" Sam asked, sure that he already knew the answer.

"Who? JoJo?"

"Yes."

"Never did like him. He's a goddamn racist, and a bully to boot."

"I know what you mean," Sam agreed. "Look at the sanctuary bill he tried to pass, protecting illegal immigrants. Thank God, the rest of the city counsil rejected it."

"Damned right. He put all cops in an awkward position, but he also victimized his own people by shrinking away a lot of jobs, especially the ones high school kids could hold down. He even screws the ones the resolution is designed to protect – the illegals."

"That's not the way he sees it, Mike. Looking at it through his eyes, he's not screwing them. With or without the resolution, the illegals still get paid seven to ten bucks an hour. He and his buddies benefit in their companies and restaurants through legitimate slavery. The city and state loose out because they don't have a legitimate tax base. If they stay here, Aragon and his cronies increase their political base."

"It's just his way of justifying slavery." A touch of anger ebbed into Mike's usually jovial voice. "He and the other bastards like him benefit. Pay salaries close to nothing, over-charge for shitty and piss poor construction, and then turn around and boast that they're doing a great service for humanity. Call me old fashion, but I still believe in honesty and integrity, and taking care of your own first. All they're doing is screwing New Mexicans and exploiting the Mexicans."

"Morally and ethically it's wrong," Sam agreed. "The problem is, the Patrons have been doing it for hundreds of years. Someday, maybe, things will change."

"Someday..." Mike said with a deeper thought. "I sure as hell hope so. There are just too many wonderful people here for crap like this to go on."

There was no patronizing in Mike's words. He loved the people in his community, and got along equally as well with the Anglos, Hispanics, and the Native Americans. His wife of twenty years was Hispanic. The people he associated with at Ray's Pub, at community and fraternity clubs, and at other groups, was made up of an extensive mix of people. He prided himself for liking their abilities and what they had to offer as people. He detested those who abused and used others. Being white or being black, or being of Spanish decent or of Native American decent did not enter into his likes or his dislikes.

"Any new leads in the Father Serrano case?" Sam asked, turning the socializing into business.

"We might have. One of the city detectives will be dropping by tomorrow. He might have something we can go on."

"I hope so. The priest's death has gotten to this city, Catholics and non-Catholics alike."

"He was popular," Mike said. "And, it was a brutal murder. Whatever comes up, we'll definitely keep you and your office informed."

"I suppose you guys have heard about the new case – a young tourist girl murdered at a motel on Cerrillos."

"Yeah, we're aware of it. Right now it's pretty much in city's hands, but whatever we find out we'll let you know."

"Thanks. I appreciate it."

"No problem. In the meantime, my friend, you've got to get your ass out more. Get yourself a good woman, and enjoy life. All work, no play, and Sam can become a sick boy."

"It's just that I got so much work to do."

Sam's reply sounded too much like an alibi to Mike. "Hey! Relax once in a while so that you can do more. Think about it."

"Yeah, well…"

"Yeah, well…my ass! I'll tell you what," Mike said as he came up with a quick remedy. "Next week Cap and his wife are coming over for dinner. Join us. We'll relax a bit…talk a little business…but mostly relax. It's next Friday night. Come on over."

Sam thought for a brief moment before he gave in. "Okay, count me in."

"Good! That's what I want to hear. Now, I better get my butt home. It's my turn to get in bright and early at the office in the morning."

Sam Dawes sat silently alone and let his thoughts take over after Mike left. He liked Mike and the commonality of their beliefs. Sitting in Ray's Pub was a reminder of it. A mix of people, young and old, from different races, ethnic heritages, and cultural backgrounds – they gathered there because they liked each other. What was more, Sam liked being there because the gathering people respected each other for what they stood for…for what they were.

6

Alex Dombrowski began his day tending to one of his favorite customers. It was customary for him to sit and drink coffee and talk with some of them after performing his pest control duties. Most of them did not need the regular monthly service and they knew it; they just wanted the peace of mind from unwanted pests, and Alex provided it. To him, it was purely black and white in taking on regular accounts, allowing textures of gray to enter only with those who needed his service on a one-time basis. Even then, if he picked up any negative cords while speaking to a potential client on the phone, he politely recommended them to one of his competitors. It was his business. He would give his clients the best, the safest, and the least expensive way to solve their problems. Malcontents were not worth it. Let another company, hungry for the quick buck, deal with them.

Over the years he earned the respect from all of his regulars. Some even had a pet term for him, calling him 'The Anomaly.' Accustomed to living in an eccentric city where workmen commonly came hours late, performed mediocre to poor service, and charged unworthy rates, his accounts deeply appreciated his promptness, his diligence and information, and the fair rate he charged. At times he felt guilty about servicing accounts that had no dire need for him, but he did come to accept that they wanted him for the sense of security against being invaded by unwanted intruders. Alex had his own rigidly defined sense of ethics and fairness, and he tried to live by them.

Like most days, it went pleasantly well until his last appointment.

He arrived on time for his next appointment at a rental triplex on Jose Street, a block south of Agua Fria. The owner of the three apartments was out in front to meet him.

"Mr. Sanchez, my name is Alex, the pest control guy you called. How do you do?" Alex reached out his hand for a greeting, and it was met with a loose and quickly removed hand.

"The people who live here are complaining about bugs."

"What kind of bugs?" Alex asked. His question was a fair professional one, and he asked it politely.

"How do I know? Bugs are bugs." The man's reply said that he did not want to be bothered with what he deemed as being trivial.

"If I'm to service properly, we're going to have to determine what we're treating for. Knowing this area, I don't think we're concerned about American and Oriental cockroaches like what are found around Cerrillos Road."

In pronouncing Cerrillos, Alex correctly pronounced the double 'l' as 'y', however…

"You mean Ce*rr*illos," Sanchez corrected him. "You gotta learn to roll the 'r's." His tone was scolding, showing little tolerance.

"I'm sorry, but I'm not from here and I don't speak Spanish," Alex replied. He immediately sensed a dislike for the man in front of him.

"Well, you're in New Mexico now. You should know how to speak Spanish," the man said. It was his last admonishment.

Alex caught eye to eye contact with the man, smiled, and made his reply. "And you should know how to deal with people. There are other pest control companies who are willing to service you. I'm not."

With that he turned, walked away, and then drove off. All the while he ignored the landlord's command and pleads for him to wait.

❦

A tear glistened in the old man's eye. He gently stroked the orange and white fur of the lifeless tabby that lay beside him on the floor.

"Good-bye. You were a good and true friend."

Alex numbly watched as Eloi Valdez, his elderly neighbor for the last twelve years, gently lift the cat and wrap it in a small blanket and place it lovingly at the foot of his bed. There it would rest until the callers from the local pet cemetery would come and carry the beloved pet to its final destination.

"It only serves to remind us of how short our time is. Someday, soon, my time will come."

"Hopefully, not for quite some time," Alex said.

"Like you, my friend, I try to be realistic. I am eighty-eight. I have seen my wife, and then my son, go before me. I have also seen my brothers and many of my friends depart. Time does not matter; it is how you live it. I've lived my life, and when he calls me I will go. I am not afraid."

Alex had little to say, realizing that the old man's words were true. "Perhaps we can find another friend to take his place."

"No, it would not be fair. But, thank you. You see, I do not want to have another friend that I can make feel lonely when my time comes."

Alex wanted to protest, but he respected the old man. In respecting him, he had to also respect his desires.

"I've lived a long life," the old man continued, "and I've seen and experienced much. I was in the Pacific during the war, and I saw the terrible things that happened there. I saw my birthplace, Wagon Mound, slowly shrink smaller when it lost its industry. I have seen many good things, too. I've watched this beautiful city grow as people came here and provided new jobs and a better economy. This is not to say that all changes were good, but they were changes and we must always make way and accept them. That is true with life. We live. We make our impressions. And, we must make way for the young ones to do the same. I have faith that most of the impressions these younger people make will be good ones. With the years…months…I have left in my life, I look forward to see it continue."

"Don't talk with so much finality," Alex said with a touch of discomfort. "You still have many years ahead of you."

"Do I?" Eloi gave a curious smile as he asked the question. "I don't know, perhaps I do, but it doesn't matter. I've lived my life, and it's time to make room for others. Maybe I will live until I'm a hundred, or maybe I'll die tomorrow. What difference does a few years make when compared to infinity? When my time comes I'll be ready. I have lived. I've tasted life's sweet offerings and its pains. I have made my little contributions. Maybe I could have made more, I don't know. But, I am at peace with myself, and while I don't welcome dying, I will not try to turn my back on the inevitable."

I wish I were able to share your wonderful outlook. Alex spoke only with his eyes. *I may be too much of a cynic to feel the way you do. Still, it is views like yours that do improve the world around us.*

Later that evening Alex clicked off the television at the conclusion of the satellite hockey broadcast. The joy of his team's victory was tempered by his thoughts of the old man next door.

Eloi walked in a different world than him. Their age, their background, and cultures lead each through different paths. Their formal education was different, but their education from life was quite similar. Both men, as they strolled along the pathway of life, seized upon the opportunity to learn as they observed themselves and the world around them. There is good, and there is bad. Eloi mostly chose to learn from the good, and for this, Alex deeply respected him.

Although the visits were never long, usually less than a half-hour, Alex took the time to talk with his neighbor on a regular basis. Usually, they would simply exchange pleasantries or share viewpoints. Occasionally the old man would treat him with tales of his younger life, growing up in Northern New Mexico, serving on active duty during the Korean War, and spending most of his life first living in Wagon Mound and then Las Vegas, New Mexico. His last thirty years he lived in Santa Fe. Pretty much a loner whose family had passed on, Eloi Valdez enjoyed the visits of any person who lent him an attentive ear.

Alex gave thought about what the old man had said about the death of his feline friend. "It only serves to remind us of how short our time is." Be it a few weeks or a few years, Alex agreed that, because of age, the tireless caller will be walking through Eloi's door. For that matter, Alex conceded the visitor could first choose him at any time upon a capricious whim. Would Eloi be ready? Would Alex, himself, be ready? Without much musing, he concluded that each man would.

More than thirty-seven years separated the two, yet Alex realized that they shared one common belief. No matter how close the end may be one must continue to grow, to learn all they can in their limited time of existence. What they learned could vary, but it could be gilded by respect and truth. Their perceptions of those two virtues may vary, limited only by their own imperfect perceptions. Still, they would strive to learn until the day they died. After that, he did not know. Deep inside his mind, he did not care. He had a strong sense for justice, and he used it to rationalize that it would not all go for naught. The thought of passing on even one sinew of his learning pleased him. After that, he could only dream.

Perhaps I'll be able to apply it all in my next life, were his closing thoughts as he turned off the bedroom light. They were tainted by a touch of cynicism in his final thought before dreamland commenced. *That's if there is one.*

7

In a modest home on Verde De Encanto, in the Palo Verde section of Santa Fe, early morning life began to stir. The fresh aroma of coffee dominated the smell of breakfast, and the murmur of the television news provided the background for the morning conversation between a husband and his wife. The occasional giggle of pre-teenage girls created the music of a happy family. Eduardo and Margarette Guitterrez loved their children as much as they loved each other.

"Come on girls, you're not getting on that bus until you've had breakfast," Margarette chided the girls in a motherly fashion.

"Sooo…?" Teresa teased. "If we missed the bus, mommy, you can take us to school."

"Yes, mommy, you can take us…please," the younger Charlene echoed.

"No way. I have to be in the office at seven-thirty."

"Ahhh, mommy…" Charlene responded in childish rejection. Then another idea came upon her. "If you can't take us, maybe popi can."

Teresa then joined her sister. "Popi can take us."

It brought a smile to their parents' face.

"Maybe…" their mother replied. "You're going to have to nicely ask him. Maybe he'll take you if he is not too busy."

"Say yes, popi…please," the girls simultaneously pleaded.

Giving a 'you got me' smirk as he sipped his coffee, their father spoke.

"Your mom and I took you twice last week. Are you beginning to make a habit of this?" His tone was gentle, with a mixture of teasing and mild admonishment in it.

"No, popi," the older girl replied. "We promise, if you take us today we won't ask you again…"

"…until next week," their father completed the sentence.

"Please, popi, please!" both girls playfully pleaded.

Playing his game to offset theirs', 'Popie' Guiterrez did not answer. He took a bite of his morning taco, and another sip of his coffee, not speaking for some time. A minute that seemed like hours to the impatient girls lapsed before he gave his answer.

"Okay, I'll take you. But, don't go pestering your mother or me about taking you to school for the rest of the week."

"Thank you, popi," the girls said while affectionately hugging their father. "We won't, we promise."

As an afterthought, Charlene added, "…not until next week."

The girls scurried off to their rooms to ready themselves for the day in school. Their mother and father had the kitchen alone, along with a moment's solitude.

"They really get a kick out of having us driving them to school," Margarette said.

"They do, don't they? I wonder if they'll feel the same way once they're old enough to drive." Cap tried to envision what it would be like in the future. "They'll probably be proud showing off, and they'll forget about us."

"Not likely, but if they do, I'll fix them by having them drive us to work." Margarette's comment generated a smile on his face. "Don't worry, though. It'll be a few more years before they'll have a car. In the meantime, let's enjoy them needing us while we can."

Finishing his breakfast, Cap felt lucky to have a family like his. He realized that there were quite a few out there who shared the same kind of moment. He also realized that, for some reason or another, there was discord in what seemed to be a growing number of those families. He tried to justify the reasons but there were many, and he knew he was limited in changing all that. All too often, through his line of work, his influence came too late.

"What should we bring over to Mike and Teri's Friday night?" Margarette asked, breaking into her husband's thoughts. "Maybe I should pick up a good coffee blend. They're both crazy about good coffee."

"Sounds like a good idea," Cap agreed. "Then again, they wouldn't care if we just brought ourselves." He instantly regretted making the comment that gave Margarette a chance to scold him.

"Don't be such a weasel. We can't go over to someone's house for dinner and not bring anything."

"I didn't mean it that way," her husband blushed. "It's just…"

"I don't want to hear it. You don't want to sound like a cheapskate, do you? If it makes you feel better, I'll buy the coffee." Knowing that Cap was ready to make a mild protest, she placed a finger onto his lips. "Now don't say anything, and give me a kiss so that I can finish getting ready for work."

It was a typical morning, one filled with love and respect. As Cap finished his last sip of coffee he gave a solemn thanks to his creator for not allowing discontent to show its presence in his home.

Much the same could be said in another house on Hopi Street on the opposite side of the city. Only in this household the seventeen-year old did not want to be driven to school. Mike Shannon's son, Adam, had his own Toyota pick-up to take him where he wanted to go.

"Sure, you can get those speakers for the truck," Mike consented. "I just don't know what good they'll do you if you can't use them."

"But, dad, everybody's got them," Adam protested.

Mike gave his son a sideways glance that said 'is that so'. He followed it with his skeptical opinion. "I don't think that is quite true. If they did, not everybody's using them."

"You know what I mean…"

"Yeah. It's just that too many kids blare their speakers. It's very disturbing, and it ain't very healthy."

"There's no law saying that we can't."

"Oh, yes, there is. It's covered under city noise ordinances. The noise those things make show no respect to people who simply want their peace and quiet. What's worse, it is very unhealthy for the central nervous system, especially for babies and the old people."

Respect was one trait that was instilled into Adam since he was a child. In this instance, invading someone's home, property, or peace of mind and health with self-indulging noise showed contempt and disrespect. By refraining from this invasion, one earned respect by showing it.

"Here's the deal," Mike continued. "You're old enough to know responsibility, so if you want them, you have to pay for them."

"Gee…thanks, dad," Adam said. Glee shone brightly from his eyes.

"Ah-ha! Wait! I'm not finished. If I hear them blasting, or if I get any complaints about them being too loud, I will personally rip them out. Agreed?"

"Agreed." Adam was too elated to let his father's conditions bring him down. It was another right of teenage passage, and an expensive one at that.

"And don't go hounding your mother to help you to pay them off."

"You don't have to worry about that," Teri chimed in. "If it were up me, he wouldn't get them."

Teri's remark was playful with her husband, not critical. After more than twenty years together she did know better, but it was just that she felt this was more of man's thing. It had to be handled as such, between a mature man and a man slowly coming of age. She had her own strong traits, ones that even Mike knew better than to cross. Like Mike, when a decision needed to be made, she made it. It often gave Mike ammunition to joke with his friends….

"Hey, I always have my wife down on her hands and knees. When we have an argument, she gets down on all fours and yells at me, 'Get out from under that bed and fight like a man'."

Fights never occurred, and the arguments were rare. Like in any marriage, they had their ups and downs, and they shared their love with each other. When the time came, they knew that Adam would find that kind of love with the woman who would someday marry him.

"I'm defrosting two romp roasts for Friday," Teri told him.

"Great! I'll make my special sauce Thursday night."

"Do you think I should invite someone over to pair off for Sam?"

"No...I don't think so. There's going to be a little homework involved. Knowing Sam, he'd get wrapped up and forget there was someone there. It wouldn't be a good way to have a date."

The morning flew by in the Shannon household, and for them a new day was just beginning.

In the year old Aragon home on Zepol Road, in the western part of the city, the morning had its unrest. The atmosphere in the solar heated house was chilled by the early morning's event.

"What the hell do you mean he's been arrested on a DWI?"

"As I told you, Thomaz was stopped at five o'clock this morning for drunk driving," Mary-Elizabeth Aragon reiterated. "That was one of your friends at the detention center who just called."

"That stupid...asshole! That's his second one this year already," JoJo lamented in anguish.

"They'll put him in jail..."

"No, they won't," JoJo cut his wife off. Collecting his thoughts and settling himself down at the kitchen table, he rocked on two legs of the chair. "That stupid...maybe he should spend a few months in detention. He won't though. Not if I can help it." He slowly let the impact of his son's action set in. "God damn it! The press will make me pay hell because of this."

There was no denying that the local press, eager to dig its claws into any type of prey, would run it as a front page column in the next day's paper. JoJo's notoriety would make it so, the same as it did with any political or civic leader. Crisis throughout the world, terrorists menacing the free and civilized world, blizzards and storms killing a hundred people, and earthquakes in California would all take second page coverage when it came to getting a scoop on one of their own locals. No matter if the article covered someone they despised or someone they supported, the gloves were off and everyone got the same treatment. It would spike sales and increase circulation.

"This won't hurt you too much. Your supporters are loyal, even if he does get jail time," Mary-Elizabeth said as she tried putting her perspective to his reasoning.

"So, you're saying we should let that dumb bastard stay where he is?"

"No! I didn't say that. In fact, I want you to call Manny right this minute and get him bailed out."

JoJo took in and weighed his wife's demand before he decided. "You're right. I'll call, but later…not now. I want that asshole son of mine to rot there for a few hours. Make him think we've forgot about him. Maybe then he'll learn about the kind of mess he's put me in."

No interludes and no rest took place in the morning's chaos. Hell was brewing out of their daughters' bedrooms.

"What the crap is the racket? You two woke us both up." The irritated voice belonged to their younger daughter, Evonne, as she came pacing heavily from her room. Her older sister, Yolanda, trailed two steps behind.

"How many times have I told you not to use that language around me?" Mary-Elizabeth complained to her daughter, her middle child who knew how to pull a mother's strings.

"Yeah, like you never use it. What the fuck's happened?"

"Your brother's been arrested for a DWI," her mother informed her.

"Is that all? We thought someone died from the way you two carried on."

JoJo, accustomed to these kinds of comments coming from his girls, especially Evonne, chose to ignore them. His wife did not.

"Don't you care about your brother? Don't you care about your father's campaign? People will blame your father."

"Pa can take care of himself. As for Thomaz, if he's stupid enough to get caught, screw him. Pa should let him stay locked up, this way he won't get in the way.'

"That's no way to talk," Mary-Elizabeth reprimanded. "He's your brother. We got to take care of our own."

"Yeah, like he'd take care of us," Yolanda joined in. "Evonne is right. We should let him rot."

"Shut up, both of you." JoJo was tired of listening to the bickering. "Go back to your rooms and let us think this out."

Neither of the two girls replied. Their stone glances did it for them. Seconds later they were back in Yolanda's room, and seconds later the booming bass of their stereo vibrated the house.

"Turn down that friggin' noise." Those were the last words they heard from their father who stood outside the door.

Yolanda turned down the volume, enough to ease the vibrations, and enough to hear herself talk.

"Do you think they'll ride the old man because of Thomaz?" she asked her younger, but brighter, sister.

"I don't know," Evonne answered. "I really don't give a crap. The same as I don't give a crap about Thomaz and his DWI. Let him rot where he won't give any of us any friggin' trouble."

The hard words shook Yolanda, and a look at her by Evonne revealed that she was taking it as a personal affront. Crossing to her, she put her arm around Yolanda and drew her close.

"I'm sorry, sis. I didn't mean any of this about you. It's meant for our stupid brother, and the old man and his political bullshit."

Silently, they caressed each other, almost suggesting an intimacy beyond being sisters. Neither of the two girls were what may be called attractive, and they both had masculine mannerisms that were accented by their stocky bodies. Sharing a same physical fate, they developed a strong bond with each other. It was the emotionally stronger Evonne who gave the most comfort, always lending a protective care to the often fragile Yolanda. As a pair they frequented the Santa Fe night and social clubs, in part to enjoy the recreations the clubs provided, and mostly in part to find something that was never there. At least not for them.

Despite their father's notoriety, their individual social life was almost nil, limited even more so by their lack of education. Attending high school separately, neither took part in extracurricular activities, finishing close to the bottom in their graduating classes. Nor did either of them show any desire to seek further education. They resigned themselves to lesser jobs as store clerks, security workers, and from time to time working on one of their father's construction projects.

Joseph Aragon's rise in the community did not affect them in their social and working lives. They sought no favors, and they got none. At times they considered their father's position in the community to be an albatross, a burden when hounded by those who sought them out for a possible social or political favor. While most of their friends came from their cultural realm, in reality friends were very few.

Bonded as they were to each other, they often played their own little games to set them apart from others. When spoken to in Spanish, they would often respond in English, or reply in Spanish if the communicator spoke in English. If their family or friends took one side of an issue, Evonne and Yolanda automatically took another. When chips were down, or if the situation arose to place either of them in awkward positions, they schemed and connived to successfully work out of them. It was their game, and their game gave them a sense of power. It was Evonne who first mastered it, and she taught her older sister how to wield it.

And…they knew how to manipulate their father's influence. If either girl took particular offense to someone, they found ways for JoJo to intercede. The offender might become victimized in a mishap resulting in a broken limb. If the offender was well to do, it was their property that suffered the costly harm.

They schemed, and they manipulated, but never each other. Whatever honesty Evonne or Yolanda possessed, they shared it between themselves.

"I know that, Ev," Yolanda said quietly. "But, Thomaz is our brother. Even if he's stupid, I don't want him to spend time in jail. He'll learn to control his drinking."

"I know how you feel, but he'll get himself killed someday. We drink, but we don't get nailed like him. We're too smart for that. When we don't find a place to crash out, we always manage. He doesn't."

Yolanda's sullen look proved to Evonne that a more cheerful approach was needed.

"What do you say we go out tonight? My treat. They're supposed to have some kick-ass music at the Tequila Club. We can do some dancing."

"I…I don't know. Maybe we shouldn't because of Thomaz."

"Come on, Yo. He shouldn't bring us down. Thomas will be taken care of, dad will see to that. It doesn't mean that we gotta stop living. Come on…let's go out and have fun."

Giving in to her sister's prodding, Yolanda nodded her approval.

"Good! We'll leave here at seven, eat out and then go to the club. Who knows, maybe we'll get lucky."

As usual, 'getting lucky' was not in the cards, and they each came to expect as much. It was a rare event for them, usually when they and their 'lucky' ones were too drunk on the concoction of tequila and beer to care who their partners were.

I hope dad gets Thomaz out, ran through Yolanda's mind. *Even if he did do wrong, he doesn't belong there.*

Screw that stupid prick. Let him stay where he won't screw it up for the rest of us, Evonne's mind raced. *Fuck him. Tonight, me and Yo are gonna have ourselves some fun.*

8

At state police headquarters the morning began routinely at eight-thirty with Guiterrez and Shannon's review of the previous day's activities. Faxed and computer copies of local police reports were among them, and one in particular caught the lieutenant's eye. It caused his eyebrows to arc a tad, and an ironic grin widened his lips.

Seeing a bit of an impish expression on Mike's face prompted Cap to ask, "Anything interesting?"

"No, not really. It's just that I know one of the names mentioned in the Santa Fe report."

"Oh?"

"Apparently nothing that he did wrong. Just accidentally got involved with some drug bust that proved to be helpful to the locals. There were also some abused kids involved. They're now in a shelter."

"Nice guy. Sounds like we should hire him on the force," Cap said in jest.

"This guy? No way. Too opinionated to make a good cop," Mike replied half in fun and half in earnest.

"Looks as though there's another tourist killing," Cap said after reviewing a few more reports.

"Yeah, I caught that one last night. Marco's coming over this morning, so he should be able to fill us in."

On cue, Cap Guiterrez's phone rang. Acknowledging the call, he instructed his secretary to welcome the visitors in.

"Well, for Christ's sake, speak of the devil," Mike greeted Marco Tessa. "I just mentioned your name a second ago."

"Goes to show you. Mention my name and you'll never know what you'll summon," Tessa greeted Mike and Cap. "I'd like to first introduce our new violent crimes detective, Detective Sergeant Francesca Madrid."

The state officers rose from their seats to welcome the new city cop.

"How do you do?" Captain Guiterrez was the first of the two to shake Francesca's hand.

"Fine, thank you." Francesca's reply was warm but it was professional.

"Hi, I'm Mike," was the next welcome to her. "Francesca Madrid…? Sounds familiar. Weren't you with the homicide division in Albuquerque?" Her nod acknowledged his query. "So, what brings you up here?"

"Oh, I just needed a change," she replied, avoiding a sob story of why she transferred. They all knew that if any of them wanted the answers they could easily find out.

"Well, change is one thing you'll get plenty of up here," Mike assured her.

Captain Guiterrez slowly broke into the welcoming for more pertinent issues, "I see you have another homicide to contend with."

"That we do," Captain Tessa answered. "As they say, no rest for the weary. Sgt. Madrid is the primary on it. It's her case."

"Heck of a way to get your feet wet," Cap said with sympathy.

"I'll say," Mike agreed.

With a smile of someone who did not expect to be felt sorry for, Francesca responded, "I guess it's all in a day's work. Captain tells me you people have accumulated your own file on several unsolved homicides."

"That we did," Mike eagerly replied. "Let me guess. You have main interest in the ones involving young females, new in the city. Right?"

"You read my mind," Francesca answered as she began to feel at ease. The friendly professional atmosphere helped to relax her.

"Hey! That's why we're all cops. Gotta read each other's mind."

"Then, you probably know…"

"…that you'd like to review them," Mike said. In his usually casual way he was playfully one step ahead of her.

"May I?" she asked, amused by his quickness.

"Sure thing."

"Thanks. When would it be convenient for you?"

"Any time you'd like." Mike's enthusiasm made her feel even more relaxed. "Cap and I are finished with our daily briefing, so I can show you what we have now if you'd like."

Before either of them could make a move for the office door, it was Tessa who stopped them.

"Mike, before you go, I have a dribble of information that may or may not help you with the Serrano case."

Mike and Cap's attention were prepared. Francesca, totally unfamiliar with the proceedings in the priest's death, listened with curiosity.

"That's right. I almost forgot that's the reason why we were expecting you. So, what gives?"

"Sergeant, I'm sure you're aware of the demise of the Monsignor John Carrol Serrano. Since it happened way outside the city limits, the state took over the investigation. But, because the monsignor was so popular in our community, we agreed to help them as much as possible."

"Actually, we share as much as possible with each other on this," Captain Guiterrez spoke with diplomacy. He could see that his city counterpart appreciated his comment.

"A few nights ago one of our city patrol guys picked up a habitual drunk. A Navajo," Tessa began. "When the cop took him down for an overnight booking they inventoried his possessions. Aside from a beat up wallet with a couple of bucks in it, they found a ribbon. The kind a priest wears around his neck during certain services."

"A stole," Guiterrez said, identifying the ribbon.

"Yeah, I guess that's what they call it. Anyway, I remember that it was not on the inventory list of things found at Serrano's crime scene. If a priest was going to give the Last Rites, I'm sure the stole is not something he'd want to leave behind. It might have belonged to Serrano."

"Quite possible," Cap and Mike said in unison.

"Where's the guy now?" Mike asked.

"That's the rub. It seems that the next day he was shipped off to Window Rock. Something about the Tribal Police wanting him for disorderly charges. It wasn't until he left that our guy made the connection."

"I assume the Native American took the shoal with him," Cap said.

"I'm afraid so," Tessa replied.

"Well, at least we know where he is," Mike said.

"Yeah," Cap agreed. "I think I'm going to contact their top cop, a Daniel Sanchez. Maybe we can arrange for Mike to talk with the native."

"No sweat," Mike replied. "Heck, I can use a little trip. You wanna join me, Marco?"

"Sure, why not. Only it's on the state's expense account," he said with a wink.

"Boy! You cheap bastard," Mike kidded. Then turning to Francesca, he added, "You better watch out who you hang around with. Cheapness can become catchy."

"From what I know, you guys can afford it," was Francesca's playful quip, one that stated that she knew where her future bread and butter were coming from.

"Oh, no! See that, Cap. My tip came too late."

They all had their little laughs before Mike and Francesca left for his office.

"How much info do you have on these cases?" Mike asked.

"Only from what I reviewed out of our files. I'm actually hoping that I can piece things together after comparing your data with ours. You might just have something we don't."

"If it's there, I hope you find it. We haven't had any luck," Mike told her. "We'll gladly share. Which brings me to what happened yesterday. All we know is what we read from the preliminaries."

Francesca went on to detail the facts pertaining to the new Georgina Becaud case. She took extra pain in telling all that she knew, knowing that Mike's department would do likewise. To Francesca it was a good way to get off to a sound and credible footing with her state colleagues. When she finished it was Mike who mentioned the certain relevant similarities.

"One: They were either strangled or stabbed. Two: From the marks around their throats, the medical examiners think at least two or three may have come from the same attacker. Three: All victims were white females, in their twenties, and from out of town."

"And the only major difference was one body was found south of here near Lone Butte," Francesca added.

"Correct. But, she was battered and stabbed. You've done you're homework."

"Thank you. I did some reading last night." She then went on. "None of the cases involved sexual assault or robbery. There is also a time lag between all cases."

"Yes," Mike replied. "Going back around eight years, there's an average of two years between each, with the closet being about seventeen months apart."

Francesca thought she knew the reason but to have it confirmed by a fellow officer would reinforce the reasoning of her question, "Why do you think that is?"

"We're not sure, but if these cases are all related, or even if some are, we can pretty much be certain that they may probably have been committed by a serial killer out to make a point. Our guess is that it's someone who kills them out of reaction. It may be something said by the victims, the way they looked, or something they did that provoked their attacker. It was very likely a sudden decision by the killer to commit the crime. Not much premeditation, but a quick decision."

"Very interesting," Francesca commented. "Aside from us, is any other agency involved?"

"The sheriff's department, only as a professional courtesy. We don't expect much help there. Then there's Sam Dawes, our District Attorney."

"Does he have any twists on this?"

"Not that I know of. He's brand new to the job. Then again, he's in the prosecuting and not the crime solving business. That's the job we're stuck with," Mike replied. As an afterthought he said, "In fact, I'll be seeing him tonight where we play darts. Why don't you join us for a beer or two?"

Almost wanting to say yes, Francesco hesitated. "I'd like to, but tonight I'm using to get myself fully moved in."

"I don't envy you," Mike sympathized. Still, it was not enough to let her off his hook. "I'll tell you what. Friday, Cap and his wife, and Sam are coming over to my house for dinner. My wife and I are putting together a little feast. Come on over and join us. We'll relax, talk some shop, and you'll get a chance to start meeting some Santa Feans."

Francesca, out of a bit of shyness, almost wanted to decline. However, it was Mike's outreaching friendliness that made her change her mind.

"Okay, I will."

They then spent a few more minutes exchanging notes and stories. When Marco Tessa was ready to go back up the few blocks to the city police headquarters, Francesca bid her farewell.

"I'll be there Friday at seven," she said in parting.

"Good! See you then."

After the two city cops left, Mike mischievously thought, *Christ! Teri's going to shoot me. I told her not to invite anyone to match up with Sam, and here I go doing it myself. Who knows, maybe they'll like each other, maybe they won't.* As a final self-satisfying thought, he added, *What the hell. What are friends for?*

"What the hell kind of trouble were you up to last night?"

Although friendly, a trace of a cop's tough tone edged into Mike's question. Alex Dombrowski was the one being subject to the friendly interrogation. Sam Dawes was also on hand at Ray's Pub, but his interest did not pique until Alex spoke.

"How the hell did you know?"

"Hey, I'm a cop. We know everything," Mike dodged to keep Alex alert. "We get to see the local police blotters every morning…just in case there's something of interest to us. Seeing your name is interesting."

"Okay! You got me!" Alex playfully threw his hands in the air in a surrender mode. With a more serious edge he then asked, "Is this on the record, or off?"

"As a friend, off…unless you did something illegal. Then I'll have to jail your ass."

Alex heard the banter in Mike's words that told him that he could speak freely. It was Sam who became a bit uncomfortable fearing that what he was about to hear might affect a case that was bound to cross his desk.

"I'm not sure I should be listening…"

"Relax," Alex said as he put a comforting hand on Sam's back, keeping him seated on the barstool. "If you shouldn't hear this, I'm sure Mike wouldn't have brought it up. The most that can happen is that you might get some reinforcement for a case that you're bound to get."

"I bet," Sam gave his dubious response.

After paying for the ordered round of beers, Alex settled comfortably onto his bar seat and recreated the previous night's experience.

It was nearly nine o'clock when he received a call from someone in need of his service. He seldom took calls that late in the day, and it usually annoyed him when they occurred. Although he considered it an intrusion, he resigned himself into accepting that other people deemed their pest problems more urgent than they did his tranquility. It was the price he paid from time to time for having a small business and operating out of his home.

The voice at the other end was female, and he could tell by her manner of talking that she was not overly educated and probably lived in a low-income section of town, perhaps within a mile from where he lived. From the way she babbled he also suspected that she might be a little high on something, but he could not be certain. After questioning her about her problem, Alex was finally able to determine more about it. German cockroaches were overrunning the kitchen of her mobile home, and based upon the information he pried from her, he knew that it was something that manifested over a period of at least several months or more. He knew that this type of roach was a difficult challenge. That, plus the over-population of the infestation, he concluded that one treatment may not likely exterminate all of the pests. He told her so.

"I don't care how many times you hav'ta come. I gotta get rid of them."

When he told her he could fit her into his next day's schedule, the caller complained that she needed immediate attention to her problem. She needed it that very same night. He became torn between acceding to her demands or telling her that another company might be able to satisfy her demand, but he already knew the answer. No other company would service the woman on such a short notice and so late at night. With more of a hope that she would become discouraged and hang up, he added more than fifty percent to the normal fee as compensation for the inconvenience.

"I don't care. I can give you cash," were her demanding words.

Trapped, and not wanting to ignore a client with an urgent need, he took her name, phone number, and address, and instructed her as to the household preparations he wanted her to accomplish before he could perform his treatment. He also told her that he would be there in exactly one hour. As it was, he had deduced correctly about the woman and where she lived, about two miles down Airport Road. The home was an older mobile doublewide, located in the middle of an older mobile home park.

Arriving at the precise time, he entered the home only to want to throw up his hands and leave. A myriad of revulsions greeted him. A home full of odors from backed up sink water, dirty dishes and pans, and unwashed clothes and garbage strewn about reeked his nose, something he thought he had previously grown immune to. The home had not only housed a thousand or more roaches, but also three small children ranging in ages of three to seven. The appearances of the two boys and a girl nearly rivaled that of the house, torn and dirty clothes, unwashed skin, and mucus oozing from the nostrils of the two youngest.

Working his way towards the kitchen his eyes roamed the wall of the living room only to confirm what he had suspected; the pest infestation was not confined to just the kitchen. Cockroach antennas protruded out from the room's ceiling molding. Entering the kitchen a further disgust made him want to empty his stomach and run. Pressed cardboard cabinets were eroding where they hung, the bare kitchen flooring rotted to a point where one could see the crawlspace below, and the filthy stove stored more pots and frying pans filled with old fats and grease. Stepping back into the living room, he made his decision. He could not in any way, shape, or form service the house. Cynically, he wanted to tell the woman that the only way to get rid of the roaches was to burn the mobile home down.

As he turned to face the woman, his eyes caught sight of something in the bedroom, a sight he had never before seen. Alongside the bed were stacks of money standing about ten inches high, and lying beside them were two clear bags of what appeared to be white powder. Not wanting to keep his eyes affixed on what he saw, he quickly channeled his sight into the opposite direction, but although he could not make out the denominations of the bills, he automatically concluded the contents of the plastic bags. *Shit! I'm in a drug den,* his mind reeled.

Gradually making his way back to where he came in, Alex started to explain that he could not be of service. At that moment a heavy-set Mexican-American man entered from where Alex was heading, blocking his path of exit. The man's macho menacing look matched his threatening tone.

"What da hell you doin' here?" he half roared.

"I told him to come. He's the exterminator. I wanna get rid of these damn roaches," the woman answered. Her fearless tone matched his, indicating that she was well used to communicating with him this way.

"I told ya, don't ever call nobody unless I tell you," he bellowed. Then turning to Alex, "If you think I'm gonna pay you, you're fucking nuts. Now get the hell outa this fuckin' house."

Easing away and facing the door from a different angle, Alex could not get straight to the door that was blocked by a pile of trash as well as the threatening man. A sense of danger started to take hold and Alex realized that he had no protection, and his five ten, hundred-sixty pound frame would be no match against the taller and much heavier menace who was not only angry but probably stoned as well. Glancing to his right, he spotted a cell phone partially buried under old newspapers on a table. Seeing his opportunity as the man and woman threw verbal barrages at each other, Alex palmed the phone and hid it behind his back. It might be stealing, but he knew that it might also be his only line of defense should he need it.

"I told you, get the fuck out!" the man again bellowed. Seeing an open passage to the door, Alex managed to move safely through it.

Having made it to the security of the street, he took a deep breath that he slowly exhaled. It served to help clear his mind of the encounter he just experienced, and it also purged his lungs of the rancorous odor that permeated the interior of the house. Now he was left with a question of what he should do. Without mauling over options his mind reacted on reflex. He knew that as a human being he could not ignore what he had seen. The condition of the house, the drugs and the money, and definitely not the children.

As he entered the additional security of his truck he punched the numbers 911 into the cell phone that he palmed. When the operator responded he quickly disguised his voice and rattled off a distress situation of a violent family disturbance, then he likewise rattled off the address of the location. Taking into account that he was using a false voice, he did make certain to enunciate the house number and street clearly. Having done so, he quickly pushed the off button, stepped out of his vehicle to toss the cell phone to the doorway of the house, reentered his truck and backed it up some two homes away. Not sure that his message was clearly relayed to the operator, he further relied on 911's ability to trace the location of the call. Finished with the call, he tossed the phone back into the driveway of the mobile home. He then sat and waited.

The wait was for three minutes. Two city patrol cars, followed by a third arrived at the scene. Allowing for the first two officers to approach the door, Alex emerged from his truck and walked to the back-up officer.

"You're here for the disturbance?" he lamely asked the officer, not knowing how else to begin.

"Yes. You the one who called it in?"

"No," Alex lied to cover himself. "But I just left that house a few minutes ago, and there are some things you ought to know."

Alex then went on to give details that he felt certain he could not do over the phone without having to go into laborious details, thereby risking the chance of not being able to convince the operator. In the past he heard police accounts of how their hands were tied by mere telephone reporting, so he chose this plan of action in order to quickly summons the police to the scene where he could give his first hand account.

With his mouth slightly agape, the police officer sought confirmation. "Are you sure of what you saw?"

"Positive," Alex answered firmly.

"If you don't mind, I'd like you to wait here. I may need to take a statement from you."

"No problem." Alex felt a sense of satisfaction set in.

The back-up officer walked up to the other two, and one of them broke away to listen about the story as told by Alex. Looking in Alex's direction to seize up the informer, the second officer nodded his head and re-addressed the man and woman who stood blocking the doorway. Using the pretense that they had to gain entry into the house where a domestic disturbance occurred, and that children may have been involved, all three officers managed to gain entry. From there, the rest of the story became part of the police report.

Alex's final satisfaction came a half-hour later when more police cars and a car from Family Services were on the scene. It was then that he knew he had done the right thing.

"…and that's about it," Alex finished telling of his experience to Mike and Sam.

"That's about it!" Mike exclaimed. Then, maintaining his ragging relationship with his fellow Brooklynite, Mike barbed his next comment. "I'd say that's enough. Jeez! I don't know, pal. For at least once in your life you did the right thing."

Hearing the intent behind the words, Alex felt humbled by Mike's remark.

"I saw an outline of the case before I left my office this afternoon," Sam said. "From all accounts, we're going to slam dunk these people not only on drugs, but also on child abuse and endangerment."

"Good!" Mike said as he took a swig from his beer bottle. "I hope you fry their asses."

"If we can get the judge not to overlap the sentences, they should be away for a long time. My guess is that the judge will give consecutive sentences because there were kids involved."

"You don't think you'll need me as a witness, do you?" Alex asked.

"Not very likely," Sam replied. "With cases like these we prefer to keep the witnesses in the background. That's for their protection as well as simplicity. Providing the cops used proper procedures, which I think they did, they gained legal entry and found the kids that opened the way for them to search more thoroughly and find the drugs. That should be sufficient."

"That's nice to know," Alex said quietly.

"So, our buddy here is a hero," Mike began his jibe again. "To show you how proud I am of you, I'm not going to take as much satisfaction when I whip your ass on the dartboard tonight."

9

In New Mexico a few warm days in the last third of winter goes a long way of ridding its ground of snow, especially on areas constantly exposed to the warming rays of the sun. Except for the Sangre De Cristo mountain range, patches of brown mixed with a little of green stand out boldly alongside white patches, lulling one into a false sense of security that spring is waiting just around the corner. To a long time resident who has witnessed many predictable weather changes, one knows better than to build hopes too high, knowing that at least one or two cold spells can darken the optimism of an early summer. To confirm this, all one has to do is to talk to someone whose fruit trees have been deceived by the fake promises of spring. Cold snaps in the middle of April will deaden apricot and peach trees, denying life to the spring blossoms that yield the summer fruit.

Driving over the rise north of Pojauque, and but nine miles south of Espanola, JoJo took delight in the absence of snow. The barren land on either side of him showed nothing but brown soil, darkened by the absorption of the moisture that recently covered it. Within a few weeks, providing that no new rain or snow fell, the soil would again brighten to light rust, thirsting for heaven's gift.

Over another rise is the beginning of the Espanola Valley, led by the small city of Espanola. There the soil is richer for about twenty miles into the eastern, northerly, and westerly directions. It is not until the land passes the Abique Dam to the northwest that it becomes barren again, dipping into a colorful stark canyon before once again turning lush as it climbs the elevation leading to Cebolla, Tierra Amirilla, and Chama. Alongside the roadway the forests and farmland grace the way. Farther north the forest and farmland still dominates until the roadway elevates, then to the left nature paints her vista of an open sky hugging the green and brown valley and an icy blue lake below. Driving slightly northeast from Espanola, and forty miles to Taos, again mostly forest will greet you on the right, while on your left you can spot sportsmen fishing year round, or rafting on the shallow river.

Ruben Gonzales' old and large deep tan adobe home stood on a three full acres in the northeast section of the city. Surrounded by open fields, the property was rich with peach, cherry, and apple trees, which were more ornamental than practical. Unless picked by the handymen or kids, the sweet precious fruit would be left to rot on the limbs from which they hung. Fruit that fell to the ground would mostly be gathered and used as compost. In all, the land did offer a peaceful setting to its visitor.

JoJo did accept the invitation against his better desires, but meeting with the two people who were contributing to his election aims was a small twenty-minute price to pay, even if one of the contributors was William Johnson.

"Some good news for you, JoJo," the elder statesman, Ruben Gonzales began. His right-hand man, Tommy Trujillo, sat quietly at the far end of the room smoking his cigarettes. "Bill, here, has arranged to make a nice healthy donation to your run for mayor. Bill, perhaps you would like to give JoJo the details."

A tall man of six foot five, his forty-six year old frame was thin. Originally from Chicago, his attire was strictly New Mexico: jeans and boots, and a bolo tie in the collar of his white silk shirt. His complexion was fair, suggesting his desires of spending more time indoors rather than in New Mexico's pure air and brilliant sunlight. His accent and his mannerisms were still that of a big city boy.

Johnson came to Santa Fe sixteen years earlier and immediately used his hustling skills to earn a small fortune. Fast food shops, ownership in a cab company, and a twenty-four table pool parlor, all combined to build his wealth. Over the last three years, however, the legitimate businesses were only supplemental to his selling of cocaine, marijuana, and designer drugs to his more elite customers. It was his attempt to build upon his legitimate image, and the opening of a new art gallery on historically zoned property on lower Canyon Road would pave the way for his newly formed association with Joseph Aragon.

"I have arranged a way to have a total of ten grand going into your campaign."

Not expecting to hear such news JoJo's mouth opened with utter surprise. His first impulse was to say thanks, but he still detested the arrogant Anglo from elsewhere, so he let his astonished expression speak for him.

"I really appreciate your swing vote for my gallery, and I'd like to repay you. Only, so that there are no noticeable improprieties that the press may uncover, I've arranged to have this money contributed to your funds through a few other individuals. They are friends of mine, and they have no compunctions about it, especially since they will be giving my money away."

Shocked at the unexpected present, JoJo took a few moments to gather his thoughts that were blown apart by the surprise. There had to be strings, and he wanted to know who was going to pull them, and at what price.

"You've already did a good deed," Ruben Gonzales said as he spoke for Johnson. "By helping Bill get the permit for his gallery you have opened up the door for him to rise to new heights with his standing in the community."

"Just for changing my vote…?" JoJo still grasped to try and understand.

"Yes, for changing your vote," Johnson answered. "It opens a door for me, as Ruben says, and the community will benefit from my contributions to various causes. Of course, I must admit that I'll benefit from the tax write-offs. But, as I see it, it's a win-win situation for everybody."

The mayoral candidate did start to recognize the thinly sketched drawing, but he did not expect to receive so much for doing so little. Ruben Gonzales then clarified the picture, enough for JoJo to understand.

"This is politics, my good man. You've been in it long enough to know how the machinery works. You oil the wheels by compromising a little from time to time, and in the long run a lot of others will benefit."

Joseph Aragon did see the picture, and it made him rue the fact that, unlike Ruben Gonzales' Rio Arriba County where one party rigidly controlled nearly ninety percent of the vote, Santa Fe was much more competitive. He had to bend a little in order to be successful, and it meant that he no longer was his own man, something that he always fancifly envisioned of himself. Yet, he knew that Ruben Gonzales made compromises, and look at where it got him.

Adding the facts together, Aragon knew he had but a slim lead going into the last weeks of the campaign. It had shrunk mainly because of the vigorous campaign staged by his despised opposition, Anthony Duran. Ruben Gonzales' visiting Santa Fe should help, and the newspaper ad his mentor promised would help some more. The ten thousand dollars from William Johnson would buy him the support that would make his lead insurmountable. What was known to all but prudently not spoken about, were the concealed voting machine manipulations that would be bound to occur at a few selected polling stations. Giddiness danced in his mind, and the euphoria lasted for several days thereafter.

"There is only one little problem that I can see," Ruben Gonzales said, temporarily tempering JoJo's high spirits. "Your son's drunk driving charge."

"Yeah...well I got Manny on it. Thomaz should be out by tomorrow, and..."

"May I make a suggestion?" Gonzales interrupted him

"Sure...but," JoJo hesitated.

"Don't fight the charge. Have your son plead guilty. Let him go through rehabilitation and jail time. It'll make you look better in the public eye, a mayor who is willing to pay the proper consequences. You know how that is."

"Yes...but, my son serving time while I'm running for office..."

"Don't worry about that. The most it will be is a few months, and I'm sure we can find a way to even reduce that."

Aragon let the idea seep into his reasoning. Concluding that fighting the charges against his son would give the perception of nepotism and it could cost him support, he came to accept it. If anything, with Thomaz spending perhaps a month behind bars would keep the young boy out of the way, keep him from getting into further trouble until after Joseph Aragon became the mayor of The City Different.

A short time after JoJo departed, returning home with more encouragement, Gonzales, Tommy Trujillo, and William Johnson returned to their more pressing business.

"Do you think he bought all that?" Tommy asked. Till now he had been silent, taking to the background of Ruben Gonzales' dealings.

"I have no doubt that he did," Gonzales said confidently as he let a smile break upon his lips.

"I'm sure he did, also," Johnson added. "Besides, the tax write-offs aren't any lie."

"That's not the way he thinks," Tommy laughed.

"So true," Gonzales said as he enjoyed the irony. "Little does he realize that my friend, Bill here, is opening the gallery as a tax-write off. Run it as a loss, but use it as a way to channel the cash from his more lucrative business. Ahhh…the beauty of stupid tax laws and imaginative bookkeeping."

"Don't forget how the gallery is going to help that business, as well," Johnson said. He allowed himself to share the delightful moments. "Just think of the wealthier people who prefer to deal through the limelight of a gallery and the art world as opposed to dealing with the low life in bars, restaurants, or on the streets."

"Yes, indeed," Gonzales said. This time his tone became more business like. "Within the next couple of days I'll have my people contact you so that you can work out new distribution systems."

"That sounds fine," Johnson replied. "Within the next week or two might be better. After all, it won't be until the beginning of May that we'll officially open. Just in time for the new season of the gallery showings. However, I'll have a private opening in a couple of weeks. It'll be for my special clients."

"Very well. Let's say we'll make it for ten days from now."

"Fair enough," Johnson agreed. "Just one question, if that guy becomes mayor, what use are you going to have for him where this is concerned?"

"As of now, just about none. It is better if we limit him to one endeavor at a time, but never enough for him to realize how he is benefiting us. It is best that we keep him in the dark, and outside."

"Afraid he'll become greedy?"

"Greedy? No, not him. People like him, who believe in their own causes, do not get greedy with enterprises like ours. They do become self-righteous, and that my friend, can be more dangerous than being greedy. No. We don't use him on one thing any more than necessary. The careful trick is to manipulate him, and that, my good man, is my specialty."

≈

Earlier that day, in a more remote part of the county, a man sat by a stream that flowed from the Abique Dam, some twenty miles to the north. His teeth clenched a pipe as the thin smoke lifted skyward, and his eyes watched the rippling water cut by movement of a fishing line. His mind of seventy years cantered through the memories of the many days gone by. Emanuel Montoya was a transplant from Albuquerque, settling northward to spend his waning years in a newly built home just south of the village of Abique.

Some two hundred feet away, his sideward glance detected three younger men in their forties and fifties emerge from a Dodge Ram pick-up. Aside from popping open cans of beer, their actions seemed innocent enough as two leaned against the pick-up and the third against a tree. Within five minutes he had forgotten about them, that is until he saw them heading his way.

"How are you doing, ol' timer?" one asked.

Caught a bit off guard by the unexpected greeting, Emanuel hesitantly returned the inquiry. "Fine. Very fine. And you?"

"Oh, we're okay. Say, I don't know if you're aware of it or not, but there ain't much fish in this here part of the river."

"Oh, I know that, but I appreciate your telling me. It's just that I didn't feel like driving up to Heron Lake, and I figured this would be a good substitute. Anyway, I'm not a good fisherman…just do it for the relaxation."

With a short laugh, the man replied, "I guess that's as good a reason as any." Eyeing the older man he went on to ask another question, "You look familiar. Where would I know you from?"

Not fazed by the inquiry, Emanuel nonchalantly replied, "I wouldn't know, really. You see, I just moved up here a few months ago. From Albuquerque."

"Yeah. I think I know where we saw you. About a week ago you were down at county hall, trying to get some movement going, or something like that."

"Yes, sir, that's correct. I was looking into how to establish a charter so that we can form an independent political party."

"Something like that Reform Party that once was. Or those Tea Parties, or whatever they are."

"Somewhere between that and a Tea or a Libertarian party."

"I don't know why you'd wanna waste your time doing that. We already got two parties, the Democrats and Republicans."

"True. But, some people might want to vote a different way. I know the Republicans are very weak up here, and even though I side with them on some issues, I don't always agree with them."

"You're right about that. That's why just about everybody like us are Democrats."

Thinking that the man had given him a friendly opening, Emanuel maintained his thought. "That is very possible. And yet, there are some people who may look for an alternative party. If they do, they're free to look into what an independent party has to offer."

"They're happy with what they got," one of the other men spoke up. The edge in the man's tone did not immediately bother Emanuel.

"Oh, but maybe they may think differently. We really don't know that."

"We know damned well what they think," the third man joined in. "We don't need any outsider telling them different."

"Now, now!" the first man interfered. "We don't gotta get excited." Turning back to Emanuel, he spoke. "What he means is, we're happy with the way things are. Ruben Gonzales and his people have done all right by us. So have the people before him for the last eighty or more years."

"Then what you are saying is that Mr. Gonzales is the Patron. Still, there are some people who vote Republican." Emanuel's rebuff was in a mild conversational tone.

"Yeah, some people vote for the Republicans. We gotta make it look good. However, we do our damnedest to convince them from messing up what we got here," the first man stated, a light caution protruding from his words.

"And we don't like the way you use the word Patron, it sounds like you're calling him a shithead or something," the third man, with ire in his voice, spoke out.

"I'm sorry, but that is a word we often use in our culture. Sometimes Its sounds hard, other times we use it affectionately."

"Well, you may use it where you come from, but not up here. It just gives the Anglos another degrading name to call us." The warning in the third man's voice became more severe.

"Again, I'm sorry. I did not mean to offend you." Emanuel Montoya's concern began to grow as the tone of the conversation grew coarser. He was alone in the area with three men, each a lot quicker and stronger than he was. His seventy years would be not a match against men twenty, maybe thirty years his junior.

"No real offense taken," the first man spoke. A warning could be heard laced within his words. "You know we don't like outsiders in this state. Well, we like 'em less up here. They're always trying to change things. Take a suggestion. Go ahead, live your life peacefully up here. You don't wanna vote with us, that's okay. We'll always get more people to do that. But, I suggest you drop your idea of an independent party. It doesn't go well around here."

Although concerned, Emanuel made another attempt to stand his ground. "Still, sir, this is a free America. Many people have died to make it so, and…"

"Big fuckin' deal," the second man exploded. "Up here we do things our way. You don't like it you can leave. Either that or join the people who keep their mouths shut around here."

Suddenly, without showing any signs of his intent, the second man picked up a rock the size of his hand and hurled it, smashing it into the headlight frame of Emanuel's Ford Bronco. The impact left the vehicle with broken glass and a dent around the frame.

"Maybe that'll give you an idea of what we're talking about."

Emanuel froze. A cold sweat overcame his outer body as a combination of shock and fear stirred inside.

"Now, now! There was no real cause for that," the first man restrained his companion. "I'm sure this gentleman knew what I was talking about without you giving him a demonstration." With that, he turned to face Emanuel. "I truly am sorry he did that, but I think you can understand how some people get worked up around here." Taking a step backward to indicate that they were bringing an end to the visit, he finished his say. "We gotta go now, other things to do. Again, I'm sorry 'bout your Bronco, and remember what I told you."

Anchored in the steps where he stood for the past few minutes, Emanuel watched with welcomed relief as the men and their Ram pickup turn onto the highway and drove back south, into the direction of Espanola.

Sergeant Joseph Cruz of the sheriff's department responded to Emanuel Montoya's complaint. He listened dispassionately to the grievance, all the while giving the old man and his wife the courtesy expected from a keeper of the peace. Later, he checked the damage to the Ford Bronco, and wrote down the details to accompany the contents of the complaint. When he felt he had sufficient data, he closed his notebook and slipped it into his back pocket.

"We will keep this information on hand in the event it's needed at a later date."

Sergeant Cruz's comment was not very fulfilling to Emanuel. It left him an uneasy feeling that this was the end of it, that the sheriff's department would not be taking any further action. He told the sheriff so.

"Well, sir, I can send you a copy of the report so you can make an insurance claim. Beyond that..." A shrug finished his sentence.

"Listen, Sergeant, the damage is one thing, but these men threatened me. You can't let them get away with that." Emanuel's demand was forceful without trying to be intimidating.

"I know how you feel sir, but without a license plate number I can't track these men down."

"But, their pickup..."

"I can't even guess at how many people in this county own red Dodge Rams. Besides, even if I did track them down, they can always file a cross complaint stating that you provoked the trouble."

"But, the damage. That should be able to provide proof."

"Who's to say you didn't have an accident and concocted the whole story," the sergeant dryly replied.

"It sounds almost as though you are taking their side." Emanuel Montoya was becoming annoyed, and he made no effort to disguise it.

"Sorry you feel that way, sir. Frankly, it's no skin off of my teeth if we wind up filing charges. However, put yourself in their boots. I know I wouldn't take a liking to someone who openly sounds off against my political beliefs."

"Hey, wait a minute, young man. Do not insult me by showing me disrespect in my home."

"That's not the way it's intended. It's just a matter of plain fact," the sheriff countered.

"I'm not the one who instigated the argument. They did."

"Your word against theirs," was the reply. "Look, Mr. Montoya, this is a big county with a small number of people. This ain't a big city like Albuquerque. Sure you got a lot of Democrats and Republicans, and even Independents down there, but up here it's different, and most people want to keep it the way it is."

"I got a right to go with my conscience," Emanuel protested. "I got a right to try to establish something where people like me can share the same ideas."

"Nobody's saying you don't have a right. You just don't do it openly. We got old values here, and our people resent people who try to change them."

Emanuel Montoya was not ready to concede. "I don't buy that. People are not robots programmed to think alike. If change is someday going to come, where people can freely act for what they believe in, then they should be free to do so."

"Maybe you're right, though I don't think so. The people are Democrats up here, and I don't see that changing. Even if a popular guy who's a Republican gets elected, he's got no choice but to do what the Democrats want. As for change, I wouldn't look for any. The Anglos who move up here are widely progressive Democrats, so they're not going to side with any Republicans. They'll simply look the other way and let us do our thing. As for the wetbacks, they'll just do as they're told. They don't want to be sent back down south."

"What are you talking about? Illegal immigrants can't vote."

"Come on now, Mr. Montoya. You're much smarter than that. Heck, they're being registered to vote all the time in places like Los Angeles, in New York. Miami. Even in Albuquerque. It's no different here."

"How can they? They're not even citizens."

"Please, Mr. Montoya. I hope I'm not giving you too much credit. In most cases, the only proof voters have to show is their driver's license. Even that's not always necessary. If someone asks the illegals for their identification, they'll simply keep coming back until they find someone who will look the other way. Most of the time they're led directly to the right people. Let me assure you, the Republicans would do the same thing, but they're not as smart. We go out and pump up these people, help them get registered. That's how we keep our party strong."

"This is unbelievable. Nonsense. Sergeant, I've heard enough, and I must now ask you to leave."

"I'll do that, sir," Sergeant Joseph Cruz complied. "If you want, I'll send you a copy of the report."

Emanuel Montoya thought for a moment before he replied. "No. Don't bother. I can see where it really won't do me any good. I'll pay for the repairs out of my own pocket."

"Fine, sir. As you wish." Sergeant Cruz opened the door, but before he left he injected another comment. "Like I said before, it would be your word against the word of those men. I guess I don't have to remind you that the same applies to our little conversation.. With that, he said 'good day' and closed the door behind him.

The Montoya's sat quietly in their living room replete of their own private thoughts. Neither had the energy to speak to the other.

Emanuel sat and contemplated, half in anger and half in angst. Although he could not fathom the contents of the dialogue, he did hear a message emanating between the sheriff's words. "Don't get involved... Don't pursue this...No one is going to help you...It's for your own good." While hashing and rehashing his thoughts, his eyes focused on his wife, absorbing the woman he loved and cherished, and needed for all of forty-five years. Age was quickly ravaging the years before them, and he knew that someday there would be the time for them to part. There may not be many years left, and as much as he needed her, he knew that her dependence upon him was even greater. She was a frail woman, and not very strong. With their children living far, far away, she would have a very difficult time surviving if she were left alone to live without him. He could not ignore this, and it prompted him into his decision.

"Come, dear. Let's make some coffee. Let's forget that this ever happened. It's not at all worth it."

10

"Well, at least they ain't gonna be able to do any development up here for a while, eh, Emilio. Still too much snow to do any diggin'," Jesus Baca nervously stated to his brother.

"Not very likely," Emilio aimlessly replied as he sat in the corner of the living room, meticulously applying a coat of wax to the stock of his Remington rifle.

Being avid deer and elk hunters, an entire section of the room stored two cabinets of fine hunting weapons, as well as a few carefully selected .45 and Glock handguns. The two brothers lived together in an old medium sized adobe left to them by their father who passed on two years before. With little to no recollection of their mother who died while each was mere grade-schoolers, Emilio and Jesus were considered as loners. They had no other relatives, and just a few friends. In reality, they only had each other.

Neither could be considered to be particularly handsome men but, unlike Jesus, Emilio was the more intelligent and the more educated man. Thought and reason defined the purposes of his life, whereas thoughtless spontaneity often dictated Jesus' action. His height and his brawn often backed up his actions. In some ways he could be Lenny playing opposite of George in Steinbeck's "Of Mice and Men." That being said, Emilio still had his perverse psychological makeup which made him similar to his brother. They both hated tourists, and the outsiders that relocated to this part of the country. They regarded these people as greedy and reckless intruders who were destroying centuries old ways of living.

The house, nestled in the rural village of Guzman and about twenty miles due north of Espanola, had six rooms, each in need of repairs. Smoke greased paneling broke its way free from the binds in most rooms of the house. The kitchen, though tidy from the every day meals cooked in it, exposed the lath and outside wall around the sink and utility areas. Still, it was the home that each envisioned would feel the warmth of their dying breaths when death kept its unknown appointment.

Money was not a main obstacle keeping them from making the repairs, for their father, Anton, left each a trust fund totaling nearly a quarter of a million dollars. Anton lived meagerly throughout his own lifetime, but when he saw that his time to depart this world neared he decided to provide for the two boys. Their earning abilities were limited, and so the monthly stipend eased the money needs. About fifty miles north spread four hundred twenty acres of pine timber, most of it standing on flat land at the foot of a mountain. The pristine forest, with a state road dividing one hundred fifty acres from the rest, remained in the Baca family for five generations. Yearly cutting of select timber furnished the meals that fed the family, but when a lodging resort sought to buy two hundred seventy acres, Anton negotiated an agreement whereby he cut and kept timber that the corporation did not need. The one hundred fifty acres on the north side of the highway remained in the family, primarily as a retreat and a place to hunt game, and to provide some timber income.

Emilio was the first to rebel against the sale, and Jesus, not one to easily follow his own path in making choices, soon joined his brother's side. To Emilio the deal was an act of betrayal. The corporation had tricked his father into giving up land that rightfully belonged within the family, paving the way for outsiders to move in. They did it in Abique and in El Rito, and in other small communities in Rio Arriba, Santa Fe, and Taos counties. Spotted development sites were always rising, and with them came the white wealth from California, Colorado, Texas, and the Midwest. They were invading his land, and he cursed them as much as he cursed other New Mexicans who sold them their land.

He looked past the wealth his people got from selling their unwanted properties at high prices, and he ignored the construction work that benefited his neighbors. He did not care about the environmental restrictions that were only for show. The presence of these outsiders, using and sharing his land, was a pollution of people he did not care to contend with. He planned on a time to come when he would take a stand, and he lamented that he knew of no one like Joseph Aragon to lead his people. He, himself, graduated from Northern New Mexico Community College, so perhaps he could learn from Santa Fe's future mayor and someday lead a revolt against the unwanted intruders. Emilio knew that the man would gladly teach him, so when Yolanda and Evonne Aragon paid the Baca home a visit later that day he could then begin to set the process rolling.

"What time are the girls comin'?" Jesus asked. He was restless, so the question was not as much of an inquiry as it was something for him to say.

Emilio looked calmly away from the rifle stock and to his brother. "When they get here," was his non-answer of a reply

For as calm of an outward demeanor often portrayed by Emilio, Jesus displayed the opposite. Calmness set itself upon him only after he made his way to bed, coming home after a night of drinking. Though they were brothers in blood, they were opposites in behavior, sharing only their love of hunting, the house they lived in, and a dislike for outsiders.

Jesus' pacing from room to room, and to the back porch, began to wear on Emilio. Over the years he witnessed the wild animal actions in his brother, and it always indicated that trouble usually preceded it.

"What happened last night?" he finally asked.

A look of surprise came over Jesus before he replied with a question of his own. "What do you mean?" Then realizing that he couldn't hide the occurrence of the night before, he changed the question to, "How did you know?"

"You told me. Every time I see you like this, you're telling me you got into some sort of trouble."

Reaching for the pot of hot coffee, Jesus recollected what his mind stored from the previous night, most of it dulled by the affects of tequila. Pouring a cup of the weak but hot brew, he blurted out, "I got into a fight last night."

He heard the story before, but Emilio sensed that the ramifications of his brother's escapade might be more serious than normal.

"Tell me about it."

"I got shitfaced, some Mexican wetback came in, started fuckin' around, so I kinda kicked the shit outa him."

It was not the entire story, and Emilio knew it.

"And…" he verbally pushed his troubled brother.

"…and I kicked him senseless. Busted up his jaw and left him out like a dead light bulb."

"Shit!" Emilio exclaimed. "How bad is he?"

"Bad 'nough," was Jesus quick reply. "I think I gave him some major damage. I don't know how bad, though, 'cause Carlos packed me into my truck an' sent me home."

"Christ…!" Emilio heaved a worried sigh. "This could really be serious."

"Shit, yeah, it's serious. I just hope the sucker doesn't file assault charges against me."

"From what you told me, you better pray your ass off that the guy ain't dead."

The comment froze Jesus. It was an idea that never crossed his mind, and Emilio could see panic settle in.

"Sit your ass down in that chair."

A fearful Jesus obeyed his brother's command and sat in the chair that Emilio pointed to.

Exhaling a deep breath, Emilio recomposed himself before he spoke. "This can be bad business, Bro. If you kick the crap outa someone, it's one thing. Odds are the cops never know about it. But, if you knock someone into a coma, or kill 'em, that's real serious shit."

Sheepishly, Jesus looked up at Emilio, imploring his more intelligent brother to tell him what he should do.

"I'm gonna give Carlos a call and find out what kind of condition the guy's really in. Beating the guy up is one thing. If it is worse than that, we gotta figure out what to do." Assessing the worried look on his brother's face, a comforting approach was needed. Pulling up a chair, Emilio placed his hand on Jesus' knee. "Look, I want you to hang low for a bit. Stay outa Espanola until we know if there's an arrest warrant out on you. Take a few days, go up to our land, and find your mind-set. Hunt a few rabbits or something, but keep away from drinking and trouble."

Mollifying his brother's concern, Jesus agreed. "I guess you're right. I'll take off tomorrow mornin'. I'll take my gear along and bunk in the cabin."

Emilio was glad to hear the words, and he nodded his head with approval. "Meantime, I can use a hand cleaning the rifles. It'll give us something to do till the girls get here."

A brisk breeze picked up, chilling the early noon sun. With the snows on the mesas and hillsides just about gone, the wind churned the loose soil, blowing it in through the window. Setting aside his rifle, Emilio rose to shut it.

"They're pulling up the driveway," he informed his brother. He could see delight in Jesus' eyes upon hearing the news, and he felt relief in knowing that the visitors' arrival would provide a welcomed distraction.

The girls brought with them treats from Burger King: whoppers, fries, and fruit pies, enough to feed several people.

"I didn't feel like you cookin' any deer meat, so I brought these. You can provide the drinks." Evonne welcomed herself in as she whisked into the house. "I hope you ain't eaten yet, 'cause Yolanda and me are hungry."

"No, just some bacon and refried beans for breakfast. They ain't fajitas or taco's, but what you got will do," Emilio replied with forced enthusiasm.

A tense atmosphere still hung heavy within the old adobe, and the girls picked up on it. After a couple of minutes, Evonne disrupted the prolonged silence, "What's wrong with you, Jesus? You don't know how to say hello?"

With a quick glance to his brother, perhaps seeking his approval to speak, or perhaps looking for him to respond, Jesus answered with a simple shrug and said, "Nothin' much."

Used to seeing a more of a hyper man who usually greeted her with a caress mixed with friendship and playfulness, Evonne could not accept his behavior. "What do ya mean, 'nothin' much'? You act as though you're on the rag. Only us women are suppose to act that way."

Sensing that Evonne might be pushing Jesus into reacting unpredictably, Emilo joined in, "Ah, he's okay. He just had a bad night with the booze."

"So, that's it. Well, crap! I've seen you tie one on many times, but you've always had enough energy to give me and Yolanda a hug. So, come on, let's have it."

This time it was Emilio who gave a quick glance. After a moment he was relieved as he watched Jesus rise, stretch out his huge arms, and beckon Evonne into them.

"That's better," Evonne said, feeling his long strong arms wrap themselves tightly around her shoulders. "Now, I think it's time you hug Yolanda."

The embracing and hugging helped to alleviate the tense air, quelling Emilio's concerns that Jesus might crack under the pressure that Evonne applied. Cans of beer were popped to wash down the whoppers and fries. Horsing around provided the ease that was shared between them. At the end of the meal, a new concern arose.

"Hey! Did you guys read about the guy who got beat up?" Evonne asked. "Seems that one of our people knocked some wetback into a coma."

Renewed tingling stirred both men. Emilio, ready to redirect the conversation, was stopped by Jesus.

"I know about it."

"You do?"

"Yeah. I put 'em that way."

The girls were stunned, as was Emilio who did not expect the admission blurted out. However, a new calm began to settle when Evonne spoke. "Good for you! That spic probably had it coming."

"I dunno, maybe he did. I was stoned at the time. But, I'm tired of these guys comin' up from down there and pretending they're one of us. Let 'em go find their own place to party."

"Amen, brother," Yolanda chimed. "The only good from them is that they take the shitty jobs we don't want. An' they're stupid enough to take whatever we pay them."

"That's gonna change someday," Emilio said, offering his view. "There'll be a day when we are gonna need them standing beside us."

"Are you sayin' that they're as good as us," the usually reserved Yolanda defended her view.

"No, that's not what I'm saying. Still, we gotta remember that our biggest problems are the Anglos. Especially the one's moving in from all over the country, stealing our land."

"You can't call what they paid your dad as stealing," Evonne opined with a touch of criticism.

"Shit, yes, I can. Even if they paid papa three hundred million dollars, it's stealing. Jesus and me were the sons of our father. That land rightfully belonged to us. Not them."

"You mean you wouldn't want all that money…" Evonne began to chide at the exaggerated amount.

"Damned right! The government would'a taken half of it when he died."

"You gotta admit, though," Evonne commented with a wistful whistle. "Three hundred mill'll buy you a lotta' fajitas."

"Yeah, it'll buy a lot of fajitas, but are how we gonna eat 'em all? Besides, you sound like you're sticking up for the Anglos."

"Sticking up for them…ha!" she responded with a bit of mockery. "All I want from those white niggars is their money. After that, screw 'em. Let them go back to where they come from."

"You got that right," Jesus agreed.

"You better be careful," Evonne cautioned Jesus. "According to the papers, nobody's saying who beat the guy. That doesn't mean somebody won't turn."

"That's basically what I've been thinking," Emilio said. "That's why I've told him to lay low for a few days."

"Maybe Jesus should go spend time with the Ayala guys up in Tierra Amarilla," Yolanda suggested.

"No," Emilio said as he squashed the option. "It's better he do some camping, like Jesus and I talked about. This way I know he'll stay outa trouble."

Jesus' immediate fate was decided. Emilio wanted to keep his brother solo, and away from others that could influence his behavior.

He went on to explain. "I want to minimize getting involved with fellow brothers like the Ayala and Luna families. They're good people, but we can't have everybody partying and getting messed up right now. We gotta stay cool 'cause we're gonna come down and support your ol' man's campaign. Then, we got the rally for Mondragon to attend in June."

"You know, I think it's great that you're supporting my pa, but I think this Mondragon guy is gonna get nowhere with his separatist movement." Evonne, being more of a pragmatist, could not convince herself to enthusiastically support Anotnio Jose Mondragon and his movement urging the formation of a Hispanic nation. Although she agreed with him, she did not believe that Mondragon could ever be successful in his goal.

Well before the birth of La Raza, and ever since the insurrection at the courthouse in Tierra Amarilla in June of 1967, Mondragon earned his reputation of pushing for the separation of American and Hispanic cultures and establishing a new sovereign nation to be called The Hispanic Republic. It would be aligned with the already fledgling of a group known as the Republica del Norte. Territory wise, it would range from the east beginning with all of the Texas communities bordering the Rio Grande. It would work westward to include all of New Mexico, Arizona, and California. Northwards, it would encompass the Texas Panhandle, Southern Colorado, Southern Utah, and the southern tip of Nevada to included Las Vegas and the Hoover Dam. Mexico was not spared from the partitioning since they would have to concede Baja California, Chiuahua, Coahuila, Nuevo Leon and Senora. The dream would be to form a homeland where the Hispanic culture would be preserved, and only the Spanish language would be recognized.

When asked how he hoped to obtain the reality of such a nation, he explained that he would create an infusion of all Hispanics, led by those of Mexican decent, into the outlined territories. There they will be able to devote themselves to their heritage and to their language without any outside interference. When advised that radio, television, and other forms of communication might pose a problem to such a design, Mondragon flatly stated, "I do not foresee any such problems. We will be controlling all forms of communications."

Many within the Hispanic communities debunked the notion of a separate nation. While many simply regarded it as a scheme for one man's ambition for fame, others were outspoken with their abhorrence of Mondragon's quest. Most, throughout the entire southwest and the west, regarded it as a move backward in their part of civilization. They sought recognition of their heritage, and while there were still many walls to scale, they saw these opportunities expanding. Some totally dismissed Mondragon, proclaiming themselves as Americans, and like many other groups, it was recognition that being an American was foremost to their ethnic or cultural background. As one newly Americanized Mexican explained, "My family never had these opportunities in Mexico. I am not worried about my culture because I honor and respect it. No outside force can destroy it. A culture's death can only come from within. If my children choose to someday ignore it, it will be for them to decide. I pray they'll choose to preserve it, but I cannot and will not force them. To do so, to make them believe in what does not appeal to them, would be violating their freedom. That is not the reason I brought them into this country."

Yet, Antonio Jose Mondragon drew many idolizers, with Joseph Aragon being one of them. Emilio and Jesus were others. Others were sprinkled throughout central and Northern New Mexico. All would someday be the kindling to a new revolution, a revolution that would spawn a new homeland where the harvesting of old traditions, of a mentality dating back many centuries, can be reborn and spread.

"It will not happen overnight," Emilio conceded, "but within ten, or at most twenty years, we can reclaim the land which is rightfully ours."

Antonio Jose Mondragon occupied thoughts of another. Ruben Gonzales was daunted by the 'revolutionary' ever since the latter's slow rise to prominence began. Neither man took part in the armed takeover of the courthouse in Tierra Amarilla almost a half-century ago. In the background, both men chided the New Mexico State Government when it called in the National Guard to quell the growing violence. Gonzales, on the other hand, used it as a blessing in disguise as he seized upon the opportunity of being a peacemaker in the ordeal that lasted several days. At the time, he was a new state representative. After the next election he became a state senator whose aim was to become governor.

Appeasement, resulting in the taking of an outward stand against developers and wealthy out-of-towners earned him the love of those who, at all costs, wanted to preserve their land from change. The same appeasement ran into disfavor with the clout behind progress, and ruined his ultimate political goal. Accepting the small defeat, Gonzales made the most of his senatorial seat, gaining chairmanship of the agricultural committee that most affected his constituents. Through tenure, he gained and wielded major influence throughout the senate and the state, but very little of his gains trickled down enough to improve the lives of the people who voted for him.

Though their immediate goals were similar, the end objectives were not. Mondragon wanted control of a new nation; Gonzales wanted control of his and his neighboring counties. Under the leadership of a man like Mondragon, no room existed for the kind of control that Gonzales possessed.

Over the years, Ruben Gonzales came to assess Antonio Jose Mondragon as a threat. A silent adversarial relationship grew during that time, and while he seriously doubted that Mondragon's dream would ever meet with reality, Gonzales concluded that whatever dreams came to fruition would have to be dealt with. If not the man's dreams, then the man himself.

"We are less than a mile away from Miguel Martinez's home," Tommy Trujillo said, knowing that he was interrupting the private thoughts of his boss.

Ruben Gonzales nodded his acknowledgement. He pushed the button to lower the car window, and dropped his unlit cigar from it. "This meeting should take less than a half hour."

"No problem," Tommy replied. "I have pretty much all day."

The Cadillac eased its way into the driveway and parked in front of Miguel Martinez's old, but carefully kept home. Apple orchards covered over an acre of the property, while peach, plum, apricot, and cherry trees covered the other two acres. A small vegetable patch used for family meals lay to the right of the house. The fruit trees provided a meager income to the household.

"The Agriculture Department has prohibited the use of the chemicals I used to kill the bugs attacking my trees," Martinez began. "I don't know what we are going to do if we have another bad crop like last year."

Sipping the hot coffee Mrs. Martinez served him; Gonzales studied the concern on the orchard farmer's face. "I know what you mean," he said with sympathy emanating from his voice. "As you know, I tried to get the ban lifted, but those Green Party folks put up a pretty big fight. They even had the governor on their side."

"I know, and I thank you, Mr. Gonzales, but…"

Miguel Martinez went on to tell his beloved state senator of other plights he and his fellow farmers faced, plights that Gonzales knew a lot about, the majority of which either met defeat or were tabled by the agriculture committee.

"…I am sorry, Mr. Gonzales. I should not be bending your ear with all of our problems. I'm sure there are lots of other things you have to worry about."

"Think nothing of it," Gonzales said, humbly comforting the elderly orchard grower. "You elected me as your senator. The least I can do is to listen to your concerns. Listening helps me to find ways to better serve you."

"Thank you, sir," Martinez replied with a bowed head.

Both Gonzales and Trujillo rose, signaling the end of the visit. After all-around handshakes, they were escorted to their car by their hosts.

"I saw what you did back there," Tommy Trujillo commented as they drove back into Espanola. "Leaving fifty bucks on the table like that. They must believe that you have a heart of gold."

"Don't I?" Gonzales smiled, testing to see Trujillo's reaction.

"Well...you must have. I don't know how many times in the past I've seen you do the same thing."

"Think about it, my good friend. What is Miguel Martinez going to remember more? What I did not do for him in the senate, or the fifty dollars I left for him on his table."

11

Having a spontaneous change of mind on Wednesday night, Mike decided to scrap the rump roast menu and instead treat his guests to his Italian cooking. Disturbing a butcher friend of his, he picked the man up, drove him to his shop, picked out the veal cutlets, prime ground beef, and some beef neck bones. He paid handsomely for the meat, not so much because he imposed himself on his friend, but because the quality was the best and not available at any supermarket in Santa Fe. As far as his friend was concerned, fulfilling Mike's off-hour request was a grateful repayment for all of the business Mike steered his way. By midnight the veal was placed in the refrigerator to marinate in his special sauce. In the morning he would call his Italian friend, a recent transplant from New York's Little Italy, and order his favorite homemade pasta.

After spending half his life in New Mexico, Mike still longed for the special cooking so notable in New York. He greatly enjoyed the New Mexican dishes, but when it came to Italian food the state took a back seat. Even the best of New Mexico's Italian restaurants only faired a bit better than New York's poorest. And, there was nothing like his own home cooking.

The one thing Mike continued to miss was authentic Italian bread, with its sesame covered crip exterior and delicate white inside. Real Italian pizza, New York style, was another treat he missed dearly, but only a visit back to Brooklyn or Manhattan would ever satiate the hunger. He shied far away from national chains, turned off both by their poor imitation of pizza and their stupidity of not being able to pronounce the Italian ingredients correctly. **M_azz_arella**? What the hell was that? It's as a cow would say…M**oo**…as in M**o**zzarella. Simply pronounce it the way it's spelled. Damn those Hollywood and Madison Avenue pretensious intellects.

"How does an Irishman ever learn to make such excellent Italian food?" Eduardo Guiterrez complimented Mike.

"It's all in the luck of where I grew up. Mostly an Italian neighborhood, my pop married an Italian girl. and I learned about cooking from her."

"I grew up in the Midwest, and I can say that I've never had anything this good," Sam Dawes said, joining in with the accolades.

"If only all husbands could cook this way," Margarette said as she turned and teased her husband.

"I make good hamburgers. You and the girls always gobble them up," Cap barbed back.

"Big deal! You flatten out some ground beef and slap it on the grill. And, that's only in the summer. I should send you over here and have Mike give you some cooking lessons."

"Please! Everybody…" Teri chimed in, "…stop! You give Mike any more praise and I won't be able to live with him."

Only Francesca, who was seated alongside of Sam, remained quiet. Feeling a bit shy in unfamiliar surroundings, she let her pleasant face speak for her. While everyone else overlapped each other talking about the fine food, it was Sam who prodded her into speaking.

"Have you ever tasted such good food?"

"I've had Italian food, but nothing like this. The sauce is so rich, and the meat…it is out of this world."

Overhearing the small conversation between Francesca and Sam, Teri joined in. "I'm glad you enjoyed it. Do you cook?"

"A little, but nothing like this," Francesca admitted.

"You'd be surprised how easy it is for Mike. All the preparations don't really take much, it's the slow simmering that really takes long. If you want, you can come over someday and I'll have Mike give you the full recipe. Then you can try making it at home, and maybe you can use Sam as a guinea pig."

Allowing for herself to be interrupted by Margarette, Teri refocused her attention hoping that she may have dropped a seed. A little red, Francesca did not know what to say. Sam did come to her rescue.

"Teri means well, but she knows that I'm a bachelor so she always tries to get someone to cook for me."

Something about Sam's voice had a comforting quality to it, easing Francesca's mild embarrassment. It even provoked her to make a comment that almost made her feel red again, this time by her own words.

"I'm sure you don't have to worry. You probably have a lot of women cooking for you."

"No, I don't really," Sam casually replied. "It's me…I'm the one who usually does the cooking."

"Oh?"

"Yes…hamburgers, hot dogs, sometimes a quick steak."

A smile came across Francesca's face as she thought Sam's way of commenting to be cute. Flippant perhaps, but cute. It set the stage for their private conversations for the rest of the evening, nothing serious, just an occasional give and take at each other's attempt at being friendly.

The main course of the dinner was complete, and the coffee and cheesecake was the next course, Margarette helped Teri bus the table, and Francesca felt obliged to assist.

"No, no, no, Francesca," Teri scolded her. "You're a first time guest. The next time you can help. For now, you go inside and join the men with the chitchat. I'm sure they'll be talking business which most likely is of interest to you."

Francesca started to protest, feeling that she should at least do something in payment for a fine dinner. The look on Teri's face told her not to, that her hostess would be pleased to see her join in the conversations that were bound to follow. With Mike and Cap already relaxing in the two lounge chairs, she sat on the sofa with Sam.

"Tessa called this afternoon to say that he can't join me on my trip to Window Rock," Mike began.

"So you'll be going up by yourself Monday?" Sam asked.

"Yep. No problem. I figure about a three-hour drive each way and maybe two or three hours in Window Rock. If I leave here about five in the morning, I should be back by the middle of the afternoon."

"Sounds like a long day," Sam said.

"Nah. On these roads it'll be a breeze. It sure would have been nice to have Tessa along as company, though. What's he got going on?" Mike's question was directed at Francesca.

"Several things…a rape, two separate brutal assaults, and a robbery. Plus he has a deadline on some reports due for the chief."

"Jeez! This keeps up and you're gonna have to hire more assistants," Mike directed his comment to Sam.

"Not in the budget," Sam said flatly. "Only if the state legislature allocates the funds, and that wouldn't be until next February when they go back into session."

"We sure as hell have a back-ass way of doing things in this state." Cap's openly critical comment was not characteristic of him, usually reserving the thoughts to himself. As a native, a New Mexican comes to think of the state as something special and through whatever faults, the state usually found the right way. But as one gets to know it, one eventually gets to know the politics. He then sees the flaws created by the demagoguery of those in power. Within time even an objective witness, one who studies the preaching of the demagogues, finds his own views become tainted.

Cap, although not a student of the arts, was always taken in by the words once stated by New Mexico's adopted acclaimed artist, Georgia O'Keeffe. When asked why she always painted landscapes instead of people, she replied, "I came here for the scenery, not for the people." At times, Cap felt the same way. He loved the beauty that the Land of Enchantment had to offer…the vistas, the sense of peace and tranquility…but, it was people who left it scarred and disrupted. He did love his fellow meek, gentle, and passive New Mexicans, but to him it was their passivity that condoned the crimes of the few, marring the good of others.

In his mind, the people had to adjust their way of thinking, but Cap doubted that this would ever come to pass in his lifetime.

"I think I know what you mean," the other native New Mexican, Francesca empathized.

Teri and Margarette served coffee inside the living room. Place mats were set out on the coffee tables, and neither Teri nor Mike ever even hinted at having the after dinner dessert in the dinning room. The living room was just what the name implied – a room to live in. Whatever crumbs or spillage that occurred could easily be cleaned.

"What do you guys have on William Johnson?" Sam began.

"You mean in the way of drugs?" Cap asked, seeking clarification.

"Yes."

Cap and Mike exchanged glances, and it was Mike who answered.

"In a word, nothing! Everybody knows he's got his fingers in the funny business, but nobody can get enough on him to nail him. Our guess is that he might be going upscale with the new gallery."

"Do you think Joseph Aragon has a hand in it? It seems strange that he suddenly changed his stand on issuing a permit."

"I don't think so," Cap answered. "Aragon's been around for a long time, and he's never been associated with drugs. He's a misguided troublemaker who thinks he's helping people by attacking outsiders. His forte is unrest. A guy like him doesn't suddenly get involved with drugs, especially if his past records show him to be as clean as it is."

"Then why did he change his vote?" Sam pressed on.

"Most likely pressure from one of his supporters," Cap replied.

"Who?"

"Who else? Ruben Gonzales," Mike offered his opinion. "The man has made a lot of money by backing deals. Don't take me wrong, the guy doesn't get his hands dirty, but there isn't a deal that goes down up here that doesn't have his blessing."

"I also think he's broadening his base," Cap added. "Within the next couple of years he is going to be forced completely out of politics, and as a result he is going to loose a lot of power. It's something the man thrives on."

"Too bad you can't nab him at it," Francesca said.

"I wish we could," Mike agreed.

"I'm afraid we may never do that. I can think of only one way to weaken him a bit," Cap said.

"What's that?" Francesca asked.

"Keep legalizing marijuana."

"What!" a stunned Sam said with a bit of incredulity in his tone.

"Hey, don't look at me," Mike laughed. "My boss and I have different opinions on this matter."

"Mike's right, we do," Cap said. "The way I look at it, it might do some good."

"How?" Francesca asked, never quite sure of her own stand on the issue. She welcomed someone else's thoughts.

"Let's look at all the losses," Cap began. "Literally thousands of lives every year are lost because of drug deals that have gone sour.

"There is also the corruption angle. People in politics, law enforcement, and the every day John Doe, are being tempted by easy money. Then there's the Feds who keep it as a high priority issue, won't even relax their stand when it comes to using it for medicinal purposes. For now, I think we should let state laws prevail. Let's wait four or five years to analyze the outcome, and we can make adjustments and changes from there.

"And, there's resources. The Mexican mobs are getting rich pushing it across our borders. Legalize it, and we slash their profits drastically. We spend billions of dollars a year in a losing war trying to break marijuana trafficking, taking away what we need to combat the cocaine and heroin trade. Think, also, about our prisons and that every year we incarcerate well over a hunkred thousand marijuana users."

"Someone on marijuana can kill you while driving a car," Sam said, injecting his opinion.

"So does someone on alcohol. It's the old argument. When I say legalizing, I also mean regulating it. We regulate alcohol, and we can regulate grass."

"Still, that brings us to the addiction factor," Sam Argued.

"Tell me something, Sam, and be honest. Have you ever smoked a joint?"

"Yes, I have."

"Once? Five? Ten or more times?"

"Ten or more times, but none in the last several years."

"You never became addicted?"

"No, I haven't."

"Has it ever led you, or anyone you know of, to use other drugs?"

"Me, no. A couple of other people I know, no. As far as others, I don't know."

"There are differences of opinion on addiction in the medical community. Then again, people become addicted to alcohol, which is legal. Quite a few of them wind up straying to hard core drugs."

"I'm curious. How does your feeling affect your job?" Francesca asked.

Cap took a deep breath before he replied. The question did deserve an honest answer.

"As long as marijuana is illegal, it's my job to uphold the law. However, I will admit that when I have to choose between directing my resources on a marijuana bust or on a coke or heroin bust, I put coke and heroin as the priority."

Exchanges of ideas on law and crime, and of politics, carried on for a couple of more hours before Margarette came in to break things up.

"Eduardo, dear, we've got to get going. I promised our babysitter's mother that we'd have her home early."

Like a respectful husband, Cap rose from his seat and kissed his wife on the cheek. "You're right. I have to get up early and do the garage work I promised to do."

"Why can't you be like that?" Teri teased Mike.

"Sure. But, you've got to build me a garage first," Mike playfully replied. Noticing that Sam and Francesca started to stir, Mike stopped them. "You guys just sit where you are. Just because my henpecked boss has gotta leave, doesn't mean you got to. Finish your coffee first."

With the night still being relatively early the two remaining guests heeded Mike's invite. After Cap and Margarette were gone Teri took to Cap's chair, but she was content to just listen in on the others' conversation.

"You two should get together soon and review some of those open files," Mike suggested. There was a hint in his voice that getting together should be more than for professional reasons. If either Sam or Francesca caught it they chose to ignore it.

"As a matter of fact, Francesca and I were talking about it before," Sam answered. "She's coming up to my office on Monday."

"Good, I'm glad to hear that. With Francesca on board, maybe you guys can get somewhere. It'll take at least a monkey or two off our backs."

"Tell me, Mike...." Francesca prodded "...give me you gut reaction on the female deaths."

"It's a little hard to give you a anything solid, aside from what we went over the other day. However, my gut reaction is that everything wraps up too tightly to connect all of the deaths together."

"What do you mean?"

"On every case, that's to include the newer Becaud one, each little piece seems to match pieces on the others too neatly."

"You're saying that one or two might possibly be copycats...?" Francesca asked.

"Uh, uh. I'm not saying that's happened, but I am suggesting it." Mike paused for a moment to group his thoughts. "The big trouble is, these cases are spread out over several years, and they've been bounced around from your department to ours and back again. Sorry to say, even with our more advanced technology, we haven't had the sufficient manpower to help you guys out. However, with your experience on board, there might be a chance in solving them."

"Can you give me any suggestions?"

"You're doing step one by reviewing all the files. As I said before, there's a large time period involved. I, for one, was never on the investigating scene of any of the murders. So, for step two, I'd suggest that you interview all of the investigating officers that were on the prior ones. There's always the possibility one of them may recall something that never got into the files."

It was Sam's turn to smile. "You know, I'm embarrassed to say this, but that is something I haven't thought of."

"Don't sweat it," Mike said. "You've only been on the job for several weeks. You've barely had time to get your feet wet, especially with all the other things you've got to contend with as DA." Then with a little friendly jab, Mike added, "To top it off, you're not a cop in the true sense of the word. Francesca and I…our noses have been trained to sniff out things lawyers don't even think of."

Midnight tolled in a new day, and both Sam and Francesca were ready to leave. Mike and Sam escorted her to her car. She said goodnight to Sam and thanked Mike and Margarette for the wonderful evening, then turned the ignition to be on her way. The key turned, the generator cranked, but the engine did not start. After a couple of more tries she got out of the car feeling frustrated.

"Now what?" she moaned.

"Don't look at me, I'm a klutz when it comes to fixing cars," Mike confessed. "Maybe Sam knows something."

Feeling slightly embarrassed, Sam admitted to his own lack of automotive knowledge.

"I'll tell you what," Mike came up with a quick idea. "Sam, why don't you drive Francesca home. I've a neighbor who's an expert. I'll have him look at it in the morning."

"But…" Francesca started to protest.

"Sam doesn't know anything about cars, and I don't. So unless you're able to fix it, take my advice and let Sam drive you. Don't worry, I've driven with him and he's safe."

Convinced that it was the best alternative, Francesca again said good night and drove off with Sam. After watching the taillights of Sam's car turn a distant corner, Mike turned to Teri who came out to join him.

"Come on, kid. It's cool out here. Let's go inside where it's nice and warm."

"What are you going to do about that poor woman's car?"

"Oh, that. Don't worry about it. I'll reconnect the distributor cap in the morning."

"I would never think that someone like Mike could be such a good cook." Francesca still felt the delightful comfort of a meal eaten a few hours before.

"Yeah," Sam agreed. "He even has a magical touch with something as simple as a steak. To think, all I'm really good at are hamburgers and franks."

"You're really serious. You can't cook, can you?"

"Stop by sometime, and I'll prove it."

Francesca reflected on her own life style as a single woman. There were many evenings when a day's work made her feel like eating nothing at all, but she usually did find the energy to at least make a salad. Her morning meal usually consisted of a yogurt and later a doughnut, and her lunches consisted mostly of salads, tacos, or hamburgers. She concluded that in some ways her eating habits were not much different than Sam's.

"You know, we both can improve our diets," she advised.

"Maybe so," Sam conceded. "Looking at you, you seem very trim and fit. I assume that you take care of yourself."

"Why, thank you Mr. Dawes. That was a nice thing to say."

"Well, you can always return the compliment and say the same thing about me."

They sat quietly for the next few blocks until they approached Francesca's home.

"Take a right at the next corner. The house will be the third one on the left," Francesca directed her chauffeur.

Sam pulled into her driveway before he asked, "You working tomorrow?"

"I am, providing my car's okay. I'm going in late in the morning just to catch up on some things. And you?"

"Naw. I'm staying home, but I have a ton of work on the computer." Pausing for a moment, he finally spoke up. "We were talking about eating right before. How would you like to join me at the El Dorado for brunch on Sunday? They serve a wonderful buffet with champagne. You might enjoy it."

Giving him at first a sideways glance, she then turned to fully face him. "You know, that sounds like a fine idea. It'll give me a chance to try some nicer restaurants in town."

"Oh, this is a fine place. Good food, with an eye appealing layout."

"Okay. We'll see you Sunday then."

They set the time that Sam would pick her up, and he drove off on his way.

An interesting man, Francesca let her mind wonder as she unlocked the door. *I'm interested in what he really has to say about those cases when we meet Monday. I can probably probe for information on Sunday, but I won't. I'll just enjoy the brunch and, if he wants to, he can bring up the subject. I hope he doesn't, after all I don't want to talk business on what I think is a date.*

A sharp woman, and attractive, Sam thought as he drove home. *Maybe I shouldn't be getting together with her like this. What the hell, though. Just so long as we don't talk any business.*

12

Setting the cruise control on eighty-five once he was west of Albuquerque, Mike Shannon glided along Interstate 40 towards Gallup. He was in an unmarked Chevy Capri, so to play safe, he radioed ahead to warn his fellow officers that he'd be flying through. The roads were usually clear in the early morning hours, and except for a heavily loaded semi tractor-trailer that might pick a hill to pass another slower moving semi, the roads would remain unimpeded until he reached Gallup. He could remedy any slow moving traffic in the left lane by flicking on his alternating head beams, forcing the wrong lane driver to the right. He humored himself when he thought about the chronic problem the state has with drivers moving slowly in the left lane. It was like having an unwritten law in New Mexico which stated: slow moving traffic must keep left.

Mike liked speed, but his continuous awareness of road conditions kept him a safe driver. Yet he often wondered how many times he would have been written up if he were not a cop. That is not to imply that he never got pulled over while in his own car, something that happened a few times over the years. Most of the state cops, and quite a number of sheriff or reservation cops knew him, so that solved most of the problems. Showing his badge and identification, with a quick explanation, convinced the others that he was one of their own and that a citation was not in order. More often than not it never got that far. A license check by the pursuing officer identified Mike, prompting a wagging finger accompanied with a grin, as his only punishment.

Reaching Gallup in less than three hours, he headed north. About fourty miles later he turned west toward Window Rock that is but a few miles past the Arizona/New Mexico state line. Driving these northerly miles was cautiously slower. The two lane roads were not in the best of repair, and the drivers were usually ones who had no particular place to go with a focus only on the immediate road ahead. Never sure of what to anticipate from others on these roads, an aware driver learned to increase his attention for any unpredictable turn without signals, unexpected slowdowns, or sudden stops. These people needed some form of transportation to get from point A to point B, but it did not keep Mike from rationalizing that New Mexico would give anybody a driver's license, including someone who is blind.

The reservation office of the Navajo Police for Window Rock stood off to the side of the road. Not wanting to waste any more time than necessary by taking in the landscape of the local surroundings, Mike entered the building, pulled out his identification, and asked to see the police chief.

"So, you're the Mike Shannon I've heard so much about. Come on in. Come in and have some coffee." Police Chief Daniel Sanchez greeted Mike with genuine interest.

With his usually brilliant smile, Mike walked up to his colleague, shook his hand and said, "Thanks, I'd love some. I hope what you've heard about me wasn't all bad."

"Bad? Hell, no." Sanchez spoke as he released his tight grip from the handshake. "Hell, you've got a reputation, even up here. It is all good."

The reservation cop was not buttering up his visitor just to make him feel good, and his comments were sincere. After pushing two decades on the New Mexico State Police force, Mike did build up a honorable reputation that transcended not only all of New Mexico, but also with cops along the border lines of Arizona, Colorado, and Texas.

"You might not remember me," Sanchez went on to inform Mike. "But, I remember you from about eight or nine years ago when you were stationed in Gallup. That was before they got smart and promoted you to sergeant."

A sense of familiarity began to be recognized by Mike. Speaking to Sanchez, he knew that he met the man before, but he had to honestly confess that he did not remember the circumstances or the occasion.

"But, I remember very well. One of our people got mixed up in a vehicular homicide investigation in Gallup, and since he was here when the complaint was filed, we got involved in the investigation. I was the investigating officer representing the reservation, and I must say, that out of all the New Mexican cops, you were the most helpful. In fact, the info you gave us helped us to exonerate the man."

"Jeez, I can barely remember that. What you've told me is just now beginning to jog my memory."

"Well, I can remember, and I really appreciated it," Sanchez said as he handed Mike a cup of coffee. "Now, it's time to reciprocate. So tell me, how can I be of help to you?"

Mike sat back in the comfort of the chair and relaxed as he gave details of the Monsignor Serrano death. From the beginning to the end, a clear picture formed from his oral accounts of the murder and of the ensuing investigation, which led up to the reason for his presence.

"After Cornelius Toohey was released into your custody, one of the city cops remembered seeing a stole, a priest's sacramental ribbon, among the personal items belonging to Toohey. I think you'd agree that it's a strange item for a layman to carry around, and we'd like to question him about it."

"I see your point, and by all means, I think you should question him. Fortunately, you don't have to go far to do that. Our cells are right behind my office walls."

"Great!"

"I'll have him brought to the interrogation room." After a brief pause, the police chief asked, "Do you mind if I sit in? He might be more responsive with one of his own people present."

Without any hesitation, Mike agreed. He knew that it went a little beyond being helpful to a fellow cop, for despite the good regard the head of the reservation police may have had for him, it was certain that he did not want a bum rap pinned on one of his own. In the police chief's shoes, Mike admitted to himself that he would do the same thing.

The interrogation room was basically just an office with a desk, a table, and a couple of chairs, and no two-way mirrors or intercom system as would be expected to be found in larger police stations. Reservation crimes were mostly excessive drinking, altercations, and some occasional thefts. From time to time there were trespassing arrests, usually by non-Native Americans unfamiliar with the reservation laws. Rarely was the room needed for more serious matters such as the one that brought Mike there.

Cornelius Toohey was seated in front of Mike, facing the glass of the southerly exposed window where a white glare shone through. Daniel Sanchez stood in a corner to the right of the window as an observer.

"Man, from what I heard, you really turned one on in Santa Fe."

Toohey looked to Sanchez, quietly seeking his advice. The police chief answered with a stoic silence.

"You don't have to worry about that, though," Mike continued in a light casual manner. "From what they told me, you're a happy drunk. Shi…it, before I joined the force, I had a few of those nights. Heck, one night I got so bad a cop found me with my head in a trash barrel. When he asked me what I was doing, I told him…puking. At least, that's what he claims happened. I was too shit-faced to remember."

Mike could see a thin smile etched on the young Indian's face. It cued him to ease further on with his questioning.

"From what I learned about that night, you probably don't remember much about it, either."

Toohey answered with a slight shrug of his shoulders.

"Do you remember if you were drinking solo, or perhaps you were with some friends?"

This time Toohey did answer verbally. "I remember startin' off with a couple of friends of mine."

"And…did you guys hang out together all night?"

"Nah, we met up with some of the local girls. Didn't know 'em, but they were okay."

"Ah, so you partied with them. Get lucky?"

"Heck, no…at least I don't think so. They were some locals, an' they invited us to a local get together."

Eyeing Toohey, Mike shook his head with disbelief, all the while keeping his broad smile. "Jeez…I don't believe it. You don't even remember if you got laid. Man, you must'a been blitzed."

"Yeah, I was out of it."

Mike decided to steer his questioning into a different direction. "Tell me, Cornelius, are you a religious man?"

It was now the interrogated's time to smile. "Me?" Toohey said with almost a laugh. "Hell! I don't even believe in the native mumbo-jumbo. Just ask this guy here, he'll tell you how holy I am."

Mike allowed himself to join in on the levity. While doing so, he observed how much at ease Toohey had become. The question of being religious did not faze him in the manner Mike was looking for. It prompted him to ask a more direct question, but still with a relaxed approach.

"So you're not religious. Ever have any friends that are religious?"

"Nah, I try stayin' away from those kinds. They usually start preachin', tellin' ya you must become a Jesus freak, to quit drinkin', and all that crap."

"I think I know what you mean," Mike pretended to agree. "So, I guess it wouldn't be likely you made friends with any ministers or priests."

"You gotta be kiddin'," Toohey replied with some laughter behind it. "No way one of those guys and I would get along. No, can't say I ever even spoke to one of them."

Mike took in the response, noting that the man still showed no signs of being fazed, and it answered some questions he had about Toohey. He pressed on a bit more.

"You ain't even talked to one?"

"That's right."

"Tell me something, Cornelius. When you were picked up, you had a priest's stole on you."

"Stole? What's that?" There was no observable change in his demeanor.

"Stole? It's something priests use when administering sacraments. It's like a ribbon, purple…"

"Yeah! Now I know what you're talkin' about. Matter of fact, Sanchez here has it locked up with my other personal stuff."

The reply caused Mike to raise an eyebrow. "Oh? If you don't mind, tell me where you got it?"

"From one of the girls."

"What girls?"

"You know. One of the bimbos I met up with the night I got busted."

The answers were forming in Mike's mind, but he did not want to jump to conclusions, so he still pressed on.

"You say one of the girls gave it to you. Tell me, why do you think she did that?"

"I saw it sticking out of her sack, and I liked the purple color and asked her about it. She took it out, showed it to me, an' said she had it for a while. She saw that I really dug it, and so she gave it to me."

"Did she say where she got it?"

"Nah, an' I never thought about askin'."

"I see." Mike did understand. Only a couple of more questions remained. "By any chance, do you remember the girl's name?"

"Remember her name? No way! Heck, I wouldn't even recognize her if she was standin' right beside you."

The response was understandable, Mike concluded. The guy was wiped out on booze, so it was reasonable that Cornelius Toohey could draw blanks while recalling his memory.

"By any chance, is there anything you can remember?"

"Nah. That night's only a foggy vision."

"Well, that's about all I can think of asking you," Mike rose while he spoke, and while doing so he reached to shake Toohey's hand. "You've been a lotta help. Thanks."

Taken aback by Mike's cordiality, Toohey could only reach out his hand in response and say, "No problem, man."

"Say, maybe you can do me a favor. Do you mind if I take the stole with me?"

With a curious expression, Toohey eyed Mike. After a brief moment he replied, "Sure, why not. Listening to your questions, it seems you need it more than me."

"Thanks, I appreciate it."

A few minutes later, after Cornelius Toohey was escorted out of the room and back to his cell, Daniel Sanchez asked his own questions.

"You get what you needed?"

"After I get the stole, I will."

"I mean with the kid. He tell you anything that was revealing?"

Mike gave a quick mental assessment, enabling himself to reach a conclusion. Cornelius Toohey was open, frank, and he gave absolutely no indication of being thrown off guard by any of the questions thrown his way.

Again smiling, Mike answered the police chief's question. "Yeah. It's safe to say that he is at the bottom of my suspects' list."

A pit stop, a bite to eat, and refueling lay ahead before returning home. The first two he would take care of in Gallup at a restaurant favored by cops, and a place where he might run into a couple of old familiar faces. It served as good relations to get some first hand input, even if it was a hundred and ninety miles away from the center of things. He would add to that input when he stopped off for gas at the Gallup state police facilities at the east end of the city.

Various topics would occupy his mind during the return trip, but the Monsignor Serrano case took up most of it. It may have been easier if Cornelius Toohey turned out to be 'the man'. After spending about forty minutes questioning him, Mike became convinced that the young Native American, with a penchant for trouble after over imbibing, was just an added spoke in the wheel. What it did do, helped. Even if it added another spoke, assuming that the stole belonged to the priest, Mike now had a piece of physical evidence. What use it might be, he wasn't sure. But, at least it was something.

Mike also had a fraction more of information in the form of a some of girls, with one young woman in particular. She was a local, meaning

Hispanic in New Mexican jargon. If, as Toohey claimed, she gave it to him then the question shifted to, where did she get it? No stole was found among the priest's personal affects at the crime scene, yet several weeks later some girl turns up with one. What are the chances of that happening? Better yet, he wondered what the odds were that this baby belonged to Serrano. He let his mind search farther before he concluded that the best bet was, if they found the girl they may wind up finding the killer. One big question remained. Who the hell was she?

13

In Santa Fe, Francesca only had to travel three miles to meet with Sam Dawes at the District Attorney's office and begin their first day of actually 'doing business' with each other. Their conversations during the Sunday afternoon brunch managed to completely elude cases of murder, of holding down an elected office, of contending with political hacks, or of making adjustments with a new major job at a new location. They did, each in their own way, use their professional interrogating skills to delve into the more personal aspects of each other's private life. If either of them became suspicious of the other's subtle questions, neither of them let on.

The brunch date was genuinely a quiet and relaxing Sunday get-together, and the food at the El Dorado was exactly as Sam promised... all prepared to appeal to the eye as well as to the palate. Afterwards, they took to the patio where she sipped on wine and he on cognac. The mild outside air teased at an early spring while the man and the woman found ways to tease at each other, at times subtle and at times overt, but at no time would either admit as to where it all could lead.

A stroll through The Plaza, and past the Palace of the Governors where all of the history of New Mexico is kept, took them up to the historic end of Old Santa Fe Trail.

Turning right at the corner where the old and famous La Fonda hotel stands, took them past the centuries old Lorreto Chapel with its haunted spiral staircase. They crossed Alameda and the Agua Fria until they reached the narrow DeVargas Street. Another right took them past an old adobe community theater, and then to Gallisteo Street where the state law offices and other state building sit, all standing out in bold antiquity for all the visitors to see. One more right again took them across the ancient Agua Fria with its faintly flowing stream, shielded on both sides by manicured firs. They walked back to San Francisco Street, taking them past more quaint shops and galleries, a multi-purpose movie theater, and finally to the underground parking in the El Dorado Hotel. It capped a small sightseeing tour.

Francesca had taken in the Santa Fe sights several times in the past, but never with her own personal tour guide. Sam over the years learned a lot about his adopted city, so he managed to fill her in with historical information she never knew before. There was much more to be seen in the small hub of the city, but he would save that for another time.

The evening ended early as the sun began to set, both agreeing that they were to meet at his office the following day. Neither gave any indication of prolonging the day, both acknowledging quietly that a step had been taken, and that others may follow.

"I'll be at your office at ten in the morning. We can then get started," Francesca said as she eased out of Sam's car.

"Good," Sam replied as he escorted her to her door. "I'll have all the files waiting for you."

A handshake and a peck on the cheek provided a quiet good night to a delightful and peaceful day.

For Sam, Monday began with business as usual. A staff meeting with his aides restarted the wheels for that week's agenda, a review of the previous week's wins and losses, and finally the laying out of individual case files on each of the homicides that he and Francesca would jointly review.

It was exactly ten o'clock when his secretary announced his visitor from Santa Fe Police Department. After the formal entrance, and seeing to any of Francesca's requests, she left her boss and the guest to attend to her other duties. Allowing a moment to pass, they both made themselves comfortable in their chairs.

Sam welcomed her with a formal handshake, both acting as professionals and neither one hinting at the previous day's 'date'. He then complimented her for her punctuality.

"Thanks for noticing," Francesca replied with an appreciative smile. "I guess you can say that I'm not your typical New Mexican. I never did agree with our interpretation of manana."

In a land where schedules are loosely adhered to, where morning appointments often did not occur until the afternoon if at all, manana lost the translation of meaning 'tomorrow'. It took on its own meaning of 'whenever'.

"So! How shall we approach this?" Francesca asked as she eyed the stack of cases on the desk. It was obvious that the stack meant that they had about three or four hours of work ahead of them.

"Well, since I've had them, I've gone over each of them at least two or three times. I know that you've been on the job for only a short time, but I assume you've pretty much done the same thing."

"In the couple of weeks that I've had them, I've done pretty much the same."

"Okay, then. What do you say that we go over each of them together, one at a time," Sam suggested.

Francesca agreed, pulled up her chair up alongside of Sam's, took the top folder, and said, "Let's get to it."

Methodically searching the first of the fifteen case files, each within the last ten years, they formed two separate piles upon review, one covering isolated incidents were the names and the dead victims of apparent robberies, of fights, or of possible executions. The other pile consisted of victims that in some way may have been linked to other victims' modus operendi; manner of death, personal backgrounds, time frames, evidence, and more. Out of the first five files reviewed, two already fit into that category, both within the last three years. Georgina Becaud's murder was the most recent of these files.

About an hour and half later, and halfway through, they came upon the file of Monsignor John Carrol Serrano.

"This one I think we should keep separate and by itself," Sam suggest as he laid it to the front of the worktable.

"Any special reason?" Francesca inquired.

"A couple. It's one of the newest, not related to anything else. It's perhaps the most bizarre, and it might be the most political. This, and the fact that Guiterrez, Shannon, and the state police are giving it their special attention."

"I see. Perhaps we can still review it to see if we both have the same kind of information."

"Sure, why not."

Together, they examined the contents of the folder and found that they both had the same information. Mike Shannon would further update their files upon his return from Window Rock. Completing their review of the Monsignor's file, Sam placed it on the desk and apart from the others.

Tapping the Monsignor Serrano's file, Francesca said, "I suppose you're also getting political heat on this."

"That I am," Sam acknowledged. "But, it's a different kind of heat. Unfortunately, a couple of weeks after the press has its field day with the murder of one woman, the murmur dies down until the next one. With the priest, it's a different story. Not only is his murder a strange one, but the diocese and the parishioners are all clamoring for the case to be solved. The people are all appalled that it happened to a man of the cloth."

"That's understandable," Francesca said.

"Yeah, well…some fear religious persecution, which I don't think is involved here. Either way, the church wants some assurances that their priests are safe. Other ministries have the same concerns."

"Are they?"

"What?"

"Safe."

Sam gave Francesca a bemused glance. "I don't know. You're the cop, so maybe you can answer that."

"I don't know. This is a state case, and I'm not sure of what kind of profiling they may have done. I don't think I have enough particulars to confidently answer the question."

"Well, based upon your instincts, give it a stab."

Francesca slipped back into her chair, and curled her lean body into a more comfortable position. The sensuality of her feminine body caught Sam's eye, but before he could dote upon any lavishing desires, she interrupted his momentarily distracted mind by giving him her reply.

"Considering that a motive has not been established for the slaying, I'd have to cautiously say, no! It's been a few months now since Monsignor Serrano's murder, and as time passes chances of this happening again to another man of the faith becomes slimmer. But, as you said, the strangeness…or bizarreness…of this murder, it does not preclude that it will not happen again."

As Sam nodded his agreement, they both accepted the special importance wrapped into the Serrano investigation. The file folder was special, justifying the need to keep it separate from the others.

The next to last case file read:

Julie Fletcher…Age: 30…Caucasian, Female…5 foot, 4 inches… 112 pounds…

Cause of Death: Strangulation.

The case went back a little more than seven years, fitting into a possible time frame of the other females that constituted the one pile. To Francesca, it seemed proper to group it with the others.

"No…not this one," Sam stopped her.

"But…"

"This office clearly has a primary suspect on this." A hard edge wove its way into Sam's words. "The DA at the time put up a great case, but the evidence against the suspect got thrown out because it was tainted by some rookie cop during evidence gathering. They dropped the charges against the suspect, however we are still convinced of the suspect's guilt. We don't have any other suspects to go with, just this guy."

Francesca noted the harshness in Sam's tone, but not wanting to push the matter she dismissed it.

"What about any link to the others…?"

"None," Sam interrupted. "This guy has since left New Mexico and has been living in Dallas for the last four years. Unfortunately, there's no way that we can tie him to any of these other cases."

To change the atmosphere…to lighten it…Sam suggested, "We have one more file. What do you say we review it and then take a long lunch break?"

"Can't. Got to meet with my boss at three. It's almost two o'clock now." Catching a hint of rejection in Sam's eyes, she boldly ventured, "I can do dinner if you're interested."

Both were slightly taken aback by her suggestion. Sam, because he was not used to women doing the asking, and Francesca, because she never before had the courage to ask a man to dinner.

The work was done, the unsolved murder cases were reviewed, and opinions were exchanged. Five out of the fifteen cases were classified as being possibly related, leaving open the door that one man…one person…might be responsible for the deaths of five young women. Both investigators, a cop and a district attorney, had their own files to work with. Now, they shared a concept that could help them.

"All right then," Sam said. "What time do you want me to pick you up?"

~~❧~~

Before-dinner drinks were sipped in the Dragon Room before they crossed the driveway for dinner in the Pink Adobe. The quaint Old New Mexican dining rooms of the adobe building served to endorse the finest of the New Mexican cuisines.

"My, you seem to have an exquisite pallet," Francesca teased.

"Oh? How's that?"

"Yesterday, brunch at the El Dorado. Today, here. I didn't know the district attorney's job paid so well."

"It could be that I'm trying to make an impression."

It was her turn to express a surprised, "Oh?"

"To balance things off a bit, maybe our next date should be at Burger King. Drive-up window."

"That's sounds fine by me. Just make sure that they give us plenty of napkins. I wouldn't want to mess up your car's upholstery." She made sure she caught his eyes before she completed her say. She then coyly added, "Besides, I didn't know we were dating."

With a chauvinistic sparkle, his eyes caught the daunting tease of hers. "I don't know. Are we?"

Dinner, deserts, coffee and cognac were accompanied by banter tossed from one adult child to the other. Inhibitions were disrobed as they indulged in their own verbal innuendoes. It would remind an outside observer of two teenagers stealing the moment to be young, and to have fun. It did not end there.

"When's the next time…?" Sam began as he slowed the car into the driveway of her rental adobe.

Anticipating, knowing the question about to be asked, she invited… "Come on inside. We can talk about it over a cup of coffee."

The living room light was dim, and the kitchen light was low, low enough to watch the glistening water from the tap filter enter into the mouth of the beckoning kettle. It reminded them of what they should be doing, feeding the hunger of one mouth to another. Reaching from behind, his left hand gently pressed down upon hers that was loosely poised upon the faucet handle, together uniting, stemming one flow to begin another. Her other hand quietly settled the kettle into the base of the sink, then rose to meet his free hand as it embraced her below the breasts. She let his warm breath awaken the excitement in her ear as she eased her body around to face him. She let his searching lips meet hers. From there, with their anticipations coming to a peak, they entered their night of ecstasy.

The night of love was all too brief to satiate either one's demanding hunger. Then again, they realized that even a week of nights could not completely satisfy the newness of their splendor. They knew that within time the craving fires would slowly subside, ebbing into a warm perpetual glow. Until that time, the woman and the man strove to feast upon the broiling of that fire.

But, practicality dictated it terms.

"God! We don't even have time for a cup of coffee," Francesca lamented.

"I wish we did," Sam replied, sharing her feelings. "I've got just enough time to go home and make a quick change of clothes. I've got to be in by eight and prepare for the daily briefings with the assistant DA's."

Francesca noted how he used the word 'the' instead of 'my' in referring to the assistant district attorneys. It suggested to her that Sam did not put himself above his colleagues. Would this follow into their newly born relationship? She did not know.

"Be sure you get something of a breakfast before you go in," she said with a caring tone.

"Oh, don't worry. I'll stop and pick up some take-out pastries and coffee. What about you?"

"Me? I'll just have the usual cop's breakfast. Providing the others don't eat all the doughnuts before I get there."

Sam gave a slight chuckle before he gave Francesca a farewell kiss. He then left for his own home.

"Bye," she quietly wished him as she watched him drive away. The joy of the night now past was slightly dampened when she realized that he didn't ask about seeing her again.

The joy rekindled later that morning when her cell phone rang.

"Hi. It's Sam. I forgot to ask. What are our plans for tonight?"

14

The first couple of days in March brought with it temperatures reaching the mid-sixties. Overlapping the cool thin air one could feel the sun's rays warming the exposed skin of the face, the head and the arms, and for the few who donned short pants, on the legs. Yet, no Santa Fean expected the spring prelude to last. Tomorrow, or the day after, reality would set in as the temperatures would again dip back down into the forties, and into the mid-twenties at night.

As beautiful and as uplifting as these days are, the native and long-time resident of Santa Fe and Northern New Mexico is wary of early warm spring weather, especially after having new record winter storms. Quick melting snow, along with a couple of rainy days, can combine to create sudden flash flooding through the usually bone dry arroyos. Even nature herself can be fooled as precious plant life, coaxed into early budding, will be frozen by the sub-freezing temperatures that still lay in wait. This game of tag played by the weather would last another six or seven weeks. Even in the month of May, the game can be played.

Changing of weather mattered little to Karen Daughtrey. Her visit with her brother, her sister-in-law, and her niece would last only four more days before she returned to her St. Paul, Minnesota home. At twenty-five, this was her first vacation since graduating Michigan State and taking on a computer design position in her home state. Warmer temperatures like these would not come until late April in her northern state, so she welcomed them here as a temporary blessing.

Karen made her plans to spend the day peacefully on her own. Her brother had to work, and she gracefully declined an invitation from her sister-in-law to join her and her daughter to visit the Albuquerque zoo. There would be plenty of time to enjoy their company, and Karen preferred watching animals roaming freely within the woods. That was on her agenda for later on in the day, but first she would have breakfast at the Downtown Subscription, and then she planned to take a soak at a local spa on Hyde Park Road.

The spa where she planned to soak the aches out of her body was located about six miles up the road from the city, and about fifteen miles below the Santa Fe Ski Basin. Nestled among trees of fir, pine, and pinon, it offered soothing massages, relaxing soaks, and juices for those who wanted to supplement their bodies from dehydration. Private rooms, a women's pool, and a general pool were all available for the clients to choose from. Not wanting to spend the extra money for a private chamber, and being too modest to soak nude in the general section, Karen opted for the partitioned women's area. There she felt confident that ogling eyes would not harass her as she soaked away the tightness in her muscles.

A little more than an hour and a half lapsed, split between the water and lounging on a blanket, before she decided she had her fill. The next trek on her agenda was a few miles up towards the ski basin where she would park her car, find a secluded spot, read her magazine, and let her mind get lost in the peaceful solitude of the forest.

Although the city temperature was warm, the air in the higher altitude shielded from the sun by the tall trees, was somewhat cooler. She was glad she brought along a warm jacket, and a blanket upon which to lie. The spot she chose was some seventy-five yards from where she parked her car. The trail, etching its way up from the roadside, around the ridge above her before fading into who knows where, suggested to Karen that it may well be a favorite location for others seeking to escape the claustrophobia of living in the city. However, she suspected that no one had visited the area for quite some time, at least not since before the snows fell. The icy clean patches of snow atop of the trails showed only hoof prints of deer that traversed the terrain. Hers would be the first human footprints imprinted upon the snow.

Karen stretched back on her blanket and faced skywards, studying the brilliant blue that filtered through the treetops to provide luminescence to the stark green and brown surroundings. She let her mind wander away from the rancor of her job, and of the man whom she lived with for the past two years. The relationship was not one that would go beyond sex and a few good times, and within time she realized that it would lead to nowhere. Still, a hurt remained as she reminisced upon the time she lost spending it with someone she did not truly love. The breakup became a good reason for her to take a long needed vacation, albeit for all of only nine days.

Closing her eyes, she listened to the rustling of the breeze, cascading its way through the trees. She heard the pita-patter of tiny feet of a rock squirrel rummaging through the old dead leaves of the previous fall. An occasional sound of tire threads, wheeling to its destination, carried up from the road below. Aside from that there was quiet, a peaceful stillness.

She lightly dozed, only to be alerted by the heavy trashing of leaves and brush nearby. Startled, she rose to find what the intrusion was, perhaps a deer, and hopefully not a bear. Searching into the direction of the noise, she was dismayed at the shape of a human form, circling around and away from her.

At least it's not a bear, she comforted herself.

Lying back down she once again closed her eyes, trying to recapture her thoughts of moments before. She could not. The image of the person in the woods also disturbed her.

There's something familiar… She broke her own thought train, and tried to alleviate her questioning. *Forget about it. You're being paranoid.*

She again reached back searching through the recesses of her mind, conjuring up images of her recent past.

I've got to come to grips that there will be someone else. There will be someone new out there. Someone with whom our interests are similar, and someone to share my life with. Someone…

Once more, nearby thrashing disrupted her thoughts. Only this time it was closer, and there was a frantic air to it.

Bolting up, she was annoyed by the disturbance only feet away.

"Look, I don't feel like…"

Before she could finish her say, and before she could turn to face the intruder, she felt the strength of an arm wrapped around her neck, and a hand clamped over her mouth and pinching the passageway of nostrils. Fighting to break free, she clawed with one hand at the arm choking her, while the other tried to pull away the powerful hand that deprived her of air. Terrorized, Karen tried to struggle to get to her feet, but she was unable. Her body was bent forward, a heavy weight was pressing from behind, and her hands were grappling with those of her attacker. She had no leverage and no strength. She could only try to squirm out of the hold that began to paralyze her. She struggled, and she squirmed, and she could feel her own strength burning out of her muscles, and the lack of oxygen exploding in her lungs. She struggled, and she squirmed, but soon there was no more fire with which to fight. Soon, life had ebbed its way from her body. Soon her concerns were gone, never to be known by any other living being.

It was a little past eleven that morning when Francesca Madrid arrived on the crime scene, only to be stopped by the county sheriff, Tico Talavera.

"Sorry miss, this is a crime scene. It's off limits."

"I'm with the city homicide division," Francesca said decisively as she produced her credentials.

"I'm sorry, but this is not your jurisdiction. We have to limit the number of people so there is no contamination."

"But…" But before she could explain, she heard a familiar voice intercede from behind.

"It's okay, Chief. I invited her to come here."

The voice belonged to Mike Shannon.

"That's fine. But, as I was telling her, this is not a city matter," Sheriff Talavera protested.

"I realize what you're saying," Mike said with his usual disarming smile. "However, since the body is on state land, it becomes a state investigation. To top it off, Detective Sergeant Madrid is already working on cases with similar profiles. She might be of very valuable assistance to us on this."

The sheriff again wanted to object, but realizing that any argument with the persuasive lieutenant would be fruitless, he backed off. He also accepted the fact that Mike could be helpful some time in the future should he need it.

"Okay, Mike. Just keep us informed," Talavera said, trying to show that he still had a commanding image to protect.

"What's his problem?" Francesca quietly asked as she and Mike walked to the taped off area.

"Ah, don't worry about him. He just has a bug up his ass because he and his force don't have the competence to handle this kind of situation."

As they approached the area she saw the body lying beneath a white coroner's blanket.

"Do you mind if I take a look?" Francesca asked, not wanting to be assuming.

"Sure, by all means. That's what you're here for," Mike told her. "I must warn you, though. The crows already made some pickings upon her. I'd have to surmise she's been dead since sometime yesterday morning or early afternoon."

"What does your Doc think?"

"After his on the spot examination, he thinks pretty much same thing. You can speak to him once he's finished."

"Do we know who she is?"

"That we do. A Karen Daughtrey…from Minnesota. That's her Toyota down on the road. It seems her brother called your people last night to report her missing."

"Who found the body?" she asked as she knelt over the body.

"Some guy from the state forestry division. I can give you the details later on. When we finish here we can both question him. With a little luck he might be able to give us some more info."

"That'll be fine. Thanks."

After studying the immediate area, she reached forward and pulled back the blanket and thanked God that Mike had warned her about the condition of the corpse. She took a brief moment to refocus, to look past the facial tears dug there by the birds. A couple of moments later she rose and walked back to where Mike was standing.

"There're not many footprints nearby," she stated.

"No, the ground is still too hard to absorb any prints. The only human prints in the snow appear to be hers, and there are also a lot of leaves around which the killer may have walked on. Don't worry, forensics is going to do a complete sweep of the area, of her clothes, and of her blanket. If we're lucky we might find something."

"I hope so." Francesca let a moment pass before she again spoke. "Based upon the abrasions and contusions around her neck, I'd have to guess she was strangled."

"That's what we suspect." Mike agreed. "Tell me, what do you find interesting about the position of her body."

Francesca gave Mike a thin smile as she answered his question. "It's something that sticks me, too. Lying there on its side, the body is bent forward. If she were facing her attacker she might not be on her back, but her body would not be bent into such a pronounced position. I'd have to conclude that she was attacked from behind."

"I agree," Mike nodded. "Given the overall circumstances, I think it's very probable that the attack was sudden and fast. She's been in Santa Fe for only three days, almost all of that time with her brother and his family. He claims she didn't have a chance to know anyone. I think it's very probable that she did't know her killer."

As she listened to Mike Shannon, Francesca gazed blankly forward letting her mind work. When she assembled her thoughts she told Mike of them.

"There are too many similarities to the Becaud and other cases to be a coincidence. I believe we are dealing with the same killer. Only he changed his time schedule. There's no year and a half or two year gap."

"I'm not going to argue with that. Now, to figure out why." He then asked, "You have a chance to go over the older cases with Sam?"

"Yes, we did that Monday. Two files in particular fit these two. A couple of other cases may qualify."

"That's what I expected."

"It seems we have the makings of a serial killer."

Again Mike agreed. "I think I'm going to arrange for a profiler to meet with us. Maybe we can develop a background on this perp."

"Sounds like a good idea."

Altering the direction of the conversation, Francesca inquired as to the jurisdiction of the case.

"This one has to be ours, but I promise, we're going to work jointly on this. You're gonna get a complete duplicate of the file, and we'll share all info." Mike put a special emphasis on the word 'all'.

"That sounds fine with me. I'll make sure that my division does the same. The only question is, how does the sheriff's department fit in?"

With a wink, Mike answered her. "Those assholes? There'll be something for them…mostly likely grunt work. Just enough to keep them happy."

Mike's reply generated a snicker from the detective. In its own way, it also assured her that their working relationship would be an open and honest one.

They questioned the state forestry worker, but the input was not enough for them to do anything with, and having completed her tasks, Francesca informed Mike that she was heading back to her office. Escorting her to her vehicle, they went over other bits of information that might be useful.

Before he let her drive off, Mike let his curiosity take over. "So, tell me, how did it go with you and Sam?"

"Oh, we work well together," Francesca replied evasively. She had an idea of what Mike was up to.

"Is that all. I mean you guys haven't had dinner or lunch together?"

This time it was Francesca's turn to coyly smile. "You know, if I had to guess, I'd have to say that you're trying to be some kind of matchmaker."

"Who? Me?" Mike pretended to be amazed.

"Yes. You!"

Mike's affective smile broadened as he responded. "Well, you know me. I'm just trying to do my part."

15

Later that same afternoon Cap Guiterrez sat in his office, studying the reports from Espanola and other satellite districts on his computer when Mike walked in. Mike said 'good afternoon' and motioned to his boss to finish what he was doing. Meanwhile, he settled into his comfortable chair and perused through his own report of the murder scene.

"Damn!" Cap mildly uttered as he clicked the computer key closed.

"Sounds like you've seen enough," Mike said with sympathy laced into his comment.

"Yeah. They had three more drug busts, between one and five o'clock this morning. One guy was stopped because of erratic driving. When our patrolman pulled him over, he made no effort to conceal the joint he was smoking."

"Probably knew he gonna get busted anyway," Mike reasoned.

"Probably," Guiterrez concurred. "But a search through his car turned up a half-kilo of cocaine. Either these guys are becoming more brazen, or else more stupid."

"Both," Mike grinned. "What we got to do is one day nail that prick Ruben, and the guys who pal up to him. Do that, and we might start making a dent in the flow."

"It would be nice, but he's like a oily eel," Guiterrez said in disgust. "The son of a bitch himself is clean. He doesn't even touch the stuff, allowing it to pass through everyone else. What's worse, even if we do bust him we might wind up with an all out drug war up there. Everybody will be fighting for control."

No simple solutions were at hand, and the civic meeting the captain was scheduled to attend the next morning did not hold any good promises. The only promise was, people will attend and ask their mundane questions, and they will be demanding answers. Afterwards, they will then go back to their everyday lives. The drug problems would still be there.

"The trouble with those meetings, Cap, is that one-third of the people attending are either dealing or using, or both," Mike complained. "Two thirds of the attendees, including the users and dealers, are on a power trip. That leaves maybe a third that really care. They're the ones I feel sorry for."

"I know what you mean. If it's at all possible to get through to them, it might be worth while."

Mike shook his head in mild disagreement. "Yeah, but you know as well as I do, the problem we face is that it's a closed community. Even some teachers attend class stoned, and they get away with it, much like in the big cities where the teachers' union protects their own no matter how much harm they bring to school. Most people are afraid they may get their heads blown off if they protest too loudly. It'd be nice if someone with a giant pair of cajonnes stepped up, but that's just wishful thinking."

"You might be right. In the meantime we have to at least go through the motions. Between that, and the occasional busts by us and the Feds, we might someday get lucky. For my part, when I'm up there tomorrow, I'm going to make sure that Lieutenant Cordova and his boys don't become frustrated."

Mike mentally wished this captain good luck. He knew the guys up there were knocking their heads over the problems every day.

"How's your day been?" the captain inquired. "Any major leads in the Hyde Park slaying?"

"Just got back from there, and it doesn't look good. Sergeant Madrid and I both agree we have the makings of a serial. Lots of things connect to the Becaud case and some others."

"How are we handling it?"

"On a joint basis. Our forensics has been instructed to keep her informed of everything. I got a request in for our profiler to come up from Albuquerque. The only problem is, he's out for a couple of weeks for medical reasons, and his assistant is up to her ass covering for him."

"Do we have time for that?'

"If it's the same killer, he's moved the time factor up, so I don't think so. Madrid and I are going to have to rely on our psych courses, and try to fit pieces together. If things get bad enough, we might have to request a loner from the FBI."

"Maybe we should do it now."

"Let's wait a few days. I have confidence in her. I got a feeling she might come up with something."

The next morning, after the weekly briefing with his small criminal affairs staff in Espanola, Captain Guiterrez asked Lieutenant Cordova to remain behind. Cordova was the district's head, and he too was scheduled to attend the community meeting.

"Are you all set for this?"

"Yes, sir," Cordova replied. "I'm gonna stress our concerns about the youth. There is not much more to appeal to but the kids. It's about the only thing that matters to most of the people. The eighteen and nineteen year olds are usually considered as write-offs by them, but if we can put emphasis on the younger ones, we might give them a bit of a fighting chance."

Guiterrez thought about the kids. Yes, aiming at the young ones up to sixteen or seventeen might reach the people attending the meeting. And, no! He could not accept the write-offs of the older ones, the ones on the threshold of stepping into a new life, of starting a new family, and of possibly making a positive difference. Eighteen and nineteen years old, and they were already being discarded like rotting dishrags. He could not accept disregarding people so young, and yet he could understand the comment of writing them off. Many of those late teenagers have already crossed a different threshold. If they were not already hooked, many were dealing. In his mind he agreed that the younger ones had to be protected, to be educated against the pains of getting high on the crap being sold there. Still he wondered, what will happen to those young ones within a few years, when they make the transition from adolescence into adulthood. Will it then be time to write them off as well?

What would happen if we crossed our own threshold, and began to reprioritize the drugs to target and crack down, by legalizing marijuana and…

No! Cap thought more clearly. *It'll still take the U.S. Congress to enact the necessary legislation. The drug czar and the rest of the know-better bureaucrats will do their damnedest to see that that doesn't happen. After all, they know what's best for the people,* was his sardonic last thought before he spoke.

"Good. Go ahead and try to reach them through their children. But, whatever you do, do not talk about writing anyone off."

As expected, the meeting had its wide share of disruptions. There were those who complained that law enforcement was not doing its job, that the schools were not educating the children properly against the use of drugs, and that the city council should pass more laws regardless of how ineffective and how unenforceable they were. No one dared to mention that two of their council-people reputably had drug connections, as did their beloved political leader. Nor did anyone dare to mention their own cherished family members who had drug ties. In the sum, no one dared to admit to their own lack of carrying out their own personal family responsibilities.

Captain Eduardo Guiterrez was the last guest speaker. He took to the podium and took the time to study the crowd before he addressed them.

"I have heard your laments…your concerns. I have also heard your anger, your frustrations, and your criticisms. I agree and sympathize with most of them. Many of you have voiced general criticisms and general suggestions as to who should be more involved." He paused briefly, refocusing his attention to selected members of the audience. "But…let me ask you this. Keeping in mind the budget restraints, protection of constitutional freedoms, and of keeping within the framework of the laws, is there one of you who can make one specific suggestion, one that is fully detailed, and one that may help to bring this crisis to an end?"

He again paused and waited, and he saw no hands nor heard any voices. Feeling the timing effectively, he continued in his even and controlled tone.

"I am sorry to see that no one is responding. However! I believe I have one." Once more he paused, this time to ascertain that he had captured his audience. "Let me be your mirror…your reflection. When I come home at night, I greet my wife and my two wonderful girls. We have dinner and relax. Before my children go to their rooms to study, my wife, Margarette, and I listen to what they have to say. If either of my children have done something wrong, we talk about it. If they have problems, we try to solve them. We may not always have an answer, or a correct one, but we try. When they ask us about social dilemmas out there such as the wanton rampage of drugs, of violence, and even the corruption in politics and in business, we try to explain it to them. Again, although we may not have all of the answers, we try not to be bias or prejudice in our explanations. We try to motivate them to use their most precious God-given talent…their mind. And, above all, we try to teach them the essence of respect…for us…for society and others…and for themselves."

Once more he paused, and once more he was assured he controlled their attention.

"One of the things I find hard to come to grips with is the attitude of people on a whole. There are many, many people who complain that government and society are interfering too much in our daily lives. On the most part, I agree with them, but I won't get into specifics here. Unfortunately, there are many…many…of those same people who look to government and society to solve all of their ills. There is a contradiction in that type of logic. I won't deny that there is a need for government, through legislation and law enforcement, to help stem the subject of this meeting. But, let me ask you. What are you…each of you as individuals…what are you doing to help thwart the menace which plagues us? Are you cooperating with your elected officials and law enforcement, or are you merely complaining? Are any of you speaking out in public against the use of drugs, but when you're alone do you allow yourself to indulge – not only with drugs, but with excessive use of alcohol as well? Are any of you discussing this matter with your friends, or are any of you befriending instead of shunning the culprits who are feeding drugs to your children and to the rest of society. Making these people an outcast, albeit a small step, can assist in resolving this problem. It is a way of letting them know they are not wanted, that there is no place for them in a healthy society.

"Lastly, let me ask you. Are you, yourself, talking to your children? Are you counseling them about the evils that they are exposed to? Are you listening to their reply?

"I have asked you these questions, but I am not asking you for your reply. I have posed these questions for you to reason with…to think about. The answers you derive are for you alone to ponder."

That night, lying awake beside the warm sleeping body beside him, Cap's restless mind kept repeating the nagging issues. Did he get through to them? Will they understand what he said to them? He really did not know. He only hoped that he reached at least one of them.

"Who the fuck does that guy think he is," an angry Jesus Baca grumbled. "He's got no fuckin' right tellin' us how to think."

Emilio Baca simply smiled at his brother's tirade. He listened to many of them in the past, and they often amused him. When he knew Jesus was finished, he spoke knowing that he would throw his brother off guard.

"Actually, I agree with a lot of what he had to say."

"What?" Jesus was dumbfounded.

"You heard me." Emilio mildly admonished Jesus as the two brothers walked from the assembly building toward their old pickup truck. Jesus would drive. "Drugs, and the people who deal them, are not going to be part of the revolution. They don't give a damned about how it's killing our people. They just want the money."

"Yeah, but still…"

"Be quiet for a moment, Jesus. Let me talk. I'm not finished."

The truck headed northwards, out of Espanola and towards their Guzman home.

"We have to get rid of these types of people who think only of getting stoned, and making quick bucks by killing us with their shit. To get drunk once in a while is one thing. To get a little high on some good grass isn't bad. To keep snorting the white stuff and frying the brain, or to shoot that milk into your veins…well, that's gonna kill you. At the very least, it'll turn you into a zombie. You and your family are going to suffer. That's what the rich fuckers want. They want to see you get so screwed up so that you'll sell your possessions, your land, and your soul. They'll then come along and give you pennies on a dollar as they steal it all away, and you'll be grateful for what they give you."

"I still wanna bash his face in." Nothing could change Jesus once he determined he did not like someone.

"I wouldn't be too hard on him, Bro. Once the time comes, and the changes are made, he will make a great soldier. All we have to do is to make him see things a little more clearly."

The next few miles were driven in silence before Jesus broke it.

"What do ya think we should do about drugs?"

Emilio thought for a moment before he replied. "The captain is right. We gotta disconnect ourselves from the people we know are selling it."

"Yeah, but we know them people most of our lives."

"That's true, Jesus. But, are they our friends? Have they ever been our friends? Think about it for a bit. None of them want anything to do with us, or our kind, unless they can get something from us. They care about nothing but getting shitfaced and stoned."

Jesus did think about it, and it made him wonder. "I don't really understand. I don't understand how we can separate them from us. Even if we don't mix with them, they'll still be around the places we go to. We can't pretend they don't exist."

"We'll have to ignore them." Emilio then turned to give his brother a comforting hand on his arm. "There are more ways of separating those people than by just ignoring them. In our revolution there will be small battles. When there are battles, there will be casualties. These people are no different than the Anglo elite who made them the way they are. If they become casualties, then so be it. One by one, we are going to make them disappear."

The light began to shine. Thanks to his wiser brother, he began to see. He began to learn. One by one his enemies would have to disappear. He began to relish his part of the coming revolution.

Jesus interrupted his own fantasy when he spoke. "Man! You're right. I can't wait until we tell the girls about what we plan to do."

This caused Emilio to order his brother to pull the truck over to the shoulder of the road. Emilio was angry, and more so, he had a new concern.

"Listen, you dimwit." Emilio's tone became strongly emphatic. "You don't tell no one of this. Especially them. I don't want them to have anything that they can hang over us."

"They're our friends, our buds..." Jesus protested.

"I don't give a shit if they're our wives. You tell them absolutely nothing. You tell no one nothing. When things are right, I'll choose the people to tell. Christ! We're on the verge of beginning a revolution, and you're ready to get us killed before it begins. Use your brains, Jesus. Don't do or say anything unless I tell you."

Jesus drove quietly the rest of the way to Guzman. His pride and his feelings were hurt. He loved his brother, and he admired him. He just wished Emilio would not be so hard on him. That he would lighten up.

He strenuously thought about what his brother had told him about the Anglos, and about the guys who pretend to be their friends. He knew they had to get rid of those suckers, and make them disappear... one by one.

PART 2

16

"Where the heck is Sam tonight? You could have used him on your team?"

Alex beguiled Mike with the same banter that they usually exchanged, only this night he savored even more since his team beat Mike's in an unusual seven to zero drubbing. He sat on a barstool that seemed to have his name on it, and sandwiched himself between Mike who sat to his left at the corner of the bar, and Gregg on his right.

"I don't know. Probably getting laid," Mike said glibly with his usual impish look on his face.

"Getting laid!" Alex responded with mock incredulity. "There's no sex when it comes to playing darts. His team needs him. Besides, how do you know this?"

The question opened it up for Mike to proudly boast, "Because I'm the guy who set him up."

"You set him up!" Alex again pretended to be incredulous. "The poor guy. Who with?"

"Some female cop, just transferred up from Albuquerque. She seems like a nice kid who might like someone like him."

"I don't know," Alex shook his head. "All these years we've known each other, and not once did you try to help me get laid."

"Shit! You couldn't get laid in a cathouse full of horny whores."

Gregg was in the process of taking a slug of his beer when Mike made his comment. Caught between swallowing and laughing, he showered the beer over the bar. All the people sitting nearby found the episode funny.

"Easy, Gregg. Easy," Mike tried to comfort him. "This sucker's the one who should be choking on his beer."

"You come out with some of the craziest things," Gregg replied. "We never know what you'll say next."

"I'm right though, ain't I?" While speaking, Mike patted Alex on the back. "When they see this guy coming in a cathouse, they put up a sign, 'Sorry, closed for the night'."

Playing to Mike's ribbing, Alex raised his right hand and stroked it with his left. "All right, so don't fix me up. Hell, I won't want my sweetheart here to get jealous."

"Hell, she'd try to leave you if she weren't so attached."

"There's an old adage that I've modified to suit me, 'beggars can be choosers'," Alex told him.

"You can say that again," Mike commented. "You know that old lady wino who usually sits at the other end of the bar? Well, he once walked over to ask her for a date…she beat him over the head with her purse."

After some of the buddy humor wore down, Gregg let his curiosity take over. "I know you were married twice. Why didn't you stay married?"

"Because neither of my ex-wives and I turned out to be suitable for each other. We all had the good sense to end it at the right time."

"Any kids?" Gregg asked.

"No…none that I know of." The response brought a little chuckle from the others sitting with him.

They sat and exchanged opinions and stories before Gregg recalled a question he needed an answer to.

"Hey, Alex!" he called, commanding Alex's attention. "What do you do for brown recluse spiders? My cousin was bit by one."

"I don't do anything for them. They're not indigenous to New Mexico," Alex told him.

"Then tell that to my cousin who got bit by one. The whole area got swollen, and the skin began to die. When he went to the doctor he was told that it was done by a brown recluse."

"Where does your cousin live?"

"In Tesuque."

"Did the doctor have pieces of the skin analyzed?"

"No. He just looked at it and told him what it was."

"How long was he ill from the bite?"

"Maybe a couple of days."

"Then tell him the doctor may have given him a wrong diagnosis," Alex again advised. "If is was a recluse, most likely it fell off a truck or a car from another state like Oklahoma, Missouri, or maybe Arkansas or Texas."

"Then how did he get that kind of bite?" Gregg asked skeptically.

"My guess is it was a yellow-sac spider. They leave the same kind of symptoms, only the venom's not nearly as bad. Have him thoroughly vacuum the room, and to use screens to help keep them out. That's much more effective than general spraying. If he does this he won't have to spend money on someone like me."

"Are you sure?" Gregg remained dubious.

"I'd believe what this guy tells you," Mike said as he came to Alex's defense. "When it comes to bugs, he knows what he's talking about."

"Are you sure?" Gregg repeated his question to Mike.

"Damned sure of it. A couple of years ago he helped us with a dead body."

"Uh?"

"We found a body along the roadside on Highway 14. He was a Native American, but aside from that he had no ID on him. When we had the autopsy performed, the pathologist discovered two things. One, the guy was a diabetic, and that he died from a lack of insulin. Two, they found a spider bite just below his calf. The doctor performed some tests and determined that the guy was bitten by a brown recluse. He said the bite can make you very sick or even cause some people to loose limbs, but it's generally not a killer. He speculated that the guy got delirious from the bite, started walking, went into shock, and died. That still didn't tell us who the guy was. So, the next day, out of curiosity, I called this guy here."

"That's when I told him what I told you," Alex joined in on the story telling. "It is not native to this state. I speculated that he was bitten elsewhere in another state earlier in the day, or that a brown recluse was in a car he was in and bit him."

"Sure enough," Mike continued. "I run a check and discovered a report of an abandoned car at the outlet mall, just two miles from where we found the guy's body. The car had Oklahoma plates. So, I have my guys aerosol the hell out of the interior before they go in. An hour later they find the guy's ID, along with some insulin, in the glove compartment. They start taking the car apart and they find it…a dead brown recluse under the driver's seat. The sonafa bitch must have been there all the time, and it must have crawled up the guy's pant leg and bit him, and then fallen out and went back to its hiding spot."

"Jeez!" Gregg exclaimed.

"So when Alex tells you about spiders and things like that, listen," Mike concluded. "He'll bullshit you with his philosophy and dart playing, but he won't bullshit you about bugs."

"Thanks," Alex stated as he lifted his beer. "That was a nice left handed compliment. Did I ever tell you how your use of the aerosol was an overkill? You guys are a danger to the environment."

"Screw the environment! If it means one of my guys not getting bit, or spraying a little extra pesticide, take a guess which one I'll choose. Every time!"

The hour was pressing midnight. Most of the dart playing regulars had left, leaving Mike and Alex as the only two dart players still in the bar. They were on their last beers for the night before calling it a week till the next comradeship. Occasionally they got together in between, usually when the bar held a Friday night mini-tournaments or when Mike held one of his out door barbecues.

"You still haven't answered the question from the last time," Mike picked up the topic from a week earlier.

"What's that?"

"Why we never see you in here with some chick. We see you getting hot to trot, necking and playing around with some girl that pops in out of nowhere, but we never see it go beyond foreplay."

Alex sensed a cop's interrogative quality in Mike's probing. He knew Mike, and he liked him. He also knew that Mike's intentions were genuinely sincere.

"Well, crap, I've always been waiting for you to hook me up, like you did for Sam."

"If I wound up matching you with any women, I'd wind up losing them as friends. So, get off it."

That was the last bit of banter before the conversation took on a more inquisitive and serious tone.

"I guess you weren't listening to what I said before."

"Oh, I was listening all right. My question is, when do you get it?"

Alex paused for a moment before he answered.

"Basically, Mike, that's between me and the woman I'm with."

Mike heard the reply, and he respected his drinking buddy's need to remain private. Still, he knew Alex to be intelligent and sharp, and as one man evaluating another, to be moderately handsome. He suspected that some women probably found him sexy. In fact, he saw the positive response he got from them when they came in the bar. All in all, it just didn't figure.

"I guess you're too independent." Mike said it more as a question than as a statement.

"That may be true. There is also the fact that I don't like burning or being burned."

"Look, pal," Mike replied. "You can't boil water for fear of being burned. If you do, you may never eat."

"I know what you're saying, but it goes beyond that. I have my likes and dislikes. Aside from liking lean women with a lot of smarts, I like them considerably younger than me."

"Big deal! There are plenty of them out there."

"There are; and there aren't."

"Oh, give me a break, for Christ's sake. What the hell kind of an excuse is that?" Mike shot back.

"Look! This may be a well known little city, but it's still a provincial one. There are many women who are into old local ways that don't appeal to me. Then there are many who come here from California,

Texas, and other places. Most of those are here on a la-la trip, thinking that it's chic. To me, that's too damned pretentious, and I'm not into it."

"You're trying to tell me none of the women meet your bill of fare."

"There are some. To be honest, a few that I met were not interested in me. A few others were single women with kids, and I don't want that responsibility. And, there are quite a few others who definitely appeal to me, but they are already spoken for. I have absolutely no intentions of getting into the middle of someone else's relationship."

"That's very noble of you." Mike intended it to be sarcastic, but in his own mind he considered it a thing of honor, something that he respected.

"I'm not trying to be noble. I'm just me. I've set up my own grounds rules; the ones I got to live by. Let's face it, there just aren't many women in Santa Fe for me to choose from."

Mike shook his head as he drank towards the bottom of the bottle. As he thought about it, the more he found he could not disagree with his friend. He, himself, was a very happily married man. He had been for more than twenty years, and probably would be for many years to come. He conceded he did not know what it was like to be in his friend's shoes, but knowing his character, and comparing it to his own, Mike also conceded he might very well be the same way. But, just not with so many restricting ground rules.

He chugged the last drops of his beer before he rose to say goodnight.

"Gotta go, pal. Got a tough day ahead for tomorrow."

"See you soon," Alex replied.

"Yeah." Mike started to leave but stopped. "Last week you told Gregg and Dennis you were with eighty to ninety women. Were you?"

"Nah. I'm no Wilt Chamberlin, not by a long shot." Alex smiled with his own impish grin. "You forget that while I was married twice, overall for about eight years, I was a very good boy. The number is actually more like a hundred, or maybe a hundred and ten."

In an old renovated house on Tano Road, Sam turned his body to snugly fit within the contours of the soft warmth beside him. His arm securely wrapped her frame into his.

It was their sixth straight night together, taking turns into whose bed they would satisfy their needs. Except for the demands made by each person's career, more and more times they did things as a pair. Except for work, seldom was either alone without the other.

"Sam," Francesca softly beckoned. "Are you still awake?"

"Ummm…" was the only sound to crack the otherwise silence of the night.

After letting a few still moments pass, she closed her eyes, saving her anxiety-laced curiosity for another night. In life, as in her career, she learned the art of patience. She decided to not test it now knowing that tomorrow, or perhaps the night after, she would have the opportunity to have that curiosity fulfilled.

"I think I'm awake. What is it?" Sam finally replied.

"Ssh…go back to sleep."

"No, no, it's okay. I'm awake, so you can tell me what it is." His soft reply softened Francesca's concern.

It was her turn to take her time, and she wanted to convince herself that it was the proper time to ask.

"Where is this going?" A hint of feminine uncertainty was woven in her words. It was a question that was asked a billion times in a billion bedrooms throughout the years of man, and throughout the world. The numbers never depleted the meaning.

"I'm sorry," Sam said drearily. "Where is what going?"

"Our relationship."

Other moments of night silence followed. Francesca was ready to relinquish his reply and try to sleep. Sam's low and tired voice kept her from doing so.

"I'm not sure, Hon. I'm not really sure." Another moment of quietness followed before he added. "I do know I really enjoy the moments I spend with you."

He felt her hand tightly squeeze his as it lay perched above her breasts.

"Tell me more about yourself. Why were you never married?" Francesca asked.

"I don't know." His voice was distant and uncertain as he reached into the depths of his mind to find a reason. "I guess I never met anyone. Maybe I was just too tied up in my work." "Have you ever loved anyone?"

The distance in his voice did not change, but the timber suggested a hint of pain. "Yes, I think so. But, that was some time ago."

"What happened between you?"

There was a hesitance in his reply, but when he did he said, "She went away. She simply went away."

Francesca waited for Sam to explain the meaning of what he said, but when none was forthcoming she let it go. She did not want to push him into telling more than he was prepared to do, knowing that in time he would probably confide in her. For the next few moments they laid quietly holding each other, feeling the warmth of each other's body.

"What about you? You never married." Sam took his turn to prod.

"No, but I almost did get married once."

"And…"

"We lived together for a year. He wanted me to quit the force, stay home and have children."

"And you weren't ready for it."

"No, I wasn't," Francesca admitted. "I love my work, and I'm good at it. I wasn't ready to give it up. I'm still not."

"Then don't. One of life's purposes is to be happy. If police work is part of your happiness, then by all means, stick to it."

"Then you'd never ask me to quit?"

"No, I wouldn't. Providing you never ask me to give up practicing law."

His reply moved her, and she squeezed his hand more tightly, moving it downwards to the top of her bosom. Currents of body electricity began to generate, intensifying as he kissed the lobe of her ear, his warm breath stimulating an excitement within her. She turned to meet his lips, and to touch the tool that would fully electrify her body. Guiding him, she welcomed him. Soon their bodies were fully charged, and another night of happiness extended into the waking hours of sunlight.

17

Joseph Aragon did not like the articles written in the New Mexican and in the Journal North. Both covered stories of two of his now former opponents in the mayor's race, both of who dropped out to support his closest opposition, Anthony Duran. Although neither of the candidates showed anything above two percent support in the polls, it still irked JoJo that Duran was the beneficiary of their quitting. This was not what he planned on, and so far, it was not what Ruben Gonzales told him would happen and a dwindling four weeks remained till that final day.

An item in one of the newspapers that disturbed JoJo the most was in the commentary section. It lauded Duran as a unifier of all the people of Santa Fe, while at the same time the writing derided Joseph Aragon for being 'a disrupter of civility, peace, and harmony'. The article came a few words short of calling him a xenophobic feeding upon the fears and ignorance of but a small portion of the city's population. It criticized him for wanting to institute old philosophies that kept 'his' people suppressed for many decades in the past.

He wanted to know what the hell the writer knew about suppression since the bitch who wrote the article wasn't even living here at the time. He fumed that she couldn't make it in New York, moving to Santa Fe to stir up trouble by writing her trash.

His critical thoughts of the newspaper writer faded as he switched back to his worrisome thoughts about the election. He damned those idiots who refused to understand that to support Duran only makes it more difficult for their people...JoJo's people. Duran will only be helping those from the outside. He had proven time and again that he doesn't give two shits about his own kind, just big money and those who are out to destroy the people's way of life.

His mind raced as he kept harping on what he read, and the consequences it could have upon his candidacy. Within three hours he would be going out, knocking on doors in his district, and drumming up voter support for his campaign. These were mostly his people, but he did not want any of them slipping away to support Duran or any of the other remaining candidates. His district was the primary base of his support, and as a polished campaigner, he worked hard to keep that base solidified.

A couple of quick phone calls helped to allay JoJo's mounting anxieties.

"I wouldn't worry about a thing," Sheriff Tico Talavera consoled him. "These two guys are nobodies. No one really cares who they support."

"You're wasting your time worrying about what's written in the newspapers," Magistrate Judge Julio Maestas told him. "Take it from experience. For years they've tried to destroy me. But look at me, I'm still serving on the bench."

A third phone call was even more important.

"You should learn to relax more, my friend," Senator Ruben Gonzales admonished him in a fatherly fashion. "Learn to take things in stride. These are little setbacks that will correct themselves, especially since I promised you that Montoya and Ruiz will drop out and endorse you."

"I can't understand why they haven't done so yet," JoJo respectfully pressed.

"It is timing, my friend. Timing. If either man had already dropped out, everybody would have forgotten about it. If it is done closer to election it will be fresher in every voter's mind. First, Ruiz will make his announcement next week. For dramatic purposes, we will wait five days and then Montoya will withdraw. Both men will enthusiastically support you. That will happen with a little more than two weeks left before the vote, and you can build momentum. It will be fresh in the mind of their supporters who will, without question, be voting for you."

Less than an hour later JoJo felt more at ease. He was further comforted when he received a return call from Judge Maestas.

"I have some very good news for you, Joseph," Maestas greeted him.

"Great! Let's hear it. I can sure as hell use some."

"I just learned that your son's DWI has been designated to Frank Rodriguez. As you know, he is one of your backers."

"That's good. That's very good to hear." JoJo was pleased enough to dance.

"Ah, but that's not all. The trial is not scheduled until April 23, which is well after the elections."

"Then it won't have any affect on the outcome. That's fantastic."

"I'd say so," Maestas agreed. "The trial won't directly affect you. If I may suggest however, so that you can stonewall the press for a bit, you come out reprimanding your son's misconduct. It will also make it easier for Rodriguez to render a light punishment."

"Yes. Yes, you're right. I can come out strongly against drunk drivers which can improve my image."

After the conversation, he gave just a little more thought about it. As far as he was concerned, Rodriguez could throw the book at him. Let Thomaz do some time. At least in jail he wouldn't be in any position to embarrass the new administration.

Another two hours remained before he would go walking off on his door-to-door neighborhood campaign. The morning had so far been a series of valleys and peaks, and hearing Evonne's voice as she came through the door prepared him for another dip in his emotions.

Entering the kitchen to pour himself a much deserved cup of coffee, he noticed that his daughter had brought home a male guest. The young man was lean, and it made his enthusiastic smile seem wider.

"Where's your sister?" he asked Evonne.

"She's off around town with a friend," came the flippant reply.

"Well, your mom's gonna be home soon. You and Yolanda were supposed to help her post some signs around town."

"Stop worrying. She'll be here when mom gets in."

Evonne did not say anything more as she waited for her father to acknowledge her companion. When she noticed that he seemed to be oblivious to the presence of another person, she took the lead.

"Pa, I want you to meet a friend of mine. He's a big fan of yours."

"Is that so?"

The young man stepped forward, stretching out his hand as he did. In a bubbling voice he introduced himself.

"My name's Emilio. Emilio Baca."

Hesitantly, JoJo accepted the hand. Cautiously, he introduced himself, not that he needed to. "My name's Joseph Aragon."

"Yes, I know. I just wanted to meet the man who will lead our people when he becomes mayor."

Warming up to the younger man, JoJo firmly shook his hand. "Thank you. I guess then I can count on your vote."

"Well, I'm sorry to say, I can't vote here. I live in Rio Arriba County." Before he could let his idol's enthusiasm wane, Emilio quickly added, "I'd still like very much to help you if I can. Anything that can help you win."

JoJo was gratified by the offer, and his beaming eyes showed it. After evaluating him for a moment, he decided that he liked Emilio. He seemed well spoken enough, and although not sharp, his appearance was very presentable."

"After I finish my door to door visits with my constituents, I'm going to The Plaza for a small rally. Maybe you can join me and work the crowd."

"I'd be very pleased to, Mr. Aragon. Just tell me what to do," was Emilio's excited reply.

"There's nothing to it. Just pick out some people and talk to them. Tell them of all the good things I'll do for them. I'll introduce you to my campaign manager, and he'll tell you exactly what to do."

"I'll try my best to help. Thank you, sir."

"It'll be my pleasure. I'll see you at The Plaza this afternoon, a little before four."

Getting ready for the neighborhood trip on foot, JoJo found comfort in the unexpected upscale slide of events that were falling into place.

As he slipped into his favorite walking boots, he was glad that his daughter had for once brought home someone who was not a bum.There might yet be some hope for her.

It was a relatively mild day, so JoJo opted to wear a corduroy jacket over a light sweater. A bolo tie was visible through the V-neck and, along with a pressed pair of blue jeans, it gave him a natty appearance; clean cut and well groomed without being overly dressed, typical of the southwestern image. He wanted people to immediately recognize him, so he shunned wearing a hat feeling that it would only cover his wavy black hair and his low forehead. Both were distinctive traits of his.

There were a few cool responses from those answering the door, and that was to be expected. As a city councilman he carried his district by a comfortable percentage, and he obviously accepted the fact that not everyone endorsed his mayoral candidacy. His reception by most, however, was one of an enthusiasm that grew as he knocked from one door to the next. The main target was winning over those who seemed to be undecided, and then trying to get a feel of what their major concerns were so that he could cater to them during his visit.

"You're absolutely right to feel that way about traffic congestion. That's why, when I become mayor, I'm going to push through new zoning regulations. We can't have outside companies building factories on Airport Road and causing more problems. I also propose that the business here pay for all the road work in their areas."

When the less fortunate complained about having to live in an old Hud Housing complex that were in need of costly government repairs, JoJo had the solution.

"Almost all of the contractors are building homes for the rich. As mayor I will force them to invest more in the construction of low income housing units. Unless they comply, I will have the city manager deny them permits for building luxury homes."

Some complained about the soaring crime rate and the chronic drug and alcohol use in the district.

"That's because the big companies are not willing to educate and hire these people. The people who own these companies are all rich and educated, and they don't care about ours. Because of that, some of our young people wind up getting into trouble. They are our people, and we must take care of them. As mayor, I will mandate that the businesses provide our people with education and training. If the businesses don't comply, we'll go to court and file discrimination law suits against them."

The answers were there, and JoJo took satisfaction in knowing he had swayed at least a few of the undecided.

His first challenge came towards the end of the touring day, outside on a porch in a well-kept mobile home park.

"Please, don't even waste your time knocking on my door," a firm voice spoke to him from the other side of a screen door.

JoJo could make out the image of a man through the screen, but he could not clearly make out his features.

"My name is Joseph Aragon. I'm running for mayor."

"I know who you are. Now please leave."

Practical common sense told him that he should walk away. However, an inner urge raised his growing contempt for the man who was being rude to him. It compelled him to make a deliberate stand.

"You are not being very polite, sir. After all, I am running to become mayor."

"I really don't give a damned if you are running to become God. Please leave."

"Why must you be so offensive?" JoJo demanded.

His question spurred the man to step out from behind the screen door. JoJo could see that he was a middle aged Anglo. It was a no wonder that he disliked him.

"I'm sorry if you find me offensive. Then again, I find people like you who practice racism to be even more offensive."

"How dare you?" JoJo protested as anger began to flush in his face. "I'm not a racist. It is people like you who…"

The man, with a harder tone in his voice halted JoJo's retort. By now a couple of neighbors were milling in front of their own homes.

"People like me? You mean 'Anglo'. Isn't that another convenient term for you to call someone a nigger?"

JoJo's mouth gaped.

"Even if it is not your intent," the man steadily continued, "you widely misuse it. Call an Irishman an Anglo, and you might offend him. A Frenchman might laugh at you. Surely people of Italian, Greek, or of Eastern European backgrounds are not Anglos. Hell! If you wanted to call me a white Polish-American bastard, I would have to at least concede that you are technically correct."

"But..."

"But nothing! You want political correctness, but you're not willing to render it. For people like you the term is a matter of convenience, to be used at your own whim. You, my not so good sir, practice divisiveness, dividing one group of people against another. You preach that you're out to help your people. You want to be mayor, but you favor one group of people at the expense of all others. To me that's being a racist. You claim other people are destroying your culture, but do you show any respect for others and theirs? You have the audacity to call Santa Fe a multi-culture city, yet one culture dominates at the expense of others. You wouldn't know about multi-culture if it bit you in the ass."

"Nonsense!"

"It's not nonsense when you place your culture above all others. You're contributing to its demise. Any culture that is so arrogant is inviting that destruction and looses respect. Groups of people cannot destroy another group's culture; not unless they're extremists preaching hatred. Culture cannot really be destroyed by others. When the people of a culture abandons its tenets, and the good thing that makes up its structure, it starts to crumble from within."

"You don't know what you're talking about. We are a people who love our children, our families..."

"And others don't? Then you're saying that Italians do not? Or the Jews? Or any other people in the world? The Europeans? The Asians? Africans? Americans? None of these love their children?"

"That is not what I am saying!"

"You are at least implying it," the man cut him short. "When one group of people puts itself above another group without giving them the respect and recognition it deserves, you're inviting conflict. If you don't believe me, then look at the root of the problems in areas like the Middle

East. That way of thinking gave rise to Nazi Germany, the Taliban and bin-Laden, and despotic governments. They recognize their own, but are not willing to recognize others. I assume you are willing to see that happen here in New Mexico."

"Of course I'm not," JoJo vehemently denied. "I want to see justice done for my people, that's what I want."

"By whose interpretation of justice? Yours? Will it be based upon morality? Equality? Fairness? And, at whose expense…everyone who does not agree with you? Wouldn't it be wiser and more honorable to work with all other groups as opposed to making them your enemy?"

"Ridiculous!"

"You're entitled to believe so," the man calmly replied. "I just hope that if you become mayor, it doesn't come at too high a price. For everybody, your people included."

Joseph Aragon wanted to push his argument further, but he noticed that other people were focusing their attention to the direction of him and the man. He had a few more doors to knock upon, and he did not want to loose more time stalemating his argument with someone who was narrow in his beliefs, someone he knew would become more of his enemy in the future. Maybe, in the future he can confront this man, but not right now.

"Well, my friend, I must be going. Good bye," JoJo said before he turned and walked away. The last words he heard came from his adversary.

"Good bye. And, no! You are not my friend."

With a nod to his neighbors, Alex Dombrowski climbed the steps of his porch and entered his home.

The Plaza of Santa Fe is in the heart of the city. It is where the Old Santa Fe trail begins, or ends, depending upon one's point of view. It is surrounded by ornate western style buildings, most with balconies, across the streets on three sides, all providing a home for art galleries, rug shops, nice restaurants, and a few other retail stores. Law and business offices occupy the second floors of these buildings. While not equivalent to Los Angeles' Rodeo Drive, the rents are high and the retail prices paid by the willing tourists are even higher. With the inflated prices, some businesses with both fine and artificially reproduced merchandise make tremendous profits. Others with modest offerings barely make enough to exist, while still many others go under.

On the north side of The Plaza is where the Palace of the Governors stands, a museum that records much of the rich history of Santa Fe and of New Mexico. Beneath the museum portals, and from spring through late fall, Native Americans display their exquisite arts and crafts, designed mainly from turquoise and silver, awing the out of town shoppers with its majestic beauty.

During the warm weather months, lovers and casual strollers occupy the wood and iron park benches. There they sit to watch other strollers pass them by, or to be amused in watching the young teenagers lounging on the closely cropped grass, or playing hacky-sac as a means to spend their abundant energy. The mood is mostly serene, but is often disrupted by the boom-boom of a low-rider driving his car in macho fashion, staking his disturbing right of passage claim to The Plaza. From late fall through early spring the tourists have all but disappeared, and the young people are in search of a new locale to play their youthful games. The lawns have been denied to them by slat fencing, there to protect the grass from what the city considers destructive intruders. And yet, to the annoyance of shopkeepers and tourists and citizens alike, the unnerving disturbance of a fool's boom-boom box music persists year round.

On this particular March day the fencing had been taken down three weeks earlier than normal, and the streets around The Plaza has a blockade against any vehicular traffic. A political rally is to take place, and as a city councilman, Joseph Aragon used his pull to make it so.

With an anguishing fire still raging through him, JoJo arrived at his rally fifteen minutes later than scheduled. He had another ten minutes before he would take to the platform and address the crowd. He wished he had more. He originally planned to work the crowd, to shake a few more hands, and to pass on some individual words to some of his supporters. He also hoped to have more time to extinguish part of the inferno blazing within. A passionate speaker, with touches of anger emoting from his lips that could excite a crowd, JoJo knew that uncontrolled vehemence would serve to turn off some of the meeker elements of the crowd.

The amplified Mariachi music blared through the speakers reaching all four corners of The Plaza. It provided JoJo with a soothing sensation, and unable to hear or speak easily, it gave him an excuse not to spend too much time with any one individual. He decided that it was better that way. His rallying words would only be drowned by the music, but it gave him an opportunity to shake more hands and to personally touch more people.

Inching closer to the platform from where he would address the gathering, he was stopped by a hand on his shoulder. Turning around he faced Evonne. Yolanda, Emilio, and Jesus were with her.

"Glad to see you could make it," he greeted them, almost expecting them not to be present. Then softening his tone, he smiled at Emilio as he spoke. "Have you been introduced to my campaign manager yet?"

"Yes, sir, I have," Emilio told him, returning JoJo's smile. "He gave me little gifts to pass out to the crowd."

"Good. I'm glad to hear that."

"My pleasure. Are you ready for the people?" Emilio inquired as he motioned to the platform and the podium.

"You don't have to worry about me. Just a little nervous, but I always feel that way before addressing a crowd."

"Moi chevalier sans peur et ians reproche," Emilio confidently stated.

Puzzled, JoJo looked at him with a blank expression before he asked, "What the hell is that supposed to mean?"

"It's just something I learned while studying French at the Northern New Mexico Community College. It roughly means, 'my night without fear or blemish'."

"I think it's a nice thing to say," Evonne spoke. "You know, he's teaching me and Yolanda to talk French."

Eager to get away, JoJo replied, "Good. Okay, I gotta get up there and get ready for my speech.

"Good luck?" Emilio wished him.

"Yeah, good luck!" the girls, almost inaudibly, echoed.

"Thanks."

God damned French, went through his mind as he approached the steps. *Who the hell needs it? He better well speak our language if he's to be any good to me.*

As he approached the podium, JoJo removed two folded pages from his jacket. They were the contents of his speech, one written in English and the other in Spanish. His eyes surveyed the crowd from his heightened viewing point, and he saw many white faces honing their attention for his words. These were Anglos mostly from California and other progressive sections of the country who moved here, hoping to encourage the abused indigenous people of New Mexico. They were here, in their new home state, to support those who were rebelling against the establishment of big business and outsiders corrupting the old way of life. They were here to rally for the equality of those they perceived as being taken advantage of. Acknowledging this, and knowing that he needed their support, JoJo made his decision. He knew that he wanted to reach these people who would someday be his constituents. He had wanted to address the people in Spanish, instead he chose English.

"Greetings, my fellow Santa Feans."

The crowd applauded and cheered when he began. He took the moment to acknowledge the accolades, and to let it subside before he continued.

"For over four hundred years, this land has been ours. We cultivated the land, and we protected the forests. We established the roots of our culture, and we provided for our own. Today, we have those who wish to destroy all that we have obtained. The rich have come here, had us build their homes and then complain that we did not do a good job. The over-educated elite complain that our schools are inefficient and ineffective, and yet they do nothing to improve them. Instead, they want to replace our people with their own on the school board. They build shopping centers and more wealthy homes that they live in for only three, maybe six months out of the year, and then they want a say as to how we should use the property tax money that we collect. They say they want to raise our living standards, to teach us the ways of the outside world. What they really want to do is break up our families, to destroy our way of life, to destroy our heritage, to destroy our culture…"

18

Taking Mike's advice, Francesca set upon the task to interview the cops who worked on the related murder cases. Part of it was easy since one of the investigators was within her command. The difficulty lay with the three who were no longer on the force; two were retired and one was dismissed for driving under the influence.

She took the option of meeting with those no longer on the force first. An unorthodox approach, she used a couple of reasons to influence her. The ones still working would still be around, but uncertainty hovered around the men no longer cops. They might be getting older which gave concern about the memory factor, or they might up and move away, or, if she just wanted to be cynical, they could just suddenly drop dead. She opted on the dismissed cop first, if for no other reason, he had the same last name as hers.

"Yeah, I guess I can say I really screwed up," ex-Santa Fe Police officer Manny Madrid admitted with agonizing remorse etched in his voice. "I threw away eighteen years of being on the job, a job that I really loved."

Manny Madrid became a bail bondsman after his dismissal, and a half-year later he earned his license to become a private investigator. Much of his free time he spent counseling others on the perils of excessive drinking, especially taking aim at those who were served with DWI's.

"It's unfortunate," he continued, "but, per capita, this state leads the country in DWI arrests. Most of them are from here, Rio Arriba, Taos, and Bernalillo counties. Needless to say, while I was with homicide there were way too many cases of deaths caused by drunken drivers."

Francesca Madrid listened sympathetically to a man who might have become a good colleague in her division, but for a twist of fate dictated by his actions, he was reduced to becoming a mere witness on a couple of cases now under her scrutiny. She began to wonder if the day-in and day-out perils of the job influenced his poor decision, and if some guardian angel kept her from making the same mistake. She thought about it for a minute before the realization set in that she was not there to sympathize with anyone. She had homicides to solve, and hopefully, Manny Madrid could give her information that would be of use.

"Basically, my memory coincides with the file information of two of the cases I worked on, the ones that might very well be related to each other."

Manny Madrid fully cooperated with Francesca's questions, something she did not fully expect from someone kicked off of the force. In appreciation, she thanked him for it.

"No problem. On the most part, the same applied to the Julie Fletcher case, the one we separated from the others."

"Why was that case separated?" Francesca queried.

"We pinned it on a Chuck Gentry fellow, a Texan who moved up here and was Fletcher's neighbor. We found some of his hair in the bed she was dead in. He had a key to her apartment that he used to feed her cat whenever she was away. According to some of her friends, he made some loving overtures that she rejected. We speculated he got frustrated, and one night used the key to get in and attacked her. Unfortunately, as the file shows, one of our young guys screwed up, and the case got thrown out."

"So, he became your only suspect?"

"On the most part, that's correct."

"That is the second time you said, 'on the most part'," Francesca reminded him. "It sounds as if there was once some element of doubt."

Letting his mind drift back to the days of his investigation, Manny spoke slowly as he tried to recall the facts. "Until we tied in the evidence, the Gentry guy was not our immediate suspect."

"You mean there was someone else?"

"That's correct. I believe he was a lawyer, or a doctor, or something like that. I didn't interview him. My partner at the time did. If I remember right, he's the one who told us that Gentry had an access to the woman's apartment."

"Can you remember the guy's name?" Francesca asked.

"No way in hell I could do that. I never met him, and the case dates back nearly a decade. It's just that when we nailed this Gentry guy, we totally dismissed all other possible suspects. Most of the names, including his, never made it into the file."

Francesca left Manny Madrid's office with one more question than she went in with. It may not have any relevancy since Chuck Gentry was never formally charged. Plus, there was still a small but similar modus operandi that could be related to the other cases. If it was related, Francesca concluded that it might very well have been the first of the series. Knowing the name of the lawyer, or doctor, or whoever was the friend of Julie Fletcher, might possibly help to fully classify the case.

The second ex-cop, Jake Sarabia, was not available to be interviewed. He retired a week after Francesca joined the force. Enjoying retirement, Jake was in Las Cruces playing golf. Unfortunately for Francesca, he would not be back for another few days. That left one more ex-cop, and she called upon him without phoning beforehand. For as cooperative as Manny Madrid was, Jim Webber was very confrontational.

"So you think you'll get these solved, uh."

"That's the goal," Francesca cautiously replied.

"I don't know why you're wasting your time. Most of the guys on the force got their heads up their asses. Besides, you're a woman. I don't know what you expect to accomplish."

The remark did not sit well with Francesca as she took it to be exactly as it sounded… sexist. The temptation to snap back was quelled by her logic, knowing that if she did she would loose any chance of digging out information from the antagonist. That took precedence over any seeming insult thrown at her.

"You were an investigator on a couple of the cases. I'd think you'd like to see them closed."

"Hey, I'm no longer a cop, so it doesn't concern me."

"Am I to think then that you won't cooperate?"

"About as much as anyone you're working with. As I said before, you're a woman, and most of your cohorts resent that."

"Is that how you feel?"

"I don't give a crap," Jim Weber replied. "When I was on the force many resented me being a white guy from back east, afraid I might show 'em up. I was told more than once they didn't need an outsider telling them how to do things."

"That's not the way I look at things. I just…."

"Maybe not," Jim Webber cut her short. "But, you're a woman, and they don't like women leading 'em."

"So far, I haven't had any problem," Francesca mildly protested.

"And how long have you been with them? A month, maybe two months?"

"About that. I transferred up from Albuquerque, and…"

"Then you should know what I'm talking about," Jim Webber again cut in. "They're no different up here. Maybe a bit worse. Just wait until you start producing. That's when you'll see what I mean."

Francesca realized that she would get nowhere with the course of the conversation, so she decided that she would have to take control and steer it back to it's intended purpose.

"Mr. Webber, what I came here for is to find out if you can help me with any information."

"Look, detective, I was a thorough cop. Whatever I knew I put into the case files. So I can't help you there."

After a few more questions Francesca accepted the fact that Jim Webber was not going to be helpful. From the tone of his demeanor, she concluded that he was the type of cop who did not overlook things, that all of what he knew lay written up in the reports. As she started to leave she did ask one more question.

"I know you didn't work on the Julie Fletcher case, but do you know anything about it?"

"If I didn't work on it, there's not much if anything you can expect me to tell you."

"I understand. Well, thanks for your time." Francesca then imposed one more question. "Did anyone who worked on the case ever mention another suspect, a professional such as a doctor or a lawyer?"

"They did, but damn, that was several or more years ago. I don't know what he was. Besides, the guy they pinned it on was more than likely the perp who killed her."

"That's the way it seems. Well, again, thanks."

Francesca was glad to leave Jim Webber's home. His brusqueness made him an uncomfortable person to be with, giving her reason to want to dismiss his accusations of prejudice. She suspected that whatever hard times he had with his working partners might well have been the result of his own personality. Then again, he was right about the sexual harassment on the Albuquerque force, and although she as of yet had not experienced any such behavior in Santa Fe, the threat was still there. She also accepted that some truth might lie in the fact that they resented him for being a white outsider. She had seen a little of it in Albuquerque, but that was quickly corrected. This was Santa Fe, and the old minds still were dominant in parts of the society. It was exemplified by what was looming in the mayoral race.

Erasing away the thoughts of prejudice, she focused her mind more to the questions she had posed to the former cop. His lack of cooperation, willful or otherwise, did not help, however he did vaguely reconfirm what Manny Madrid told her. There was once, ever so briefly, another suspect in Julie Fletcher's murder. It might be nice to know who he was. One investigator who might know was still on the force, so upon her return to the office she decided to question him.

Matt Abeyta, a fifteen-year veteran, was a mild mannered cop with little ambition other than putting in his required time for retirement. With only two years of college he resigned himself to being no more than an everyday detective assigned to homicide, but that was not to infer he was not good at what he did. A keen eye for detail, coupled with a sense of executing his responsibilities made him a par above average. In the short time she worked with him, Francesca acknowledged this, and she hoped it would help her make some progress with the cases he was attached to.

"As you know, Sarg, I was not the primary on any of them," Matt Abeyta explained.

"That's not important," Francesca stated. "You worked on them so you might be able to shed some light, or at least solidify what we do have."

"Okay. Just pound away. I'll be glad to help whatever way I can."

"Thanks."

They spent about a half-hour reviewing the particulars of each case. In the end just one bit of light was shed, a faint beam that was not noted previously in the Georgina Becaud case file, her first assignment as a Santa Fe homicide investigator.

"The only thing that surprises me is that Sarabia was incomplete with the facts in the file."

"How's that?" she asked.

"Well, you see here where a witness claims that he might have seen Becaud talking to someone in the restaurant?"

"Yes," Francesca answered. "The stomach contents reveal that she ate just about two hours before. I asked Jake and you to question the people who worked there. No one could recall seeing her. Just a vague account by another customer."

"That's true, and it may not be relevant, but Jake does not mention that the customer stated he heard someone speak to her in a different language."

"Oh? Not English or Spanish?"

"No. I remember distinctly the witness saying that someone struck up a conversation from a booth across from her. He claims that he never got a good look at the person because of the way the seating was laid out, but he heard the Becaud girl speak in some foreign language. He said it could have been Italian, or French, but since he speaks Spanish, he knew it wasn't that."

Using her own sense of reasoning, Francesca deducted that unlike French, Italian and Spanish has a lot of similarities that the customer should have been able to distinguish. This left her to lean to the fact that the language spoken may very well have been French. This was backed up by the fact that the girl came from a French speaking background, and there was the sketching in her pad depicting a perfume bottle and a French slogan. She kept this information stored in her safe called memory. Very likely it might not have any bearing on matters, but if it did she could not create a scenario where she could make it fit.

By the end of the day, with the exception Jack Sarabia, the retired cop who was out of town, Francesca finished interviewing each of the active and non-active cops that had anything to do with any of the cases. No new illumination on any of the information offered any brightness. Basically, the detective was still at ground zero, the place where she had begun the day. Still, something kept cawing at the back of her mind, disturbing the clarity that she wanted to find. Perhaps a break such as taking the night off, spending quiet time with Sam and a fitful night's sleep, would relax her thinking process for the next day.

A half mile south of the Santa Fe Police Headquarters on Cerrillos Road, Lieutenant Mike Shannon and Captain Eduardo Guiterrez burned a little extra oil in their own headquarters. The hour pushed past six o'clock, two hours past the normal shift rotation. They were ranking officers on duty twenty-four hours a day, so normal schedules did not apply for them.

"Then, all we have to do is find out is who gave Cornelius Toohey the purple stole and we may find who our prime suspect is," Cap said, as both men tried to find a resolve to the force's most demanding homicide case.

"It seems that way," Mike answered. "The other two priests confirm that it belonged to the monsignor, and that he would have taken it with him when he responded to a call for the last rites."

"So the killer might then have taken it after he killed the priest?"

"Quite possible," Mike tentatively agreed. "Why the hell he, or she, would do that isn't clear. It could have been a prize or a trophy, or perhaps he didn't take it at all."

"How's that?" Cap asked.

"It's very possible the monsignor dropped it somewhere between the rectory and his car. There's a smudge of motor oil on it, something we didn't find at the immediate murder site that was probably covered with snow. But, the rectory parking lot has several spots where cars leaked oil. We can guess that snow already covered the spot where he was killed, and according to the two priests, there was no snow accumulation when he left the rectory. Just water and ice."

"But, it's not conclusive."

"No, it's not. It doesn't mean that the oil spot wasn't on it when he was murdered. It does, though, give us a couple angles to look at."

"You think the female is the key."

"I don't know if she is *the* key, but I'd say she is definitely *a* key."

"Was forensics able to lift any traces off of the ribbon?"

"A couple. One was a thumbprint where someone must have touched the oil spot. However, since it traveled through so many hands up until I got it, we don't know what to think. They are running a trace on the print, and no match has yet been made. The lab did however confirm that it's female."

"But, we don't know for sure if it's the one we're looking for."

"That's right," Mike confirmed. "At least we do have something. It might turn out to be valuable when we find out who she is."

"If we find out who she is," Cap said, mildly correcting Mike.

"Com'on, Cap," Mike rebutted his superior with a twinkle in his eye. "I said when, and I'm sticking by it. What do you think we are? Some numbnuts sheriff's department?"

Cap enjoyed Mike's enthusiasm, a positive attitude that said, 'we always get things done.'

"I don't know about you, but I'm ready to wrap things up for the night," Cap said as he stretched back in his chair. "I promised Margarette and the kids I'd take them out to dinner, and it's nearly six now. What about you?"

"Hey, I'm right behind you. Teri's taken the boy over to visit her mom, and this is my dart night."

"You should have left earlier," Cap said.

"Nah. Besides, we'll have a couple of late nights coming up, so we better get used to it."

Contemplating, Cap agreed. "That's true. Maybe we can get some resolve on some of these cases. In the meantime, we've got a top brass inspection in Espanola late next week. A few of the state representatives, and I'm sure the press, will be there."

"You're right, I guess we've got to get ready for that. You want me there?"

"Only for image sake. You're the second in command in criminal affairs, so it's best that you attend."

"You got it," Mike said. "I just hope that the civilian reps don't muck things up finding faults that aren't there."

"It's nothing to be really concerned about," Cap replied. "Most of them are there just for the photo-op."

"I hope you're right," Mike said while rising from his seat and prepared to leave. "On that note, I'm taking off. See you in the morning."

After Mike left Cap made a quick call home to tell Margarette that he was on his way. While gathering his personal items, he thought about Mike's comment about the civilians possibly finding faults with his men during the inspection. He hoped he dispelled the concerns by telling him that they would be there for photo opportunities, to spread their own exalted visions to the media.

He reassured himself that that will be the case. Most of the legislative people wouldn't even know what to look for. The only way they'd know is if Chief Ebner cued them in, and he was damned sure the chief wouldn't do that.

19

A routine common to most lovers, from the young to the mature, became established. In some ways, the pattern of the days and nights they shared with each other became predictable. Still, for both Sam and Francesca, the weeks they spent with each other were treated somewhat as a new experience. They each had previous lovers, and they each previously had long relationships, but neither had ever before fully felt the attraction that kept drawing them together, magnetizing emotions that previously lay dormant.

Francesca did nearly marry her last love, a rising top executive at an Albuquerque satellite division of one of the country's largest computer chip manufacturers, and a man who wanted her to be his wife, his lover, and his homemaker. He wanted her to surrender her career to meet his needs. At least that is what Francesca felt she was getting out of the relationship. Clues like 'you can travel with me all over the country while I attend corporate meetings' or 'you would be a perfect hostess for the cocktail parties we'll give to entertain business guests' contributed to her feelings. Never did he show concern about her work as a police officer, nor about her attitude regarding her career. Never did he give any signs of recognizing her love for her job. He just made assumptions. Even at the end he assumed she wanted everything he mapped out for her, that she would find happiness being the proud wife of a man who someday would become president or even CEO of his corporation. When she told him that she wanted out, he assumed that she would change her mind and grab what he was offering her. He never assumed otherwise.

At the beginning, Francesca made her own assumptions; that she could freely fall in love with a man of dominating ambitions, that she could always maintain her own identity, and that she could continue on with her career as a cop. That was based upon naïveté on her part, and later she lamented being foolish enough to cling to the belief that her desires would win out over his. In the end she made two decisions. One was to make him realize that she would never be able to fulfill the wifely role he designed for her. The second was to accept the opportunity that awaited her sixty miles to the north.

Sam had his own romantic imbroglios, but never did marriage get a chance to enter the picture. He was already married to his mistress, his love since graduating, his wife who supported him, who occupied most of his waking hours, and fulfilled his dreams. Law was his love. It was his mistress and his wife.

Several years earlier, while still in his mid thirties, he met someone with whom he thought he could grow especially close to, someone who could fill a looming void in his future life. Friends egged him to marry, to have a wife and a mate who could help him as he shaped a career that might include politics. He scorned their encouragement, reminding them that he saw no foundation in a marriage based upon exploitation. He reasoned that if he ever did marry she would be a woman of independence, someone who loved him for his personal traits, and not as someone to potentially roll out a red carpet into the world of politics or public affairs. He could always hire a 'girlfriend' to elevate him in public and social life. It was a thought that, although still repugnant, had more honest merit than using a woman as a wife just to raise his stature.

His relationship with the woman developed slowly. They dated, they spent time together, they made love, and a mutual bond sprouted from the seeds planted by his nurturing love. She kept a distance by not fully committing to the closeness between them, but he went on to cultivate the soil, and delighted at the green growth that stretched its way skyward. Then one day a very sudden and much unexpected dark storm cloud appeared, and by nightfall an evil icy rain fell, killing the bud of a promising future flower. He painfully mourned the loss, but within time he came to accept that she had permanently gone away, never to be seen again except in his memories.

Over the next years, after time managed to ease the pain of the loss of a hopeful life of sharing, other women walked into his life. None stayed long enough to replant in, or to trample on, his garden. None, until Francesca.

For Sam this relationship was different, one that he never tasted quite the same way before, and one that he gratefully savored. Nothing one-sided hampered their feelings, and although not often spoken, each came to accept that which existed between them would only become enhanced by the love melding them solidly together. No demands were made, and none were given. They acquiesced to each other's need, be it independence, career challenges, or simply some moment of undisturbed solitude. So, when either required their own little space, the other did not hesitate to accede to the need.

On this night it was Sam who had plans that did not include Francesca.

"It's Wednesday, my dart night. I should be in somewhere around midnight."

"I know," Francesca told him. "That's why I've chosen tonight to catch up on a few things I've been meaning to do at my place. Enjoy yourself, and kick ass in your games."

Francesca accompanied Sam only once to Ray's Pub for a night of darts. She enjoyed watching him and his friends vie for wins, of meeting new people with whom Sam shared his comradeship, and of course, seeing Mike in a non-professional climate. But, she knew that her visit to the pub on those nights would be few and far between. Francesca was not into sports. She saw how the players wrapped themselves up in their games, and she realized that by being there she would only become a dart widow sitting around and watching a game she had no desire to learn. Rather than sitting around watching grass grow, Francesca used her Wednesday nights for more constructive purposes.

The matches were played, and most of the games were completed earlier than usual. Mike and Sam, and Alex teamed with Gregg were the strongest out of the eight teams that played in the Wednesday night dart league. Each had weaker opponents, drubbing them 8-1 and 9-0 respectively. The caliber of play cut the time by at least fifteen to twenty minutes. That was okay, for it allowed more time to sit at the bar and resume their attempts to solve the world's problems

Alex was the first to settle into his seat and wait for the others.

"I see you guys whitewashed Tim and Andrew," Mike later noted after completing his match.

"Yep," Alex confirmed, beaming a victorious smile in Mike's direction. "What'd you guys do?"

"8-1. Lover boy here," Mike said referring to Sam, "Let himself get skunked in a 301 game."

"You know you're right," Alex said. "Ever since he's been dating I've noticed that his darts have gone to hell."

"You noticed that, too, uh. It seems like he's one of these guys that can't handle having a love life and playing darts at the same time. He must be good at one, because his darts stink."

Gregg joined Alex in enjoying the humor of Mike's good-natured ragging. For Sam's part, he just settled back in his seat and smiled, accepting the fact that this was his night to be picked on by his Wednesday night buddies.

Several minutes of fun and exchanging good barbs passed before Gregg asked a more serious question.

"What ever happened to that DWI case on Thomaz Aragon?"

"Who?" Mike asked, slightly puzzled.

"He's talking about JoJo Aragon's kid," Sam replied. "I don't know. I think it's in Magistrate Court."

"I thought your office handled DWI cases," Gregg queried.

"Not unless they reach a first or second class felony stage. This was his second DWI but there weren't any injuries or damage, and no other crimes were committed. Beyond that, I couldn't tell you much even if I knew."

Gregg caught on to Sam's drift that in essence said that even if his office did have the case he would not be at liberty to discuss it.

"That son-of-a-bitch," rumbled lowly out of Alex's mouth, drawing everyone else's attention.

"Who's a son-of-a-bitch?" Mike asked, hoping he could stir a little banter into Alex's direction.

"That prick, JoJo Aragon."

"Come on, now. Is that the way to talk about your next mayor?"

"When that happens, I will definitely move the hell out of Santa Fe."

"Great! That gives me one good reason to vote for the guy".

Alex turned to Mike to give him his comeback. "Thanks! Just remember, one prick deserves another. I'll be gone, but you're the one who'll be stuck with him."

"And so will the rest of us," Sam said, joining in the conversation. "It'll be one sorry day if he wins the election."

"Amen," was said by one, but heralded by all.

"If that guy wins he'll only split people further apart," Gregg said.

"There's no question about it," Mike agreed.

"It's unfortunate," Sam commented. He then added, "From what I hear, he's going to get a big boost after this weekend. A close friend of mine at our local newspaper told me that he'll be getting a full-page endorsement from some nationally known musician. The musician is footing the bill for about twelve thousand dollars."

"Wow!" two or three of the others mouthed in a show of exasperation.

"Does this guy live here?" Gregg asked.

"He spends maybe a month out of the year here. He's got a home in one of those new developments near the opera house."

"That's not even in the city limits," Gregg said.

"True, but that doesn't prohibit him from supporting Aragon."

"Doesn't he know what kind of guy Aragon is?" Gregg then asked.

"I doubt it," Sam answered. "I think that being the humanitarian that the musician is reported to be, he truly believes he's helping disadvantaged people."

"I'm not one of those who believe that people should mind their business when it involves what goes on here," Gregg spoke up, showing disgust, "but this is one guy who's stupid. He backs a guy like Aragon without realizing that even a lot of Joseph Aragon's people can't stand his guts. That includes me."

"It's what I call the Milagro/Beanfield War syndrome," Alex said.

"How's that?" Mike asked.

"In my opinion, a lot of outsiders, not knowing the make-up of the people here, see it as their idea of good vs. evil. They don't see the full picture - just see what they want to see. The rich guys are the bad guys, buying up land, cutting down trees. However, they don't understand that many people who live here are the ones soliciting the sales of their property. They wanna' make a small fortune and provide themselves with a better life. The 'bad guys' are risking their money in the hopes making more, and while doing it they're creating some wealth and better living opportunities for the people that live in the area."

"Yeah, but that's a problem that exists anywhere," Mike said. "Take the south, or places where skinheads and other bigots live."

"Yeah, that's true, but at least they're exposed for everyone to see," Alex replied. "Nobody ever thinks of this place as being bigoted, unless they live here for a while and see or experience it."

"Maybe so, but the celebrities keep coming here," Mike offered as an argument.

"Right, but how many stay?" Alex asked. "Most come and experience things for themselves, and within a couple of years they leave. Some have managed to look past it and refuse to be daunted."

"Amen, bro," Gregg said, letting his feeling be known. "Take my people; they've experienced what Alex is talking about for some four, five hundred years. Sure, many of us have mixed with people on my wife's side, and that's because we respect for each other. Then there are a lot of New Mexicans who look at us original natives as inferior. Even my wife, whose heritage is Mexican, gets a lot of barbs thrown at her. It's been that way for a long time, and I'm afraid it might be that way forever."

"In time it'll change," Sam offered his comment. "Better education will help do that. Plus communications: radio, television, the computer. They reach more and more people."

Alex injected his opinion, "You may be right, but that depends upon the people who teach. Will they teach what history has recorded? Or, will they teach in accordance with their own bias – their own personal agenda as what is being done in many universities?"

"Well, I can only hope that Sam's right," Gregg said.

"Same here," Mike said as he drew his beer to his lips. "I'll even drink to it."

Neither Alex, Sam, nor Gregg said anything. They just nodded their heads in unison agreement, sealing a pact that each individual man knew existed among them.

The discussions had not ended. Just a pause set in to let a new topic develop. Mike ordered a round of beers. When they were opened, each man had a beer in his own hand, Alex raised his and toasted, "to all the free thinkers who sit at this bar."

"Here, here!" was the uniform response.

"Christ, Alex, you know you sound like a libertarian," Mike said.

"Isn't that what true libertarianism is all about, being free and open minded, respectful of another's right to their own point of view?"

"Why libertarianism?" asked Gregg.

It was Alex's turn to exhibit some levity.

"Why not? Communism is supposedly dead. Fascism is not in vogue. The rest of the world is either socialist, ultra-liberal, or ultra-conservative, and we all know how screwed up it is because of it. So, maybe if we develop a society where everyone thinks freely, lives freely, gives due respect for everyone else, and keeps government and society from dictating how we live from day to day, and end political correctness, it might all become a better world to live in."

"Sounds like he's on a soap box again," Mike said, but it was Sam who persisted.

"Isn't that why we have a democracy, so that people can go out and elect other people who think like them?"

"Ah, contraire," Alex quipped. "First of all, we're a Republic and not a democracy. Aristotle criticized democracy as being a means for those at the bottom to scream and yell enough so as to bring the people at the top down to their level. It deals with numbers, giving everyone a voice and a vote. The majority wins and the minority looses. It doesn't deal with what is right or wrong, and many don't realize that there is a responsibility that is supposed to go with their democratic rights. All too often the majority votes for a guy or an issue that turns out to be a disaster. Democracy might be the best thing we have going for us, but it is not the salvation everyone thinks it is."

A bewildered look came upon Gregg's face. Mike's and Sam's expressions remained fixed. They believed they knew where their philosopher friend was going with this.

"In a truly free society, democracy can never mandate how people feel and think, and the different beliefs each of us have. It often contributes to intolerance. Some groups try to dominate over others by spieling out their own pet dogmas and incorporate them into laws, oblivious to any possible harm. The winners in the popular majority often feel that they have all of the answers, and they try to impose them upon the beliefs of others.

"Beliefs are ideas. They must be individually developed and nurtured. When they're mandated, collectivist thinking develops and there is no longer individual freedom. Although it may be favored by a majority, it winds up violating the Utopian vision of democracy. It, instead, opens the doorway to Big-Brotherhood and totalitarianism."

Alex waited until he felt that his statement was absorbed. No one interrupted him, so he continued. "Democracy is a tool - well-intentioned, designed to give everyone an equal voice regardless if they know how to use it. Regretfully, it often becomes a tool where people elect other people to tell all people what to do, and how to do it.

"Take ancient Greece for example. It was a democracy. Socrates had a hand in electing its leaders, but when his philosophies ran in contrast to those he may have elected, they sentenced him to death. They even had the audacity to tell him which poison he must take."

A mild chuckle was generated from his small audience.

"On a more serious side, though," Alex went on. "We all know the evils of bigotry and discrimination, and we passed laws to eradicate these evils. Instead of enforcing the existing laws we enact new ones setting up quotas. We then penalize people and organizations for not hiring by the numbers, which in turn discriminates against others. Instead of educating and training those of limited abilities, we instead penalize those that are better capable. We award what they earn to someone who does not fully understand what's been given him. Inequity has not been erased, but it becomes compounded.

"Many people in a democracy abdicate the responsibilities that go with it. They stop voting. They stop voicing their opinions based upon reason and common sense. They all allow democracy to cater to those who yell the loudest, demand the most, but contribute the least. I might be paraphrasing Plato a bit, but it was Plato who stated that 'those who do not involve themselves in politics allow themselves to be governed by those inferior to them.'

"In principle, democracy is ideal. However, it will work much better when people are not penalized for trying to improve their lives, and when it stops just catering to those who feel that government owes them everything."

"Good luck!" Mike weighed in. "Your rhetoric is based on idealism. I don't disagree with you, but the majority of people don't vote that way."

"Mike's right," Sam said. "Most people vote along party lines, or for the candidate who pretends he knows what he's talking about. They may not understand what the candidate is saying, but they'll vote for him."

"That is part of the responsibility if you want to have a fair democracy," Alex replied. "Learn to listen to the message instead of the messenger."

"As I said before," Mike responded. "Good luck!"

"It demonstrates the drawbacks of a democracy as we know it. If people vote only along party lines because it is fashionable, or traditional, then they are contributing to democracy's demise. If they hear only what they are being told, they are contributing to its erosion. If they relinquish their rights to the screamers and yellers, they are then contributing to its death. If they start thinking for themselves, with their own minds, only then will democracy grow healthy. They will only survive when they stop trying to be altruistic; by stop trying to service everyone else's needs before they adequately nurture their own and their family's."

"So, then you admit it," Mike tried to corner Alex into a full commitment. "You are a Libertarian."

"Based upon the various conversations we've had, I'd say that each one of us here are deep down Libertarians, although not all of us realize it enough to admit it."

"We're talking about you. Are you, or aren't you?" Mike persisted with the adamancy of an interrogating cop.

"Philosophically speaking, I am. Politically, I'm not."

"Oops! Here you go again, damn it. Not committing yourself."

"I just did on a philosophical basis. On a political basis, they are dyslexic and they think the world is flat. They put the power of politics ahead of firming up and spreading their philosophies."

The unexpected comment drew snickers from the others, but the motive behind the amusement varied.

"Maybe you're right, but we have only two parties to vote for," Gregg said.

"I'm a registered Democrat," Sam commented with a light, but more serious tone. "What don't you like about them?"

"Dogmatics," Alex flatly replied. "Aside from covertly pushing socialism, they are too damned dogmatic about their views. They push their agenda primarily by viciously attacking the opposition leaving very little room for disagreement. If you do they try to make you look like a fool. It is a way of being an elitist."

"Republicans are not different," Sam retorted. "Look at the far right."

"True," Alex answered with an earnest agreement. "But, over the last twenty-five or so years the Dems have done an excellent job in perfecting the art of spin, leaving the wuzzy Republicans far behind."

"What's wrong with that?" Gregg asked.

"Spinning is an art of deception - a refined tactic where you attack the opposition, while obfuscating the intent of your agenda. You first tear down the merits of the opponent's ideas so that the public cannot see the weakness of your own."

"Well said," Mike said to Alex's surprise. "Then again, there are quite a few good politicians out there who try to sell their issues."

"No doubt about it, but unfortunately not enough. Not enough Barry Goldwaters or Ronald Reagans enter politics. Or even Patrick Moynihans who was a Liberal. They're the ones who clearly tell you how things are, they tell you what they intend to do about it, and most importantly they leave it to the people to decide whether or not to agree."

"So, you're saying most politicians are not out to do good," Gregg said in a questioning tone.

"I'm saying that most politicians, like our friend JoJo Aragon, are out to control. They enter politics because it gives them power. They don't go into the arena for the money. Most have enough already. Does being a wealthy politician mean that he or she is corrupt? No. It is not the money that's the root of all evil in politics. It is the quest for power. Money only helps to buy that evil. There are many fine Democrats and Republicans, who believe in their issues. Lots are in politics to control with power. They're the ones who open the door for the evil to walk in."

The pub's air became still with silence. Even the jukebox, playing a popular country and western song, went unheard. Each man, whether they agreed or not, reveled in their own chilling thoughts.

Breaking the ice, it was Mike who spoke.

"Let's have another round of beers. This one's on our friend, the philosopher, here."

"Amen!" chorused Sam and Gregg.

20

Canyon Road begins at the Paseo De Peralta, and winds its way eastward for nearly four miles until it hits a fork. One thong leads to a gate, blocking all vehicular traffic from disturbing the pristine forestry on state land. To the left of the fork the road turns into Cerro Gordo, a sometimes dirt and a sometimes asphalt road that loops around bringing you back to Palace Avenue, and within two blocks of Canyon Road.

Two thirds of Canyon Road, all of Cerro Gordo, and all of the capillary of streets in Santa Fe's artistic neighborhood, are made up of homes, rehabilitated and restored old adobes. New homes are built on a grander scale, and they are in keeping with the tradition of the Santa Fean scheme of earthen adobe colors. The wealthy live in the other third as well. But this stretch, a stretch that extends from the Paseo up to the end of Palace Avenue, is also home to much of Santa Fe's art galleries, specialty shops and boutiques, restaurants and cafes all catering to the city's wealthy, to the people's need for extravagance, and to the very deep pockets of the tourists.

At night there are different kinds of movement, mostly by those who dwell within Santa Fe's most affluent section. Except for those who have a specific place to go, the number of tourists dwindles leaving the area to be inhabited mostly by the residents, and by those who wish to fancifully wine and dine or to attend gallery openings. The art themes in these galleries, be it in the technique of paintings, of photography, or of sculpture, are mainly southwestern. Seldom can the term universal art ever be applied.

On this night Bill Johnson hosted a party, celebrating the opening of his new gallery. Joseph Aragon, as a city councilman, kept his word by casting the deciding vote that gave Johnson the city permit to open the gallery. As far as Bill Johnson was concerned, it was a done deal several months before he announced his intentions. He already obtained a building permit that allowed him to add an ell to the structure of his two-story home. Confident he would achieve his goal of getting the gallery permit, he went on ahead with the construction. If for some reason it would be denied, something from the outset he knew would not happen, Johnson was sure he would find another use for the new structure.

The celebrating officially began at seven in the evening, and the guests were all by special invitation. The normal gallery opening practice, which allowed any and all to enter, was ignored. This was his night to make the impressions, and the artists whose works hung on the gallery walls were just part of the show.

Champaign, wine, and hard liquor flowed freely. Hors d'oeuvres disappeared as rapidly as they were presented. Music of Jazz, alternating with the classics and with local sounds, filled the air.

By eleven, the numbers of guests declined. Most came to allow themselves to be seen mixing with others who represented Santa Fe's rich and famous. They then went home early, grateful to be away from the atmosphere and the repetitious art covering the ultra smooth diamond-glass plastered walls.

The people who stayed late were the ones who were special to Bill Johnson. They were his clients and suppliers, his users and his distributors. Frequent trips were escorted through the doorway leading to the office in the main house. Deals were done. Exchanges were made, all with happy smiles that said 'enjoy'. They all radiated until someone, receiving a package in exchange for another, spoke into the collar of a short jacket covering the otherwise bare shoulders of his female escort, "All right. Move in," and to Bill Johnson himself, "This is a bust. You are under arrest."

What may have been twenty or thirty men and women, all with guns drawn and wearing dark jackets and caps with the letters D E A sported on them, appeared seemingly out of nowhere. Johnson, and fifteen remaining guests, froze in disbelieving shock at what they were witnessing. Soon, the shock turned to fear and concern as plastic bracelets were placed around their wrists and behind their backs.

Bill Johnson always expected to be pinched by cops for lesser reasons, and he was always prepared by having his attorney on standby. He never expected to be nabbed in the claws of ravenous predators at a gala event, and he never expected that his attorney would be one of those included in the snare. For Bill Johnson, and for many of his friends, the night of celebration would be their last for several years to come.

❦

While the posture inside the office of New Mexico State Police Chief John Ebners's office was not rancorous, it was not completely cordial either.

Captain Guiterrez and Lieutenant Shannon listened quietly and attentively as the police chief addressed his concerns to John Dorset, the lead agent of the DEA task force that raided the Bill Johnson gallery and home the night before.

"We're glad to see Johnson finally taken down," the chief began. "What I'd like to know is, why wasn't state and local authorities kept informed?"

The three state cops thought they knew the answer, but they wanted the federal agent to state it clearly from his own lips. It would help to clarify the questionable trust that existed between the federal agency and the state agencies.

"Based upon our negative relationship with local enforcement in this part of the state, we opted best to go the course alone," Agent Dorset explained.

"Then you're implying that there might have been tip-offs before the raid on the gallery," Chief Ebner said with a matter of fact tone.

"That is correct, sir."

"You are also implying that the tip-offs might come from this agency. We did work with you on past raids." As displeasing as it might sound, Ebner had to push the agent into admitting that he did not fully trust the state police.

"Yes...and no," the agent cautiously replied.

"I don't understand. I assume you'll explain."

The agent showed no hesitancy in fulfilling the state police chief's assumption. "The state police is subordinate to the state's Department of Public Safety. That means an extra set of ears would have knowledge of our intended raid. We considered this a major bust, so we wanted to minimize the chances of the wrong word getting out."

"Are you insinuating the DPS may be employing someone crooked?"

"I cannot comment on that."

Agent Dorset's answer piqued the ears of the state cops in the room. Not commenting seemed to affirm that suspicions of the state's top enforcement agency existed.

"And, what about our boys?" Captan Guiterez asked.

"Aside from the one rogue cop you have in the center of the state, our office feels you have a bunch of sharp and honest people working for you."

The cop referred to was a long time state patrolman who lived and worked in the mid-section of New Mexico. For several years he was suspected of working with the leaders of the tiny villages that blanketed the area. Parking his patrol car along the roadway, and pretending to be engaged in conversation with a local sheriff or forest agent, he would lay in wait for an out of state plate to pass them by. When one did, he pursued the vehicle and stopped it, usually under a pretense of not having a valid license plate. The other official car trailed closely behind. Engaging the out-of-stater into friendly conversation, he coaxed the occupants out of their vehicle. While the occupant was still engaged in friendly talk with one of the officers, the other seized upon the opportunity to search the unoccupied vehicle. Most times up to an ounce of marijuana, very often planted, was found. Frightened, the occupants were remanded to the local justice of the peace where fines were levied upon them. A fifty-dollar misdemeanor fine was upped to three or four hundred dollars, often the total amount of cash the person from out of state carried. Upon payment, the state officer told the defendant that a hearing date to contest the arrest had been set, and followed it up with, "If I were you, I would not come back here." After the still scared defendant departed, the two officers were then paid their share of the take.

The cop in question was under investigation for nearly a year, but neither state nor federal officials were able to nab him for extortion. Top state brass wanted to transfer him, but they were dissuaded by federal agencies. With only four months left before his retirement, it was hoped that he might one day become careless. All parties were still waiting.

"I appreciate the compliment," Captain Guiterrez said with a touch of sarcasm. "However, I'm sure you realize that this doesn't dismiss concerns we may have against your office. It seems that the trust we've had seems to be damaged."

"I am sorry that has to happen, but our main priority is to break up operations like the one Johnson had."

"I hear what you're saying, but that puts us into a position of not knowing where we stand," Chief Ebner forcefully commented. "What about the operations up in Espanola? Are you going to keep us out of the loop on that, too?"

"To be honest with you, sir, I don't know," Dorset stated bluntly. "We do know the local agencies up in the Rio Arriba area will be kept out. Considering how close the personal ties are between the people that live in the area, if your department does get involved, we will probably request that officers from the outside be brought in to assist."

"It sounds like you're now making an indictment against our department," Chief Ebner replied back, equally as blunt.

"No," Dorset answered. "I don't consider it as an indictment against your people. It's just that we may have a lot at stake here. Per capita, Rio Arriba is one of the worst drug areas, if not the worst, in the entire country. If, on the federal level, we can make some inroads, we may have a chance of bringing that ratio down. But first, we have to completely trust the people we are working with before we can foresee having any success."

"And, you don't think our men up there can be trusted."

"That's not quite what I'm saying," Dorset defended himself. "In drug situations like the kind you find up there, lives will be at stake. To protect my people, we want to have complete confidence in our working partners. Till then, we will ask that only officers with no ties to that area be working with us."

The meeting came to a close with all sides having a clearer picture of where they stood. As for Cap and Mike, they did not particularly like it.

"In my mind, it's the DEA's excuse to be glory seekers," Mike gave his stern opinion as he settled back into a chair back in the captain's office. "A few of our people could have been selected to be in on it. The same for the Santa Fe Police Department who could have acted as backup control should things have gotten out of hand at the gallery, spilling out into the streets."

Cap nodded his agreement. He stood near his office window that gave him a clear view of the field below where cadet trainees were going through their exhausting routines. Recalling his days out there, he thought of the many fellow cadets with whom he trained. Most went on to become respected members of the force, while the ones who flunked out went on to become community leaders. He had no doubt that those training now would someday make their own contributions.

Another moment passed before he presented his view. "What bothers me the most is the image Dorset impugned upon our people. In one breath he implies that he does not trust us or the DPS, and in another he calls our people honest. If there is someone crooked in Public Safety, fine. Weed out that person, and get rid of him. We have good people on our force, and I do not like seeing them scared because of a lack of trust."

"The trouble is, we don't have any recourse."

"No, I don't think we do. Chief Ebner will speak up for us, but in cases like these, the feds are the ones calling the shots."

"To complicate matters," Mike said as he looked to the future, "we may not know which drug dealers to go after without fear of stepping on the DEA shoes."

"The answer to that is simple," Cap replied. "We keep going after the ones whom we set up as a priority. If we happen to step on the spit polished shoes of federal agents, then so be it. If the feds don't want to completely trust us, then screw them."

Mike's eyebrows raised as his eyes bulged with a bit of glee. Cap's expression was one Mike himself would make. It was one he never heard, or expected, from the mild mannered, always polite, and always in control Captain Guiterrez. He smiled before he playfully admonished his superior.

"You better be careful, Cap. You'll never get to heaven using that kind of language."

A frantic phone call was placed from Santa Fe to Espanola.

"Relax, my friend. Relax," Ruben Gonzales spoke calmly into the phone. "There is nothing for you to worry about. So relax."

Refusing to be mollified by the Patron's comforting words, JoJo barked with the anxiety of a beaten dog.

"Nothing to worry about! If they ever connect those donations to my campaign as coming from him, I'm dead. I'll be ruined. People will think I'm dealing drugs. I'm not."

"Stop ranting!" Ruben Gonzales' tone evoked an air of authority to which JoJo had to heed. "You sound as if the end of the world has come."

"But...but..."

"But...but...nothing!" Gonzales mimicked JoJo. "Now you sound like a dying locomotive. You have to realize that Johnson's bust in no way will affect you. His donations were turned over through independent sources, so there is no way that suspicion will be cast upon you or anyone in your camp. Please, tell me that you understand me."

"I...I...trust you, it's just that I never expected anything like this to happen."

"Neither did we," Gonzales lied. "It came as an equal shock to us as well. Now, hang up your phone and go about your business as though nothing has happened. As far as your interests are concerned, nothing did. Trust me."

"Yes…yes, sir, I will. I trust you."

"Good. That is more like it. So, for now, good-bye. I'll be in touch with you soon. Especially if I have some good news."

Ruben Gonzales hung up his phone and turned to his old friend and aide, Tommy Trujillo.

"That stupid ass acts as though he's the one with trouble," Gonzales told him. "Little does he realize that I'm the one who should worry."

Tommy shook his head, sharing his mentor's concerns.

"I'm not overly concerned that Johnson will connect us with his problems. It is the people who supply him I worry about. Just as Johnson is the go-between between his rich buyers and his distributors, his suppliers are the ones actually in the middle between him and me. If he names them, they may name us as the brokers…the one who sanctioned the deal."

"Aren't you worried he might implicate us?"

"No, I know he won't. He'd be too afraid of doing that. He'd rather do jail time."

"I can arrange for the suppliers to be taken care of," Trujillo offered.

A look, accompanied with a smile, told Tommy he had Gonzales' blessing.

"It should be done very soon. We do not know what Johnson will accidently give the feds. We do not want to give them any room to make a move in questioning the contacts."

With that, Tommy Trujillo rose and left to embark upon his mission. Ruben Gonzales was now alone in his smoke filled room. Extinguishing his cigar, he thought about the affects Bill Johnson's arrest could have upon him, his family, and his little empire.

He had worked too hard, for too many years, for some Anglo bastard to mess up what he had built. He could not let that happen. He was ready to retire, and he wanted his remaining years to be peaceful ones.

Gonzales poured himself a scotch before reaching for a fresh cigar for his new thoughts.

He had a disdain for it, but Tommy had to arrange for a job to be done. He could not let any bungled dealings, or arrests, or possible traitors take away the few good pleasures he had in life.

⁓⧤⁓

Not long into the very early morning hours, hours before sunrise, a pick up truck pulled into Echo Canyon, some thirty-five miles northwest of Espanola, and isolated from any populous. The nearest dwelling was about eight miles to the south. A vehicle with two occupants pulled into a dimly lit section of the park and waited for their contact. The rendezvous point was quiet and isolated from any other forms of activity that could possibly bear as witness. No other cars, trucks, or campers were there, making it a perfect place to conduct business.

"I just wish ta' hell we could have met in town, instead of all the way up here," the passenger complained.

"Quit bitchin'," the driver took him to task. "For the type of bread we make because of this guy, I'd meet him a thousand miles from here if he wanted us to. I just hope he's got another score set up for us."

"Yeah, man, so do I." As an afterthought he added, "Maybe he can fill us in on what happened last night."

"Maybe," the driver answered. "I sure as hell hate seeing Johnson go down. We could'a made a lot more cash from the guy."

"Yeah, I agree. He would've made us…"

A sharp crack cut his sentence short. The driver turned his eyes to his partner only to see a large red mass where a face should be.

"Shit!"

That was all he was able to utter before he felt an impact at the back of his head. He heard no sound, and he felt no pain as his head snapped forward. He had no time to realize that he was dead.

In the darkness, two men stepped from the shadows on either side of the truck. After inspecting their slain prey, one lit a cigarette while the other poured fluid over the stilled bodies. Again igniting his ninety-nine cent lighter, he lit the flammable that drenched the driver. Once the blaze began, he reinforced it by tossing in the cheap lighter. The butane contents added an additional accelerant, creating a ball of flame. Stepping back and away, the two figures took in the eruption. The fire would roar, but no one would find the remains until daylight.

"It's a little chilly out here," one man stated as he entered another pick up truck, parked closer to the entrance of the park.

"Not for them, it's not," his partner sardonically replied, enjoying his own tainted humor.

21

Jake Sarabia, the retired ex-cop, came home a couple of days early from his golfing trip to Las Cruces. His daughter's increased contractions showed signs of a premature birth, and as a loving faithful father, Jake aimed to keep his promise of being there for her at the birth of her first child.

A widower, he was unaware of Detective Sergeant Francesca Madrid's visit until he found her card under his door, and her message on the telephone answering machine. After checking on the condition of his daughter…no changes from six hours earlier…Jake left a message, giving his contact number. His next chore was to return the detective's call. He worked with her for only a short time before he retired from the police department, but he did know that she was tenacious. The message and the card told him that she wanted to speak with him for some reason that she deemed urgent. An hour later, he was sipping coffee with Francesca at her desk.

"I know I've been retired for just a few weeks, but it feels like old times," Jake said, reminiscing on the many days he spent like this as an active cop. "Now please tell me, how can I be of assistance to you?"

"I'm working on several files pertaining to the unsolved murders, some of which go back a long time. The last case you worked on involving Georgina Becaud fits among them."

She saw Jake Sarabia's eyes light up, as though he were being given a new challenge, the kind of challenge he had when he was on active duty.

"The last case I worked on, uh?"

"That's correct, Jake," she confirmed to him. She didn't want to make him feel bad, so she did not mention the little bit of information he omitted from the file. Why upset his happiness of being retired? "What I've done is to group them according to similarities. Some stand by themselves, and there are a few we've put into separate piles. This includes the more recent Becaud murder, and the Daughtrey murder which I'm sure you're read about." She noticed the attention he gave to what she was telling him, making her feel that here was a man who would help her any way she needed it. "There is also a case or two which I'm having trouble categorizing."

"Those are the ones you brought me in for," Sarabia said, as though finishing Francesca's thoughts.

She noticed the intuitiveness in Jake Sarabia, and she regretted that she never had enough of an opportunity to work with him.

"Yes," she answered. "I was hoping that you might be able to shed some light on one case in particular. Julie Fletcher. This is one you were the lead on, so maybe you can help me put it into the proper file."

"Well that case does stand by itself. As you know from what's in the jacket, we had a prime suspect who got away on a technicality. So, unless there's something new that I'm not aware of, this is not one of your related cases. I just hope you can come up with new evidence that we can pin on that Gentry fella."

"Then you're convinced that he remains the prime suspect," Francesca stated as though she knew his answer.

"Yep. About as sure as I know that eating a can of beans will make me fart."

Francesca was amused by Jake Sarabia's assertion. Looking at the man, she did not expect a folksy comment coming from the refined looking ex-detective.

Together, they discussed the various details pertaining to the case revealing nothing new. At the end of the review, she did have one last group of questions to ask.

"Julie Fletcher had a couple of close friends, one who was an initial suspect," she began.

"Yes, that's correct. But, very soon we connected Chuck Gentry to it all."

"This initial suspect, he was a doctor or a lawyer, or something like that?"

"He was a lawyer."

"Do you remember his name?"

"You mean it's not in the file?"

"No."

"Well, you should know him. Almost everybody knows him. He's our current DA, Sam Dawes."

Jake Sarabia could see the jarring affect the name had upon Francesca, the look comparable to someone being hit by a fired .45 caliber bullet. He learned over and touched the arm of her chair.

"Are you all right?"

Snapping to, realizing how odd she may have appeared, she quickly told him that there was no need to be anxious about her lapse. "I just felt a sudden rush," she lied convincingly. Then motioning to her coffee mug, she added, "It happens to me from time to time after I have had too much caffeine. It passes quickly."

"Seems like you should cut back."

"I keep intending to, but you know how it is when you feel the pressure of a lot of work."

"Boy, I sure do," Sarabia assured her. "That's the reason why I retired, to get away from the pressures…and the caffeine."

Composure gradually reset itself, and mental clarity took control enough for Francesca to pursue with questions.

"Why was he the initial suspect?"

"You mean Dawes?"

"Yes."

"Well, our DA was still an up and coming attorney back then, noted as a man to be fair and honest. His clients had nothing but praise for him. At the time, he and Julie Fletcher were at a lot of places together – The Bull Ring, The Pink Adobe, The Compound, and other nice places. It was assumed they had a special thing going, that is until she was seen with other men. Shortly thereafter, she winds up dead.

As investigators, our first suspicions turned to him as being the jilted lover. We were about ready to call him in for questioning when evidence turned up linking Gentry to the crime."

"You mean his strands of hair?"

"It would have been solid evidence against the guy, but then one of our liberal judges throws it all out because of some minor technicality."

"Did Gentry ever admit to having relations with the deceased?"

"Oh, he did all right. Claims they did it a few times, including the early afternoon of her death. Frankly, I for one didn't believe it, and testimony from other people seemed to corroborate the belief. They were absolutely two different kinds of people. She was attracted to smart and influential people, which was something he wasn't. Gentry was basically a bum who mooched off of other people. So, we figured he used the key he had access to, raped her, and then killed her."

"The file doesn't show any semen found."

"No. We believe she fought him off right after he penetrated."

"The file also doesn't indicate any bruises that could be associated with rape."

"No, but there were a couple of very small cuts near her throat. We figured he used a knife to force himself upon her, and when she was finally able to resist he stabbed her. He then made the knife disappear."

There was some vagueness in Francesca's mind about what might have happened on that night, but the collective reasoning seemed clear enough to charge Gentry with the crime. The evidence never reached a conclusive stage before the case was abruptly thrown out, leaving a shred of doubt in her mind that, perhaps, Gentry may not have been the one to commit the crime. If not Gentry, then…

A cellphone buzz interrupted her train of thought.

"That's the hospital," Sarabia said. "My daughter is due with her baby any time now, and this may be it."

"Thank you for your time, Jake," Francesca said as she rose to shake his hand. "You've been very helpful. Enjoy your retirement, and I hope everything goes fine with your daughter and her baby."

"Thank you. I'm sure it will."

Jake Sarabia departed leaving Francesca with her own disturbing and puzzling thoughts.

Sam. Sam Dawes. Her own Sam Dawes. The man who not only rose to become the District Attorney, but also the man who has become her lover, someone with whom she was daily committing her life to.

Running through her recollections of the day when they sat down together to review open homicide cases, she recalled quite vividly his reaction to the Julie Fletcher file when it came up. She recalled how intently adamant he became in suggesting that it should stand separate from the others, and how evasive he was in discussing it. Could it be that he was trying to ignore the fact that he was pictured as a possible suspect, or was he trying to cover any clues leading to his possible involvement, that there was more to the case than what was clearly visible? And…why did he insist on being so definite that the Julie Fletcher case had no connection to Georgina Becaud's, or to any of the others? Was he hiding something? Was he….

No! Stop it! Her confused mind admonished her. *You can't start regarding him as a suspect.*

Shutting herself completely off from the other detectives working around her, she left her desk and went to the women's officer's lounge. Since the other female officers were off on their own various assignments, Francesca felt certain that she would find the solitude she suddenly needed in the privacy of the room. Perhaps there she could hash out the anguish that began to stew within her emotions.

Slumping deep into the leather sofa provided for the comfort of the women, she propped her head on the armrest, and curled her legs up into her slender torso.

Rehashing her thoughts of moments earlier, she began to explore the various scenarios. What was Sam's involvement with Julie Fletcher? They were seen numerous times together, so obviously they must have been lovers, at least intermittently. Then she was seen in the company of other men. How did it affect Sam? Did he even know about it. Gentry claims that he and Fletcher had sex in the past, including the day of the murder. Could he be telling the truth? If he did have sex with her, did Sam know about it? If so, what would his reactions be like? Was he hurt? Jealous? Could he have killed her?

A shudder rankled rapidly through her body, and with shivers rattling through her drained muscles, Francesca tried to dispel the unpleasant thought. She had to painfully remind herself that she was a detective…a cop. She had to clinically analyze the facts, and to accept them regardless of what they may reveal. It hurt, and making the separation was undoubtedly a struggle.

Focusing her eyes toward the door as though the solutions to the quandary would walk through it, she searched deeper to find some other link. She could find nothing – nothing till she nearly rested her mental search. Then something came to her. It had to do with the Georgina Becaud case. A witness stated that the girl had company at her table, that they joined in conversation, and that the conversation was in a foreign language. Francesca then recalled the times when Sam spoke to her in French, while they were playing around, and when they were making love. She soon found out that he spoke the language fluently, having learned it in college and having refined it by spending a brief time in France, and later using it with his French speaking friends. Could it be…?

Stop it! You're reaching for straws again.

But, was she?

Once more she struggled to keep the woman in love's emotions separate from the cop's. Being objective in the performance of her job had to overshadow feelings of love, and not the other way around. She had to commit herself in her resolve, if not for any other reason than to eliminate the dark haze that only minutes before set up housekeeping in her relationship with Sam. Until then…she was uncertain.

The hour approached four o'clock when she rose from the sofa. Francesca had already decided on one course of action, and as she left the office she was on her way to pursue it.

The change of shift at the restaurant where Georgina Becaud was known to have dined began at four. After five a dinner trade would begin to build, so she managed to get there as soon as possible, before the hungry customers started to flock their way in. Within fifteen minutes Francesca was speaking to the shift manager.

"I know you're going to get busy soon, so I'll try to keep the questions quick and simple."

"Oh, that's all right," the evening manager, Carla Acevedo said, alleviating the need to hurry. "It'll be another half hour or so before the crowd comes in. I'll have my assistant take over for me while you ask me your questions."

Carla summoned her assistant and instructed him not to disturb her conference with Francesca. With a nod of her head, Carla indicated she was ready for a barrage of questions if need be.

"First, Ms. Acevedo, I'd like to ask you how long you've been working here?"

"Oh, nearly five years. Five years this July."

"So, you're familiar with most of the regular clientele who eat here.'

Francesca went on with several more questions, most of which were designed to keep Carla Acevedo at ease, and to gain her trust. When she felt that she had attained her goal she produced a photo.

"Do you know who this man is?"

A look of surprise overtook the shift manager's expression. "Why, yes! That is our district attorney, Sam…I'm sorry, but I don't remember his last name." It was obvious that she was not overly up to date with the names of who was who in Santa Fe.

Francesca acknowledged the woman's reply with a glance before telling her that the last name she was stabbing at was Dawes.

"He's not in any kind of trouble, is he?" Carla asked.

Thinking quickly, not wanting to reveal the underlying motive of her query, Francesca responded, "No. Nothing like that at all. It's just some routine checking for some higher government position he's being considered for."

It was a lie, but Carla showed no sign of catching on. Francesca hoped that the woman would not pursue with questions that would force her to awkwardly create more dishonest answers. The woman did not.

"He comes in here?"

"Yes."

"Does he come in often?"

"He used to," Carla replied. "But, he hasn't been in here for quite some time. Maybe two months, or so."

"Got tired of the food, uh?" Francesca said with a try at mild humor.

Carla laughed and said, "I hope not. I really don't know why he stopped coming here."

Francesca asked a few more questions that were mostly irrelevant. Timing her last one with the signs that she was ready to leave, she rose and walked to the manager's office door before she spoke.

"There's something else that I'd like to ask you, pertaining to a different subject."

"Yes…"

"Do you remember the night of the murder of Georgina Becaud? She was the girl who was killed in the motel across the road."

"I remember it, all right. I was off that night. Susan…Susan Joya was on."

"I see. When is she on again?"

"Susan doesn't work here any more. She and her husband moved to some place in California. I'm sorry I can't be more specific, but I don't know where exactly."

Francesca thought for a second before she concluded that her task at the restaurant was complete.

"I thank you, Ms. Acevedo. It was very kind of you to take the time to answer my questions."

She left the restaurant and walked to her car, all the while pondering the real significance of what she learned.

It all seemed ridiculous. Sam, first being identified as having known Julie Fletcher, and now known to have been a regular at a restaurant where it was established that Georgina Becaud dined on her final meal… her last supper. Santa Fe is a small city, so it could be coincidence of him being at least indirectly connected with two murdered women, but what about his fluency in French? It was established that the Becaud woman spoke with a particular someone the night that she died, a person unidentified, but someone who spoke in a foreign language.

Was it French? Could that person have been her murderer? Could that person have been Sam? If so, does that mean he…

For God's sake, stop it!

It was Francesca's thought, but it could very well have been the last thought of either woman before death took over.

This can't be happening to me!

This, too, could have been the last thought of either woman.

Sam! Not Sam! We have too much between us for it to be him. It was a selfish thought, but it was an honest one.

Closing her eyes and breathing deeply, Francesca sat motionless behind the wheel of her car. There had to be a rationalization behind this – coincidence, or even the shaping of a script that does not exist. She was a cop. It was her profession to create scenes that might not be real; that is the way she solved crimes. The fact that Sam has appeared in two scenes in one afternoon does not necessarily mean he was in any way involved with the gruesome slaying. It does not…

But, what if he is? She caught herself thinking. *The possibility always exists. O. J. Simpson was a national hero before he was accused. Judas could have been canonized a saint if he hadn't turned traitor. Sam's an honest DA out to prosecute crime. It does not mean he's not capable…*

She shook her head to chase away the thoughts that were deteriorating the fondness, the love she held for him. She knew an explanation lay somewhere and she knew that answers would have to be dealt with, whatever they may be.

What do I do now?

She thought for another moment before she realized she did not have any answers. Turning the ignition key, she took one more deep breath before searching the road for traffic. During the homeward drive, she tried to shun the nagging questions that had no immediate answers. Once home, Francesca kicked off her shoes, checked her messages, then shut off the ringer to her home phone and muted the cell. She had to escape to her own solitude for a bit. Afterwards, she would again have to face the revelations of the afternoon. She could not be disturbed by anyone, especially not by Sam.

22

Millicent Sherman's mood soured from petty annoyance to complete frustration as she turned on the light to her motel room. She had to settle on a room for smokers, and the heavy acrid oder immediately insulted her sense of smell, prompting her to leave the door ajar as she opened all operational windows. Luckily, there was a ceiling fan, wobbling as its blades circulated the offensive air around the room. A can of room spray was found in the bathroom, suggesting to her that the management had at least a little consideration for their non-smoking guests. With a little more luck, within a while the artificially sweetened air would replace the lingering acerbic smell.

It had not been a good evening for her ever since she drove through Albuquerque and neared Algodones as she traveled northwards to Santa Fe. A truck hauling gravel, a sight very common along I-25, had its load loosely secured, allowing for trickles of dirt and stones to escape the massive bin and bounce freely upon the highway. It is a very common hazardous occurrence in New Mexico that results in chipped body paint or cracked windshields for the car dubiously traveling behind. Milicent's car became such a victim as a stone, the size of a cat's eye, bounced from the roadway, smashing into the passenger side of her windshield. To her further agony, only seconds before she had questioned the warning statement posted on the tailgate of the truck: 'Not responsible for damages from stones kicked from the highway'. Even if she wanted to challenge the claim, to get the license number, or the name of the hauler, she became too frightened to approach within a quarter of a mile of the truck. Like so many before her, and so many thereafter, Milicent surrendered to the road terror, and prayed that her automobile insurance would cover the damage.

Only a few miles further north, as she neared Santa Domingo, a heavy and steady rain began to fall. With daylight beginning to fade, quickened by nimbus cloud cover, her hopes of driving a bit farther from her home in Scottsdale, Arizona also began to fade. Her ultimate goal, which she knew would be a half-day away, was Colorado Springs. There, she would meet up with her brother, a cadet at the U. S. Air Force Academy. Beginning late that Friday afternoon, Milicent planned to spend a wonderful weekend with her younger sibling. Conceding the desired mileage, she decided to instead spend the night in Santa Fe.

Unfamiliar with the city's outlay, she chose the Cerrillos Road exit, and she stayed on it until she reached what she reasoned to be the heart of the city. Not fussy about what restaurants were available, a motel near a pizza chain seemed to be a good choice. Passing the motel, Milicent drove a quarter of a mile, made a U-turn into the direction of a night of rest. She had not driven more than a couple of hundred feet when a flashing red, white and blue came up behind her, causing her to pull to the right of the road.

Not sure of her offense, she asked the officer about the infraction she committed.

"Didn't you see the sign which indicates no U-turn?" the stocky, medium height cop asked.

After confessing that she did not, she handed him her license, registration and insurance identification. Four minutes later, after running a complete check on the data he returned to the car.

"I decided to just give you a warning," the cop advised, and followed it with an admonishment. "It's wet out here, so drive safely. Pay attention to the signs. They're put up there for your safety."

"Thank you," Milicent said with relief as she put away her documents.

Using deliberate motions to prove to the officer that she really was a very careful driver, she went through the routines of turning on her signal, checking her rear and side view mirrors, and turning her head to check for oncoming traffic. For added measure and effect, she made the old-fashioned hand signal to indicate she was merging into the road. A few hundred feet later she made her left turn into the motel parking lot.

If there was any comfort about her room, it was the fact that it was at the end of the one-story building, and the only cars she saw were about ten rooms away. Being a light sleeper it was something she requested, hoping that she might luck out and not have overnight neighbors to disturb her rest with their loud talking or high volume on the television set.

Opting not to again drive around in the inclement weather, Milicent decided upon making use of the nearby nationally known pizza restaurant. Darting around small pools of water, and evading raindrops, twenty minutes later she was back in her room with a salad and a mini pizza. Fortunately, a PBS program on apes would entertain her while she ate, and until she was tired enough to slip under the covers and sleep.

⤜⤐

John Lorenzo was a state cop for a little under two years. He was stationed down in Socorro, but a special education seminar at the academy brought him up to Santa Fe. Before leaving his district office, John received permission from his senior officer to spend a couple of recreational days in Santa Fe before returning to duty. The only drawback was that he could not take his assigned patrol car since he was mixing pleasure with his training, but that was of little consequence to him. His per diem would increase for the use of his private vehicle.

Not foreseeing bad weather, or having the foresight to book accommodations ahead of time, John also needed to find a place to spend a couple of nights. Having left Socorro late in the afternoon, it was nearly ten-thirty when he arrived in Santa Fe. However, having spent a little more than three months of training at the police academy, he did have the advantage of knowing the layout of the city. Although the motel was three miles further from his morning destination, he knew where he was likely to book a night of rest. If he was so inclined,

John could always find a better location the next day. On the other hand, if he wound up staying for all five nights, he knew he would be closer to downtown where the good restaurants and recreation spots were dominant. In either event, driving a mere three or four miles could not make much difference, perhaps only five or six minutes in either direction.

Having a couple of manuals to check out before reporting to his first class, John did not go straight to bed. He was not very tired, but he was pretty certain that the boring texts would help him find his way to dreamland.

⚬❦⚬

Santa Fe police officer, Ray Flores, was tired, but he was also perturbed. He hated rainy nights, and he disliked having to exit his car to scold or cite a moving violator. He hated the fact that each night, at midnight, he had to report in to the cranky old desk sergeant before being relieved of his night of duty. Officer Ray Flores hated his job. If only it would offer him what he joined the force for – a bit of adventure.

The time read twelve-ten when he left headquarters to go home. He was not tired, and he was still perturbed. He would have loved to go home, change clothes, and then go out for a few beers and, with a little luck, maybe even score. For Ray it was almost a nightly urge, but by the time he went home and changed it would be one in the morning, the time when most bars were closing doors, and the few still open would not afford him the action he so desired. He would have loved to skip going home, but he was in uniform. Plus, he had his police car, and it could easily be spotted by some police brass making their early morning rounds.

Ray Flores possessed a macho self-image which would allure any female to his beguiling charm. He needed to hook up with someone for some action, and then it dawned on him as to where he might be able to get it without having to change clothes or worry about his car.

⚬❦⚬

Millicent Sherman must have been asleep for a little less than an hour before a light knock on the door awakened her. Angered at being disturbed out of her REM, she sat up and spoke with an edge in her voice.

"For God's sake, it's the middle of the night. Who is it?"

"It's police officer Ray Flores. I'm the one who gave you a verbal citation earlier this evening." His voice was low but audible. It seemed that he was trying to be considerate of others who may be sleeping in other rooms.

Confused, but cautious, Millicent did not put on any lights. Instead, she peered through the opening of the drapes to get a view of the officer. She could see no other parked cars for at least four or five rooms up, and more importantly, she could not spot any car belonging to the police department. She could not even see her own car from where she was positioned, so Millicent stepped to the other side of the drapes for a better view. She spotted her car, and alongside to the right, she made out the silhouette of a police car. Craning for even a better view, she was able to distinguish the figure of a man. Being able to make out the bulges around the belt of his waist, she could ascertain that it truly was a cop. She quietly questioned what the hell he can want from her at such an ungodly hour.

As though he had heard her thoughts, Officer Flores spoke. "I ran further check on your license, and there are a couple of questions I have to ask you."

"Shit! Couldn't he wait until morning?" Millicent verbally questioned herself. She then question him, "How did you know where to find me?"

"Easy. I watched you drive the short distance down the road before you turned left into this place. I need to ask you a couple of questions. If they pan out, you can get to back to sleep."

"Christ! All right." Realizing that she was clad only in her underclothes and that she needed to dress, she then added, "You'll have to wait a minute. I have to put something on."

After pulling up her jeans and slipping her sweater over her head, Milicent stepped over to the door, unhooked the latch and opened it. The cop, about thirty, five-ten and a husky two hundred pounds entered the room with a note pad in his hand. With a thin smile and a mustard charm, he proceeded to ask questions he previously dreamed up, all the while trying to make the young woman feel relaxed with his stab at faulty humor. Gradually, he let his improvised questioning turn to conversation, slowly warming up to his ultimate purpose.

"It seems from what you told me, things check out. There must have been a glitch in the data relay."

"Good," Millicent was glad to hear.

"Sorry to have had to roust you, but I was just doing my job," Ray Flores apologized.

"No problem. I guess you have a job to do, even at this hour." She tried giving him a smile to acknowledge that she understood, even if it was at a miserable time of night.

The officer took a step towards the door, hesitated, and then spoke.

"Look, I guess I made it a little difficult for you. Why don't I make it up? There's an all night diner nearby."

Rapidly, Millicent added things together, and the total sum infuriated her. An outspoken women, and never a person to keep her thoughts hidden, she angrily spoke out, letting her volume rise as she did so.

"I don't know what you're talking about," was the defensive reply from a man whose confidence was suddenly crushed, putting him on edge.

"Oh, yes, you do. I'm not interested, so please! Get the hell out."

Still defensive, the officer turned the handle to the door. He was about to open it to leave when Millicent's angry words stopped him.

"Don't think this is the end of it. I'm going to report this to your superiors."

His defensive mold now changed to panic.

"I was just doing my job…following up on some leads."

"Bullshit!" Millicent's voice crept higher. "Those leads were bogus, and you damned well know it."

Three rooms away, John Lorenzo heard raised voices penetrating through the thin sheet rock-walls dividing the rooms. He could not make out the contents, and he dismissed them as a lover's spat. Having spent other nights at cheap hotels while visiting Santa Fe, John knew incidents like this were very common. Satisfied with his reasoning, he turned his attention back to the last couple of pages in the manual.

"Listen, I explained to you…" Flores fought to keep composure as his mind raced as to what the next move would be. In split moments, it was decided.

Her anger reaching a higher point, Millicent moved towards the door. "Get out!" In doing so, she brushed past the police officer's midsection causing a reflex response. His arms briskly shot out as his hands grabbed the delicate shoulder of the woman, spinning her around to face him. With a look of shock, her eyes widened and her mouth opened as her voice started to say, "Get your hands…"

His large hands quickly cupped her mouth while his other forced her free arm behind her. In her squirm to release herself from his grasp, she momentarily caught Flores off balance. It was enough for him to fall forward unto his quarry, slamming both of them against the credenza, crashing the floor lamp against the wall.

The crashing sounds made its way to John Lorenzo's room. It alerted him that it was not merely a spat, and that trouble was definitely in the making. What bothered him more was that the loud arguing voices were replaced by what he reasoned to be the breaking of furniture.

Grabbing his shield and his holstered gun, clipping both to his belt, he hurriedly left his room in search of the disturbance. As he swiftly moved towards the room of activity, he saw two cars. One was a red sedan, and the other, to that car's right, was a city police cruiser. At first he thought that it was a local affair, a Santa Fe cop performing his or her duty. But, something bothered him. The police car was parked, and in a seemingly tight position and not easily accessible from where the subject room was. It had a strange appearance of trying to be concealed. It also seemed to Lorenzo that if it were a work in progress, the police light would be turned on.

Removing his shield from his belt, he cupped it in his hand so that he could easily identify himself. His next move was to enter the door already slightly ajar. There he witnessed the struggling pair.

"I'm a state officer. Can I be of assistance," he announced loudly, maintaining his alertness for unforeseen actions.

Now scared beyond whatever he imagined he could be, Ray Flores tried to think quickly.

"A local arrest. I've got it under control," he warned the state cop.

It still did not seem right to Lorenzo as he took an extra cautious step forward, remaining alert as he did so. "You're going to hurt her that way. Here, let me…"

Flores' panic turned into sudden rage. Spinning off of the female he shouted, "This is not your affair! It's local business."

Unexpectedly, they both heard the female scream.

"He assaulted me! He's trying to rape me!"

Losing it completely, Flores warned, "Shut up!" while he simultaneously went for his weapon.

"Don't reach for it!" Lorenzo warned Flores.

Undaunted by the command, but still full of panic and realizing that the situation was becoming out of hand, Flores shuffled backwards from the woman, withdrew his gun and started pointing it into the state cop's direction.

In the flurry of the following moment, fear raced through the minds of each person in the room. Only one shot was discharged, piercing Flores in his right thigh. A thud from his dropped weapon, and a moan of agony were the only sounds that culminated the end of his night for adventure.

23

Earlier that evening, Francesca curled deeply back into her sofa. The phone was unplugged, her personal cell shut off, and only a dim light in the hallway illuminated the living room. Not knowing if or when the department would need her, she kept her department issued cell nearby on the coffee table. She didn't want to be disturbed. All she wanted was to let her mind relax, but the swell of information she came upon earlier in the day would not allow that to happen.

A personal woe mixed with her professional questions. Did a link exist between the Julie Fletcher murder and the murders of Georgina Becaud and Karen Daughtrey? Was Sam the one Georgina Becaud spoke with at the restaurant on the night of her death? It was established that Sam frequented the place on a regular basis. Was it all a coincidence? Why didn't Sam ever tell her about being a regular customer at the restaurant? Surely, he must have known about where Becaud dined, and he could have easily mentioned it at the time of the initial investigation – that he ate at the same place, and that he may have spoken with her. It would definitely have diverted suspicions from his direction.

Why, for God's sake, does it have to be Sam? Francesca silently lamented.

Catching her thoughts, not allowing herself to fall into total despair, she tried to weigh each facet of what she knew. As a detective, she had to look beyond coincidence, that Sam actually did know one of the deceased, and that he may have spoken to the other on the night of her death. However, she had to allow for the coincidence factor. The population of Santa Fe, encompassing the heart and the outskirts of the city, is less than one hundred thousand. About a hundred and thirty if she included the entire county. In reality, that is not a large population, not like Albuquerque where the population, to include the nearby areas, neared a million. Definitely not like Chicago or New York, or even Phoenix and her sister cities in Arizona's Maricopa County. Santa Fe is small, and the game of numbers change. The likelihood of knowing two different dead people increases as the population number decreases. So, it was very possible for one person to know, or just merely meet, two women whose deaths were under a murder investigation.

Self-pity was not excluded from her thoughts. For the first time in her life, Francesca felt entirely comfortable with a man with whom she could spend the rest of her life. His gentleness, his compassion, and his respect for her, knitted a bond she did not have with other men. When they made love she could feel the energies that he spent, making her feel that she was the only woman to ever exist in his life. Deep inside her body, her heart, her mind, and her soul, she knew she loved him.

Francesca loved Sam, but could she stand by him? She was a cop, and if Sam in some way was responsible for either of the deaths, there was also a possibility that he may have been responsible for the death of Karen Daughtrey, or perhaps others as well. If Sam were guilty, she knew she would have to abandon him, not only because she was a cop but, also, she was a human being. In her mind, no amount of love could forgive another person's cruel and wanton disregard for life. She knew what her stand would be, but it would never heal the pain she'd feel if she ever lost him.

More than an hour passed, and Francesca wanted to escape her thoughts. Rising from the sofa, she went to the stereo and turned on the local public radio station. Fortunately, it played soothing Gershwin music, making her feel grateful for not having to listen to any unsettling sounds generated by rock or Tex-Mex. The gentle background suited her somber mood. Hopefully, a cup of tea and a sandwich would help her to focus on something new.

She had just finished slicing the sandwich in two when the doorbell rang. Looking at the clock that showed ten-fifteen, too late for any solicitor to call and not knowing of anyone else who would at such an hour, she came to a conclusion.

"Good evening," she greeted Sam with an edge of raw indifference.

"Good evening to you, too," Sam replied unaware of the conflict embroiling Francesca. With a light attitude, he entered the house. His attempt to embrace her was thwarted as she turned and walked back into the kitchen.

"I just poured myself a cup of tea. Do you want some?"

"Sure, why not," he answered. As he trailed behind her he felt the iciness and sensed that something was amiss, and he knew he would find out the reason soon enough.

They spent the next minute in silence as Francesca served Sam his tea. Not knowing what to make out of the distance that seemed to separate him from the woman he cared for, Sam spoke.

"Something wrong? I've been trying to reach you all day. Either you weren't taking messages, or you weren't answering the phone." With a touch of thought and consideration, he then asked, "Is there something we should talk about?"

Although she should have, Francesca did not expect the question. She held his gaze for a moment, her expression stoic and blank. Sam could not read what she was thinking.

"Maybe there is," she replied quietly, almost hoping he did not hear her. Gathering her fortitude, she then said, "Let's go sit inside on the sofa. There is something we must discuss."

Uncertain of her mood or her thoughts, Sam obeyed what seemed to him to be a command. He sat at one end of the sofa while Francesca settled at the other. The moments of silence that followed was broken by Francesca.

"Sam, why didn't you tell me you knew Julie Fletcher?"

She thought she saw his face ashen as he pondered the depths of her question. Sam had no immediate reply, but Francesca waited patiently till he did. In the meantime, she studied his face for any clues to what was whirling within his mind. It was Sam's turn to wear a stoic face.

"I guess it was wrong for me not to," he began. "I should have realized that you would probably learn about it."

"I did," she replied. She now had to pursue with her next question, both as an investigator and as a tormented lover who just uncovered a dark secret. "Tell me about her. You were lovers?"

He became sheepish as he focused upon her. Francesca could see a hurt in him, but she could not tell if it was for himself, for her, or for Julie Fletcher. She allowed herself to perceive that the pain was for all three.

"Yes, we were." Sam's words were solemn, as though he were showing respect for a dead woman, and for the kind of relationship that they shared together. "We were together for several months before our relationship began to deteriorate."

"What happened?"

"I'm not sure," was Sam's earnest reply. "I'm not really sure. We were happy together, at least I thought we were. It all changed overnight. I tried asking her what I may have done wrong, but she simply replied, 'nothing'. I tried pushing her into giving me some clue as to what was wrong, but she ignored me. Not long after, she started dating other men. I knew that I had to come to grips with the fact that our relationship was over."

"Did you?"

"Huh?" Becoming aware that Francesca was applying a third degree, Sam spoke forthright. "Eventually, yes. There's no denying that it took me a while, but I eventually did. I stayed away from places where I knew I might see her, and I buried myself deeper into my work. It did take some time, but I did get over her."

"How did you feel during that time? You felt pain. Did you feel rage...anger?"

Once more Sam's eyes looked into Francesca's, and again he felt pain. This time the pain was different.

"Jesus Christ!" he answered, snapping his focus away from her. "You know, you sound like a cop who doesn't believe her suspect."

"I didn't say that."

"No. You implied it."

"I'm sorry. I just…"

"It's just that you want to find out if I was capable of killing her, isn't it?"

Francesca found that she was unable to reply.

"Christ, Fran! I know that we've been together for just a short time, but I would have surmised that you'd know me a little bit better."

"Sam, I'm sorry. I'm just…"

"You're just being a cop doing her detective work," Sam harshly explained for her.

They sat at opposite ends of the sofa, each drowning in the whirlpool of their own emotions. Finally, despite the distress created by her previous question, she felt the need to push the envelope a bit further.

"Sam, have you ever been a customer at Steak-n-Things Restaurant?"

He gave Francesca a puzzled look as he nodded to her question. "Yes, I used to go there. Why?"

"But, you don't go there now?"

"No. I haven't gone there for two or three months now. Where are you going with this?"

"I guess you liked the food and all," she persisted, refusing to be distracted from her direction.

"As a matter of fact, yes. The food is good, and the price is not expensive." Testiness colored his reply.

"I guess it's a fair place to meet women?"

Francesca's leading question caused Sam to rise from the sofa, and cross the room in disgust.

"For God's sake, Fran. I didn't go to that restaurant to meet women, but if you must know, the answer is yes. I've met a few women there, some were locals, but most were passing through. I don't see where this is leading to, though."

She measured her thoughts before she replied. There was no easy way to explain the scenario.

"Sam, we know for a fact that Georgina Becaud ate there just before she died. We now know she conversed with someone, most presumably a man who spoke to her in a foreign language…quite possibly French."

"Jesus!" Sam stood frozen in place as he stared down upon the woman he felt he loved; the woman who was now conducting a major investigation, and who was now leading up to a serious accusation.

"It seems you stopped going there just about the time that the Becaud girl was murdered."

Sam briefly turned away as he angrily shook his head. A moment later he gave Francesca his thoughts. "That might be true, I'm not sure. It also coincides with the timing of my meeting you."

This time it was Francesca who was taken slightly aback. "Are…are you suggesting that…?"

"I am not suggesting, I'm stating it," Sam cut her off. "I've been going there for a long time. It's only a quarter mile from Ray's Pub, where Mike and I, and a few others get together to play darts and to chew the rag. Sometimes we go eat there afterwards. I started going to the restaurant not long after Julie died. I wanted to avoid the conversations and pity I'd have gotten at the places where she and I went to. After a while, I just got used to going there. I liked it. And…"

"It was a convenient place for you to pick up women." Like an attack from a wasp, Francesca's comment stung him.

Without any hint of denial, Sam answered, "Yes, you can say that. But that was something that happened only two or three times."

"And, it is very possible that it was you who spoke with Georgina Becaud on the night of her death."

"That's always possible. However, this is part of the investigation you haven't filled me in on. Tonight's the first I know of the encounter." Again, Sam shook his head in dismay. "I can't answer that."

Francesca's eyes widened as she registered Sam's response. "You can't answer! Is that the lawyer in you giving yourself advice?"

Once more, he felt the sharpness of her blunt words. "No. I can't answer because I don't know."

"I don't know what you mean."

"First of all, I may have conversations with people, but that does not mean I remember what we talked about, or what they look like a day or two later. I didn't get the case file for a couple of days after her death.

The press photo was an old one of her, and not a good one at that, and I didn't get to see the driver's license ID photo until much later on."

"You couldn't tell from the file photo?"

"Fran, you've seen the photo. She had bruises, and the girl had a contorted look on her face. It's not something you can easily identify as being someone you possibly may have met. Furthermore, it was several days later before your department concluded that she ate there. That time line creates more of a blur."

"Surely, you can remember if you ate there on the night she was murdered."

"Off the top of my head, no. I can't. At the time, it was not something I'd have associated. I never even gave it any thought that I may have met the girl. That was quite a few weeks ago, so trying to connect things will be even harder."

Francesca kept a mental recording of their conversation. Neither spoke as she tried to assort the data that her mind accrued. Sam did likewise with the questions Francesca pried him with.

"It's now my turn to ask questions," Sam said with a poised attorney's voice. "You have put me on your suspects list, haven't you?"

"Sam, I only came up with this information within the last day or so. I don't know what to think. I really don't."

"Just the same, you approached me with your questions as though I were. Tell me, Fran, were you, or were you not, going to give me any benefit of a doubt?"

Francesca was at a loss as to how to respond. More out of a defensive reflex, she did. "Sam, it would have been a lot simpler if you told me about your relationship with Julie Fletcher. On the day we reviewed the case files at your office, it was you who avoided going over her file. If you'd have told me then, we might not have had this scene here tonight."

Sam took in what Francesca said. His analysis told him that to a degree he agreed. "I guess you're right, I should have. Then again, it was only the second time that we were together, before we began to make some sort of commitment with each other." He thoughtfully paused for a moment before he added, "I guess this may have ruined something we dearly shared between us."

"What's that?"

"Trust."

Francesca and Sam held each other's gaze, neither certain as to what the next move should be. Both became uncertain as to what lie ahead.

Breaking the stillness that was not icy but mutually awkward, Sam made the first move. "I think it's just as well that I go home."

Dropping her gaze, unable to contribute something new to ease the unwanted entanglement, Francesca softly agreed. "It's probably best."

They spent the next moments observing each other, each trying to invade the mind of the other…to assess the discord this evening had brought to them. Neither one could make a determination as to what that would be. Only emptiness, a new void, could be mutually shared.

Sam departed, leaving Francesca alone with only her tears to keep her company, to act as her companion.

God, what have I done, she sobbed as she buried her face into her hands hiding them into the cushions of the sofa's armrest. *I accused him. I have no proof, yet I accused him. What I've learned…what he just told me…it's all just circumstantial. Yet, I treated him as though he were a murderer. God! I could have waited. I could have gathered more facts. Instead, I have just ruined the one good thing that has happened to me. I have hurt him. I have chased away the only man that I really loved.*

On a quiet back road of Della de Montoyas leading to Tano Road, Sam felt the same kind of sadness he felt several years ago, a sadness over the loss of Julie Fletcher. But, he did not think about her as he drove homeward to a house that would again be void of bliss; a certain joy brought to it with Francesca's endearing presence. His mind just kept replaying the scenes acted out only minutes earlier between him and Francesca. It felt like an improvised drama minus a director to cue them as to where the scene would lead. As much as he tried to assemble reason out of chaos, his thoughts kept fumbling the attempts. He had to get home, to sink back in his own special chair, to keep the lights down so that the darkness could match the blackness of his mood.

God! This is agony. His thoughts spoke to him as his car crunched over the driveway gravel until it came to a rest. *First Julie, and now*

Francesca. Why can't I be like other men? Why can't I hold on to any woman I love?

His anguish followed him into the house and throughout the night. No amount of contemplation would ever reveal an answer to him.

Francesca's cell rang at six in the morning, waking her from an unfit sleep. Noting the call she let it go to voice mail as she rose from the sofa where she slept for the night, still dressed in the clothes from the day before. Allowing herself enough time to fully waken, and to clear her still confused mind, she then returned the call.

Using the automatic dial, she waited for an answer. "Yes, Captain Tessa. Francesca here," she spoke with a voice having traces of sleep in it.

"Sorry to wake you, Detective. I think we may have some breaking leads on a couple of the unsolved cases you've been working on."

The news stirred her into alertness, waking her from the dreary dreams created just several moments before.

"Good," she said, trying to sound pleased. "Can you fill me in?"

"I'll give you a brief synopsis," Captain Tessa told her. After doing so, he concluded with, "You'll get the full details when you get in."

Hoping that this might be the beginning of an eventful day, a day in which she could come to again think of Sam without appalling questions, Francesca showered and dressed and was on her way to the office. She skipped making any breakfast so as to speed her arrival. Once there, she could indulge on the reputed cop's breakfast of coffee and doughnuts.

Twenty minutes later, coffee in hand, she sat in Captain Marco Tessa's office and listened to each bit of minutia concerning the previous night. Although the development of the facts was intriguing, the source of its creation was disconcerting.

"It hurts having to arrest one of our own, but the M.O. has some similarities to the Becaud file," Captain Tessa concluded.

"No question about it," Francesca agreed. "The first thing we need to do is to have a records search. We have to determine where Officer

Flores was on those nights of the murders. Was he on duty, and if so, we need a log of his activities."

"Good. I'll order records to get on it immediately," Captain Tessa volunteered. Before releasing Francesca to her awaiting duties, he added an introspective comment. "You know, Sergeant. My emotions are torn. Part of me hopes that we have the sonafa' bitch, and another part hurts thinking that one of our boys is actually a murderer."

Francesca gave the captain a sympathetic glance as she left the office. She could easily identify with the emotions since they were not much different from the ones she felt for Sam.

After tending to the pressing issues concerning the previous night's assault by a cop on a female tourist, and discussing the particulars of the case with the assigned officers, Francesca placed a courtesy telephone call to Mike Shannon.

"See that. I've always said we had one hell of a great department," Mike proudly jested with Francesca over the phone. "Cap's been in his office all morning, doing back flips."

"Pass him my congratulations," she told Mike.

Hearing upset in her tone, Mike then felt a bit of remorse for his excessive jubilation. His next words were more contrite. "I guess I shouldn't be blowing my horn so much. I'm sorry it was one of your boys who got nailed."

"We are, too," Francesca acknowledged. "Still, that doesn't take away any credit your man deserves."

"Thanks," Mike replied with more professional control. "So, you think that may open the door on some of the unsolved homicides?"

"We'll have to just wait and see. I sort of hope so."

Mike understood Francesca's choice of words. He guessed he would use the same vocabulary should one of his people ever come under such critical suspicions. "Let us know what comes up," he stated. "If you guys need anything, just tell us what we can do to assist."

"I will," Francesca assured him. "Mike…"

She stopped before she could utter another word. She wanted to talk to Mike about Sam, and about the dilemma that grew from the facts uncovered through her investigation. She built herself up to confidentially talk about it to Mike before she called. On impulse, she quickly scrapped the notion with a realization that she could not make out the full implications of the facts.

"…Yes?" Mike asked.

"Oh, nothing. It's just one of those things, when you want to say something and then you forget what you were going to say."

"A brain fart, uh? Don't worry about it; I forget things all the time. It's the price we pay for having hard working heads on our shoulders."

She enjoyed the way Mike always found a light way of coming up with replies to mundane issues. "I know what you mean. I'm just happy to be part of the thinking class."

"Atta' girl" Mike then asked, "How's Sam?"

The question was quick and unexpected, throwing Francesca off guard. Trying to satisfy the momentary lapse in her response, she answered, "Oh, he's fine." Then to try and cover the evasiveness of her reply, she added, "You know how it is. Both of us so busy, we don't always get a chance to sit back and relax."

"Tell me about it. Well, tell him I said hello, and that I'll see him come Wednesday."

"I will," she lied before saying goodbye.

As she hung up she began to wonder how much Mike knew about Sam's relationship with Julie Fletcher. If he did not know about it, she wondered if Mike ever had any suspicions about Sam concerning the woman's death. Judging from the comradeship between the two men, she surmised he did not. To top it off, Mike was a friend, a loyal friend who would put any iniquitous questions behind him. Yet, she wondered what Mike would think if he knew that Sam might have conceivably spoken to another woman just hours before her murder.

At the end of the workday she received the expected report from the records department. She was glad that they were swift to comply with Captain Tessa's request, but she was mildly dismayed that it had come so late in the day. She hoped to get an on-time departure for home, where she could begin to unwind from the eddy of events that transpired over the last couple of days.

Opening the envelope and removing the contents, Francesca went on to review the data on Officer Ray Flores. Bringing up the notes on the computer pertaining to the case files, she began to make comparisons. She went on to match up the time factors, comparing the office logs on the hospitalized and suspended officer to those pertaining to the murders. The goal was to find the time framework where the cop could conceivably be associated to any of the victims and their deaths. Within an hour she reached her conclusion. None of the information permitted her to connect Flores to any of the crimes. The incident at the motel was an isolated one, but one that would most definitely result in criminal charges being filed against him.

What was more was the fact that nothing changed concerning to the outcome of the unsolved deaths. Her prayers to fully eliminate the sickening suspicions she had developed were not to be answered. Her agonizing imbroglio had not been washed away.

24

Nearly a week passed since Alex last saw his neighbor, Eloi Martinez. Strolling over to Eloi's driveway he picked up the morning paper from the ground, all the while expressing a concerned wonder as to the old man's health. During those days Alex kept watch, at first unconsciously and then consciously, as to the lack of activity. Enough time, perhaps too much time, had lapsed and now Alex had to inquire as to the old man's well being.

A knock on the door produced no response, and he waited a minute before knocking again. Before departing to make a call to the mobile home park's manager and inquire if they knew anything, he contemplated turning the doorknob. But, he did not want to startle the elderly man should he be inside snuggled comfortably in his favorite armchair. He waited for that minute before turning around and descending the steps. The rustling of a chain lock from inside stopped him. He turned back around to greet his neighbor who was the first to speak.

"Well, hello. How are you?"

Alex could see a pronounced pallor behind the warm greeting. The old man's already frail body seemed thinner.

"I'm fine," he replied. "It is me who should be asking you that question. We were worried about you."

"Ho-ho, I'm okay. Just had a few bad days with the flu. The doctor told me I should stay home...that I should stay in bed and rest. It's my fault since I did not get a shot. At my age you sometimes don't feel like bothering with those things."

"I'm sorry to hear that," Alex sympathized. "I didn't want to disturb you, but since I haven't seen you for a few days, I figured it was about time for me to check up on you."

"Oh, thank you. Come. Come on in."

At first Alex wanted to decline, afraid that he would be disturbing Eloi from his rest. After studying the man and knowing that he did not have many people visiting with him, Alex reconsidered.

"All right, but I won't stay long. You should get your rest."

"Please," Eloi said with a smile and a dismissive wave of his hand. "Don't worry about that. One gets tired from getting too much rest. Besides, I need to take some medicine and drink some juice."

Alex placed the newspaper on the kitchen counter so that Eloi could have easy access to it. The old man picked it up, removed the rubber band, and glanced at the different front-page stories.

"I see where one of our city cops is in trouble," Eloi stated after he finished scanning the article.

"Yeah," Alex answered, "it seems he attacked some woman in her motel room. The article says he called on her in the middle of the night during which time he got physical with her. It's not clear whether or nor he tried to rape her, but she was assaulted."

Shaking his head, Eloi looked at Alex. Placing the newspaper aside, he thought for a moment when he made his comment. "It is too bad when a young woman has to be afraid of the police. What is this city coming to?"

Not sure of the answer, Alex replied, "I wish I had an answer to that. Maybe he's one of these oversexed macho dudes looking for action any way he can get it."

"Ahhh…too many of our young men think they're macho. Some have absolutely no respect for women. Just so long as they can get what they want." He again shook his head as he continued with his reply, "I don't know why some have to behave this way."

"I don't know either," Alex sighed. "It might just be the mindset of some of these guys."

"Maybe, but many of our people have had the same mentality for many centuries."

"I truly wish I had the answers for you, but I don't," Alex quietly said.

"I'm not sure anybody does," Eloi conceded as he poured some orange juice. "I can remember when everybody seemed to get along. Now...? Ahhh! It all seemed to have gotten worse after that land grant dispute and near revolution in Tierra Amarilla way back in 1967. Now, we have bigots running for mayor, and cops terrorizing innocent young women."

Alex nodded his head in agreement, but it was mainly to Joseph Aragon's bid to become mayor, and the article about the cop printed in the newspaper. He had to admit that the Tierra Amarilla revolt was one subject that he did not know much about.

"I'm sorry to say I'm somewhat unfamiliar with the incident up there. Never found the time to read about it. Maybe you can fill me in."

"Well, then, sit yourself down and I'll tell you what I remember." Eloi was glad for the company, and to have a warm intelligent body who was willing to learn about certain events.

"It was late spring, June I believe, in 1967 when the trouble exploded. That was around fifty years ago. Some people refer to it as the Alianza Land Grant Movement, while others refer to it as the Tierra Amarilla Courthouse Rebellion. In either event, it was led by a man named Reies Tijerina who was a leader of the Alianza Federal de Mercedes, which some people say is the grandparents of La Raza. Others simply refer to it as the revolution.

"A few days before the incident, the then Santa Fe district attorney – I believe his name was Sanchez – yes, Alfonso Sanchez...well, he arrested three or four members for what he called an unlawful assembly designed to cause a violent showdown...in other words, an uprising. Alianza in Spanish means Alliance. They did not like a court ruling regarding ownership of the old Mexican and Spanish land grants in that area. So, on the day of the incident, they went in and raided the Rio Arriba County Courthouse in Tierra Amarilla in order to free the arrested men."

"You mean the Alliance did that?" Alex asked for clarification.

"Yes, the Alianza. They went there…about twenty of them…to free the men. Ironically, they didn't know it, but the district judge already released them on misdemeanor charges only a half-hour to an hour earlier.

"Anyway, they seized control of the courthouse, a gun battle broke out, and a state policeman was seriously wounded. One of the gunmen then went to the officer, put the gun to his face, and pulled the trigger. It went click. The gun jammed. That was most fortunate, because the young officer would have become the only mortality of the rebellion at the time. Later that would change.

"Gunshots rang out throughout the courthouse. A couple of sheriff deputies were badly roughed up, and a number of people were held hostage at gunpoint. Meanwhile, some of the men with rifles and a machine gun fired their weapons at some state police cars coming to the courthouse. Realizing the danger they were in, the police cars backed away from the scene without any of them being injured. Some of their cars were shot up, but the cops were not hurt.

"The National Guard was called in, and they arrived just as it got dark. However, the gunmen fled the building by then and took some hostages with them. They then headed straight to Canjilon, a small village, some miles south of Tierra Amarilla."

"Yes, I know where that is. It's still small," Alex told Eloi. Knowing that the old man did not finish his story, he apologized for the interruption.

"That's all right," Eloi said lightly before he continued. "The greater majority of the people in the area are Hispanic, and they became angry when they heard of the raid. But, it was the police and the courts they became angry with. So they tried to band together and join the group called Alianza Federal de Mercedes, with the hope of retaking the land lost to them under the courts decision on the land grants."

"What happened to the people involved in the raid?" Alex asked.

"The gunmen? The state police and the National Guard rounded up most of them. Some were convicted, but they were later pardoned by the governor. Except for one young woman who was detained for nearly two years, no one really did any major jail time. That was because one of the main civilian witnesses against them, one of the neighbors, was found beaten to death before he was able to testify?"

"What about the land involved?"

"In my opinion, the few pieces of land was just an excuse," Eloi stated flatly. "I believe what they wanted was to control all of the land up there."

"I don't understand," Alex said, confused by what Eloi meant.

"It seems that many of the people up in the high lands bought land that was not supposed to be sold to them. Part of the land was taken over by the Forest Services. The locals up there used to use the land to graze their cattle."

"Much like the land problems in Nevada and places like that, then."

"From what I know about it, yes. I can't say I disagree with the people, either here in New Mexico, over in Nevada, or anywhere else. The government, influenced mostly by white collared easterners, is making it a habit of imposing new tough rules pertaining to government land. They disregard that ranchers were allowed to use the lands for many decades, and even more that a century. They do not even try to take into account the bad affects it has on the local farmers and ranchers – the people who are helping to properly utilize the land, the very same people who are putting food on everybody's table. And now, the government not only want to charge them for further use of the land for grazing, but they was want to charge them for using it in the past."

"Were there any other groups involved?"

"There was a land development group, out of Arizona if my memory is correct. They gave back some two hundred or so acres to some local group up there, and they paid one of the involved claimants a considerable sum. I don't know all the details to give you the full information. Still, the people wanted to control all of the land, and they didn't want any outsiders coming in. Not land developers, or people who just wanted to build a home up there."

"I see," Alex said as he absorbed the lesson. "I go up to Chama once a month to service a large account there. On the way back I've noticed a sign, an old one I think may have been put up a number of years ago. On it, it reads 'Tierra O Muerta!'"

"Land or Death!" Eloi said with surprise emanating from his voice. "So, that sign still stands. Heavens, it's been more than fifteen years since I've been up in that part of the state. I remember seeing it back then. It was originally put up in the 1960's."

"It's still standing. Off to the right side of the road as you're heading south."

"Well, I'll be. I'll tell you something. While most of the people of the deep south have given up any dreams of reviving the old Confederacy, there are still many people in this state who want us to become a separate homeland. Today, they are supporters of a group named Republica Del Norte. They have dreams of making New Mexico, and other parts of the Southwest and parts of Mexico an independent sovereign nation, separate from the United States."

"I've heard a little about that. What about the whites and the Native Americans? What would the group do about them?"

"I am not sure. I can only guess the sign you've seen will then be changed to read, 'Capitulate or Die!'" The old man paused for a moment to let his comment set in. "Alex, my ancestry is both Spanish and Mexican. I am, what is today called, Hispanic. Many years ago that term barely existed, and we did not care much about labels since we considered ourselves to be Americans like everybody else. Most of the people who want a revolution are my people, but I am not one of them, and neither are a lot of others. Yes, my ancestry may classify me as Hispanic, but I am first an American. I was born in this country, and I love it and all of its people. Many – no, most – of my people feel very much the same way. Being what is called Hispanic often calls for seeking special laws and recognition because of it. Other groups like the Jews or the Italians don't ask for special attention. Neither should we, or any other group. In my mind, we have a constitution that is to protect all American citizens regardless of where we originate from. When we make laws to protect, or to enhance a selected group of people, we mostly do it at the expense of others. To me, this is wrong. It is discrimination. We cannot cure one evil by creating another."

Alex sat in silence as he absorbed the words coming from someone he considered a wise old man. He could only reply, "I could not agree with you more."

Eloi nodded his head in appreciation of Alex's comment, but he saw that the younger man had not finished his say, so he remained silent.

"To me," Alex continued, "the most important things are life and mind. They coexist with each other. I am critical but I do not condemn religion, or culture. They are records of who we are, but they do not reflect what we are. That is determined by what we do. And that is determined by how freely we use our mind. It controls the influences that religion and culture leave upon it. We alone determine how to use them by creating our own destiny – our own future – and hopefully, we provide a positive influence to others who in turn will be free to create their own destiny."

"Yes, I agree," Eloi interjected. "Please, go on."

"Ethnic, social, and religious backgrounds are the basic ingredients to form a culture. Often it becomes a doctrine that states that we must obey its tenets, tenets that are said to be superior to all others. Doing so, we are then denying other cultures from making their claims, and consequently we are denying the other's right to exist. When we live solely by the tenets of our culture we have surrendered our use of reason, and the development of our mind. By allowing culture to dictate instead of guide us, we've become no different than a non-sentient data programmed into a computer. We become but one step above a zombie whose soul is controlled by another.

"We shouldn't abandon our cultures. By all means, enjoy and savor them. Just do not permit culture to rule our existence."

"This is all so very true." Eloi took his turn to agree. "It's a very sad situation. There are many good hearted, well-educated and intelligent people in this country who think they're serving humanity with new laws. Instead, they are crippling mankind. I am proud of whatever I've achieved in life, and they were not awarded to me through quotas or because of my origin. All of their nonsense makes me cringe."

"I'm sure they wouldn't be successful if the Alliance attempted to depart from the rest of this country," Alex commented.

"No, I really don't believe they ever would be, however a lot of whites, blacks, and Native Americans might get caught in the middle. So will many of my own. You have to realize, there are those who take their pending revolutions very seriously. Should they ever succeed, one of the by-products would be a Cuban style socialist government with Spanish being the official language. The man who headed the uprising in Tierra Amarilla had a commune. His children were made to be part of it, and they were not allowed to learn any English. The only woman involved in that raid was his daughter, who was only seventeen back then. After the raid ended, after she saw the brutality and learned about the murdered witness, she began to question her father's beliefs. She was detained in jail for about two years but never went to trial, and during that time she and her father became estranged. For a further sad note, the young woman eventually had children of her own, and she talked and educated them in English. No Spanish. It is a shame because she wound up denying them an additional learning tool, a tool that would help them to understand and to decide for themselves the merits of their ancestry."

"I guess that was a scar she bore from the conflict."

"It was. It was a scar from a wound that would never heal. My only hope is that it does not permanently affect her overall outlook."

"Hmmm…." Alex drew a deep breath and then exhaled. "It's a pity. Their origin. Their culture. Their religion. The things that many people cherish the most becomes their bane. Again, it is no different than the terrorists killing in the name of their religion."

"That is because they have allowed themselves to be enraptured by it. Like what you said, instead of respecting and honoring it all, they have allowed it to dictate the way they think and the way they live. It becomes their doctrine. In the process, they never learn to respect others whose origins and cultural and religious beliefs are different. A constant conflict ensues, where almost everyone believes that only their kind is right and thus everyone else is wrong. It brings about the next conundrum: who is right, and who is wrong."

"I think we are very much alike, you and I," Alex continued. "I don't hold any claim to my origin or cultural background. I have never been to Poland, and it is not my homeland. If I ever go it would only be out of curiosity, not to lay claim." As a concluding thought he added, "Also, I am not religious."

"Am I then to believe that you are an atheist?"

"No. You might call me a haphazard deist. I said I am not religious, but that does not mean that I have dispelled my belief in a greater power. There is an innate feeling that somewhere in this universe there is an energy – a force – looking at us, and allowing us to do things on our own. Maybe even allowing man a chance to better himself and to eventually unite with that force."

"Interesting."

"I detest what religion has done to man, and what man has often done in the name of religion. I detest even more the slavery of the mind which religion, or at least those who teach it, commits man to. I will freely share this belief with anyone willing to listen. But! No matter how strong my beliefs are, in no way do I reserve the right to impose it on anyone else. The day I start doing that is the day I become no different than the ones I criticize. Each person has a free and will. No one! Absolutely no one reserves the right to enslave another person's mind."

"You don't believe in religion, but you do believe there is something else. Please, if you don't mind my asking, what do you think happens to us when we die?"

"Ha! Man's oldest question to which he still does not have an answer. It's funny, man very seldom asks what happened before he was born. It almost seems that when we die we circle right around to where we started." Alex twisted his head to indicate a firm answer eluded him. "I don't know. I can only wonder, just like everyone else."

"I assume you don't believe in heaven or hell."

"Hell, no, I don't," Alex emphatically answered. He then took a whimsical approach. "The way I look at it, if God is truly all merciful, there cannot be a hell. On the other hand, it would be boring as hell to go to heaven just to fly around all day with a harp in your hands."

Old man Martinez did find the analogy amusing, but Alex could see that he wanted a more serious opinion. As he studied the elder, and he became aware of what Eloi was after. Age was taking its toll, and the years were not far from dwindling down to zero. After a little more thought, he tried to give an earnest opinion.

"Eloi, I believe in justice. One thing I have always had difficulty in understanding is how two people, both having the same background and the same opportunities, take different paths in life. One living a decent and honorable life, while the other lies, cheats, steals and kills, and they both die and go into the same abyss. Is it justice that the likes of Hitler, Stalin, Ghangis Khan, and Mao Tse-Tung in death receive the same rewards as the many good people who also die? My sense of justice prompts me to ask if it is the same justice that we are all awarded when we die? If so, then life is as unfair as death."

"I find that interesting, a different way of looking at things. One thing is for sure, we all one day will find out what awaits us. I, too, believe in justice. I just hope that it is fair to us all when we die."

Each man listened, captured by what the other had to say. Later that evening Alex kept evaluating the lessons the old man had given him, and he found himself in continuous agreement with the man's way of thinking. For the total part, it was no different from his own. An old man, with little formal education, had learned much by living and observing life. In a world that often complains about not being listened to enough to make a difference, Eloi Martinez was an exception. He did make a difference, and it was a gift he verbally gave. Alex accepted the gift, one that he would cherish for a long time into the future, and one he could, in turn, pass on to another. For this, he was grateful to the wise old man.

25

"Jesus, you gotta stop worrying about guys like Eddie Real. They yap off their mouths, but nobody really listens to them."

Emilio Baca tried to calm his brother who had just entered the house, fuming over derogatory remarks made about him by one of his drinking buddies.

"He ain't got no right saying I'm nothing but a fuckin' pit-bull who'd fuck up his own mother. Then he tells people I'm loco…that I ain't got enough smarts to fill a scumbag."

Jesus' description of what Eddie Real called him caused a snicker to slip from Evonne Aragon. With their father's election only a week away, and with Emilio becoming a more active supporter in the campaign, the two sisters were spending much more time in the company of the Baca brothers. Yolanda became especially fond of Jesus, often accompanying him wherever he went. She was present when Jesus first heard of the insults laid upon him.

"Ev, please don't laugh. This Eddie guy is bad, and he's got a big mouth. Jesus has a right to be mad," Yolanda mildly scolded her younger sister.

"You're right. Jesus has got a right to be mad," Emilio said. "But, he's got to keep it cool. Normally I'd say go on and bust his head, but not now. With your father's campaign, and with our need to get people to listen to our demands for a better homeland, this is not the time."

"Shit, Bro! I just can't let him keep bad mouthin' me. I gotta do…"

"Nothing!" Emilio firmly stated. "You do nothing! Not now, anyway. We got priorities, Jesus. He ain't one of them."

Emilio managed to silence Jesus, but he could see the hot anger kept violently roiling within his brother. For now, he was content that Jesus still respected him by obeying his command. Someday, though, it might be different. He knew Jesus to be an impulsive hothead, and someday it could lead him into serious trouble. Emilio wished with all of his heart that that day would never come, but deep down inside he knew the wish would probably not come true. He just hoped that should the day come, it would be somewhere in the distant future. Most of all, he wanted his sibling to gain calm, and to work with him and the Aragon girls on the matter spread out immediately in front of them.

"So, your dad thinks I'm doing well in working the people," Emilio said as he turned to Evonne.

"Oh, yeah, he's very pleased. He said he kept an eye on you, and he was very impressed with the way handled yourself. Said you got what's needed to become a leader. He can see you doin' good in politics, maybe even get elected to a county seat or maybe somethin' even better."

"Man! Those are very nice things to hear coming from a man like your dad. Although I never knew him till now, I knew of him and I've always respected him. It's just too bad he has to get backing from people like Ruben Gonzales."

His surprising comment stunned the girls setting them off guard, especially Yolanda.

"I don't understand why you say that. Mr. Gonzales is good for our people," she protested.

"Mr. Gonzales is only good for himself," was Emilio's immediate retort. "Wake up woman, he's just using us. He always used our people."

"I…I…don't un…understand," Yolanda stammered, a trait she often exhibited when she was confused or upset.

"Well, then I'll explain it to you. Gonzales' been in state government for, what, forty or maybe fifty years. All that time, what has he done for us? Nothing! He's paid us a lot of lip service, but he never helped his own people. He never helped our ranchers or orchard growers, or gave us better housing."

"Maybe so," Evonne spoke up, "but if he's so bad, then why has the man been so powerful?"

"Because he helps his cronies who get him votes. He smiles a lot and pretends he likes people, making them think he's a nice man. He gives money to different groups to make his image look good, and to get a big tax break. That man's become powerful and rich because of drugs. He arranges meetings with dealers so they can broker big deals, and he looks the other way when the deal goes down. No deal gets done without his approval." Emilio paused for a moment for dramatic effect. "That will all change, I tell you. When our people take power, and with people like your father to lead them, there'll be no room for the Ruben Gonzales'."

His three-person audience listened, nodding their heads in approval. Again, it was Evonne who spoke up.

"Until that happens, we gotta live with it."

Emilio gave a look that said, 'thank you for understanding'. "Absolutely correct. It hurts, but it's something we must do. We need to use bastards like Ruben Gonzales as a voice. While we're doing that, we've got to groom our own new leaders."

"You'll be one of them, Bro." Jesus now had something to distract him from his anger, so he broke his silence by following his brother on a path promising them a brighter tomorrow.

A warm brightness came over Emilio's face, and his manner took on a stately glow. "Thank you, my dear brother. Maybe I will." Adding a lighter touch, he turned his attention to the Aragon girls. "Maybe someday your father and me will walk down the aisle together. Joseph Aragon as El Presidente, and Emilo Baca as Vice-Presidente."

"Yesss…!" The three others chorused their cheers.

"I can feel it!" Emilio went on with an evangelic chant. "I can see it! It will happen! I feel it when we work the crowd. I see it when I look at our people. They want change. They want independence! We shall give it to them. Right here! Right now! Now we begin our new world… our new Republica del Norte!"

The four of them shared the good moments before heading into Santa Fe. They had campaign work to do, and they were inspired by Emilio's promise of a new independence.

Emilio allowed himself to take part in the gaiety, all the while keeping a watchful eye on his still fuming brother. Jesus had a short fuse, and the eruption was usually long and loud. Emilio did not want to see an ignition to the blast.

Not now, Brother! Not now. Emilio tried to telepathically communicate with Jesus. *Keep it cool, man. We don't want your anger to screw everything up.*

The newspaper polls were showing that Joseph Aragon's lead in the mayor's race increased slightly. With just a week left before the election the news was very encouraging. He was still not content.

Although the field narrowed by one with the dropout of another rival, JoJo expected more of a swing considering that the former candidate threw his support behind Aragon. The political and social ideologies between himself and the departed rival were not far apart, so it seemed reasonable to JoJo that the increase in the polls should have been at least by two or three more percentage points.

The specter of Bill Johnson's arrest on drug charges still troubled him. Ruben Gonzales gave him assurances that the donations to his campaign could not be traced back to the accused drug dealer. JoJo was told not to worry. But, he worried just the same. There were no guarantees a trace could not be made, and if it were, JoJo worried more about the ramifications of the gift. Not only would the perception of taking money from a criminal put an unfavorable light on his campaign, but it could also lead to questions as to why the donations were made. If that happened, then JoJo had to fear criminal charges for bribery and graft for selling his vote in favor of issuing a permit allowing Johnson to open his gallery.

JoJo wished that the issue would dissolve, that it would wash away like dirty water down a drain. He knew better. He also knew it was the tightrope he had to walk once he allowed Ruben Gonzales to negotiate for Johnson's donation. Now, all he could do was take the advice given to him by Gonzales and not worry. He just had to find a way to forget about such concerns, and pretend they did not exist. For someone like JoJo, this was not easy.

"Where the hell are those girls, and that guy Emilio?" JoJo found another avenue through which to vent his frustrations. "They should have been here by now. We got work to do."

"For Christ's sake!" Mary-Elizabeth complained. "Nothing ever satisfies you. You should be happy that you've increased your margin in the polls. Instead, you're bitching because the kids are only a couple of minutes late."

"They're ten minutes late," he told her. "They should be here."

"So, they're a little late. Big deal! You got almost an hour before you're supposed to go out."

"I just don't like people being late on my time." JoJo refused to be mollified.

"Emilio and the girls will get out and do as you ask them. I'll say one thing about the young man, since he's been around Evonne and Yolanda both have been around here more often. They've been helping out a lot more with your campaign."

"Yeah, they have," JoJo said as he softened his tone. "Emilio seems to be a good influence on them."

"He's bright. I think you should keep him around after this is over. He might become very valuable to you."

"I'm considering it. I've seen how he related to our people, and he's very good at it. He may even have a future in front of him." JoJo remained silent for a moment, thinking about a couple of questions that have been nagging at him. "What I can't figure out is, who is going out with whom?"

"Whadaya' mean?" Mary-Elizabeth asked with a bit of confusion, not knowing where her husband was leading with his question.

"I can't figure out if it's Evonne matching up with Emilio and Yolanda with his brother, or what."

"Maybe they're all just friends."

Mary-Elizabeth's response bewildered JoJo. "Uh? I don't get it."

"You know, you men got no brains when it comes to women," Mary-Elizabeth said as she chided him with her matronly air. "You think that because men and women are together they're supposed to be screwing."

"It's just...well, you know."

"Come on! Face it already, JoJo. Our girls aren't really altar material. The only way that would happen is if one of 'em got knocked up, and even that I don't think is very likely."

"What do ya' mean?"

"JoJo, our daughters ain't the type to screw around with men," she bluntly replied. "Other women, maybe. But, not men."

A scarlet hue covered JoJo's face. "You can't mean they're...they're..."

"Maybe they are, and maybe they're not. What'a you gonna do? Shoot them? Wake up, JoJo. Stop totally living in the old ways, and get used to some of the things that might be going on today."

JoJo had his suspicions, but he never confronted them before. It did not suit the macho image he had of his family. Another dreadful thought exposed itself. "What...what about our son?"

"Thomaz? Ha!" Mary-Elizabeth said with a scornful laugh. "He'd stick his dick into a dead stunk if he had a chance. I don't ever want to see him get sent up, but if he did go to prison, he'd be the fucker and not the fucked."

The redness in JoJo's face grew a little deeper as he thought about what his wife said. Whether she was right or not was not the issue. He just did not want to find out.

"Thomaz is a lot like Emilio's brother," Mary-Elizabeth continued.

"Jesus?"

"Yeah...whatever his name is. They're both macho, ready to piss on a live wire. The only difference is Thomaz has a lot more brains."

Her comment caused JoJo to relax a little and issue a rare chuckle. "You're damn right about that."

"That guy...Jesus...he worries me. He doesn't seem to have it all together like Emilio."

"You've noticed that, too," JoJo agreed.

"I have. That guy's wound too tight, and I don't like it. I look at them, and I can't believe Emilio and him are actually brothers."

"Ummm…I've noticed that, too. When this election is over, I've gotta find a way to cut him loose."

"You'd better." Mary-Elizabeth then cautioned, "Just be careful how you do it. He and his brother are very tight, so if you want to keep Emilio around you'd better figure out a good way to do it or there might be trouble."

For all the years that JoJo and Mary-Elizabeth were together, he learned to trust his wife's cautioning advice. She had good instincts, and she was right about Jesus. What he did not know was how to handle the situation. Perceiving he had time, JoJo opted to use the remaining week to find a solution to a minor situation before a problem grew.

Thinking about that, or any other problem, was replaced by the arrival of his assistants.

"Sorry we're late, pops," Evonne apologized. "We got stuck in traffic. Seems there was a crash up around the opera house."

Relieved that they finally arrived and could soon get started, JoJo for once took a gentler tone. "That's no problem. We still got a few more minutes before we get started."

They spent time reviewing the plans for the day. Yolanda and Jesus were to post more signs and hand out more fliers, while Emilio and Evonne were to hand out fliers and talk to people.

While discussing the afternoon's routines, JoJo kept a watchful eye on Jesus who seemed to be a bit on edge. He didn't want him to start anything with anyone and, hell, he would hate to get rid of him before he had to.

"Don't wait up for us," Evonne stated, interrupting her father's thoughts. "Yolanda and I are gonna head back up north when we finish with these."

Acknowledging what Evonne told him JoJo nodded his head with his reply. "Just make sure you finish up what you gotta do. I wanna see all of them fliers handed out."

As he watched them leave he still could not shake his uncomfortable feelings about Jesus, a gnawing feeling anchored in the pit of his stomach. *I just hope that fucker doesn't start anything.*

26

The day was bright and sunny, a good day for an outdoor inspection and a good day to display his officers in a positive light. The senior officers from the outlying areas of Chama, Tierra Amarilla, and other small townships within the Rio Arriba County command were in attendance, leaving a skeleton but fully capable group of officers patrolling the highways, or as backup in key township offices.

Sunshine reflected on the slick-top cars as well as on the faces of his troops. As a senior position officer in Santa Fe, the Espanola district was under his command. All of about ninety lieutenants, sergeants, and patrolmen and patrolwomen made up the force covering the county which spanned about a hundred miles north to south, and about seventy miles east to west. In his mind, they did an exceptional job responding to such a large area, and the positive responses from the inspection committee bore fruit to the captain's pride.

Pride seemed to be the order of the day that began early, at six in the morning. The usual banter of wanting popi to drive them to school led to a surprise announcement by Teresa that both she and her 'little' sister, Charlene, were both going to appear in their school's spring play.

"I'm playing the most important girl part," Teresa beamed. "And Charlene's got a big part, too."

"But it's not as big as hers, popi," Charlene issued the complaint of a seven year old.

"Don't worry, dear," her mother comforted her. "I'm sure when you get bigger you may get a bigger part, just like Teresa."

Her mother's comment did serve to appease Charlene who smiled and went to her popi for a hug.

"That is wonderful," Cap exclaimed. "To think, both of my sweethearts are going to be on stage."

"You will come, popi?" Teresa asked.

"Of course I'll come. There's no way you can keep me away. Why didn't you tell me last night?"

"It's my fault," Margarette answered. "I wanted to tell you about it, but you got home late and the girls were already in bed, so I figured that it could wait until this morning."

"I'm sorry," Cap apologized. "I got tied up with paperwork, and making preparations for the inspection up north."

"Sssh! Don't apologize. It's not like you work late every night. We understand. Besides, it's not like those days when you were working your way up. We're grateful that we have so much of you now."

A warm embrace demonstrated Cap's appreciation of his wife's understanding.

"And," Margarette said, glowing as she was about to give him more good news. "I have a meeting scheduled with the top company officials this morning. They called for it, and I'm told that I will be asked to take on the manager's role at our branch."

Feeling his wife's joy, Cap again hugged his wife. "That's great! I know how hard you've worked for it. You deserve it."

The warmth and the pride went on to build through the morning hours as his men, and the district office, flew through the inspection with high praise.

"Hell! You look like a cat that swallowed the canary." The familiar passé quip came from Mike. He, too, wore a boastful smile.

"That's the way I feel," Cap admitted. "We did well. As a matter of fact, you did well."

"Heck! I did nothing. My charge comprised of only a few people. Cordova should take the credit. He's the district's top boy."

"Just the same, the criminal affairs people report directly to you. You've got to take at least a little credit."

Using a playful attitude towards the compliment, Mike responded. "Okay! If you feel that way about it, I'll take some of the credit. Thanks."

They shared a little mirth before heading back to the Santa Fe headquarters and the different chores that awaited them.

"I feel like being a nice guy, so I'm giving you a little reward. Give me the keys, I'm driving," Cap said.

"That's not protocol, chauffeuring the junior officer," Mike joked as he handed over the keys. "What the hell, who am I to argue with the boss?"

After making a quick stop for lunch on Riverside, they headed back to home base. They drove a couple of miles through the heart of Espanola before an incident report came over the radio. Brief seconds later it was followed by an officer down alert. The incident was taking place in Sombrio, a small community abutting Espanola and the county line.

"Hell, that's only two miles in front of us," Mike stated.

Acknowledging the information, Cap nodded his head and replied. "We better check this out."

With their headlights in the alternate flashing mode, and a siren squealing as they approached traffic congestion, they sped their cruiser southward on Riverside, over a hill, and into Santa Fe County. A quick left crossed them back into Rio Arriba County, and Sombrio was in front of them. Both police officers could see police vehicles approaching from about two miles to the south on Rt. 285. Before Cap made his left, a peek into the rearview mirror told him that an armada of support was coming from behind.

Cap had very little trouble finding the location of the house where the incident was taking place. The directions over the radio were very explicit, and it was further recognized because of the state patrol car and sheriff's vehicles already on the scene.

It was just a couple of minutes after eleven o'clock, just about the time when Cap and Mike were finishing their early lunch break, when a sheriff knocked upon the door of a rundown doublewide mobile home. He was there responding to a disturbance phoned in by a worried neighbor. Fifty feet from his patrol car stood another, its occupant making a call to dispatch advising that he was also at the scene.

The response to the officer's knock was not immediate, and he could hear only a dead quiet on the other side. Glancing to his right he could see a single-wide mobile home, about eighty yards away. An elderly man stood on the porch, starring in his direction. The sheriff reasoned that it was the old man who made the call, and after waiting for a couple of silent minutes he decided his next course was to question the onlooker. Turning to step off of the stairs leading into the doublewide he was stopped as the house door flew open, and a woman's voice, full of fear and panic, screamed.

"Help me! You gotta help me!"

Alarmed, he spun around to face the woman, simultaneously letting his hand reach to his side and to the holstered gun strapped there. Before he could respond he heard a crack and immediately saw blood flying from where had once been the woman's forehead. Stunned, the sheriff froze at the sudden violence before him. It was his only mistake, and a fatal one. The next sounds he heard came almost at the same time – one being a crack and the other a thud that hit his chest. The force of the impact flung him off of the stairs and onto the ground. He could see a black crow soar through the light blue sky before a permanent darkness set in.

Startled by what he witnessed, the second sheriff again reached for the phone. "Officer Down! Officer Down!" He could not say more, and he was vulnerable. He could not reach for his gun, and he could not squirm for cover. In the next instant he too heard a crack. It coincided with the painless impact he felt above his left ear. For him, he too would fear no more sounds or feel any more contact. His body lay contorted over the front seat of his car.

Within a half minute after the third fatal shot was fired, a state cruiser pulled into the driveway and parked on the far side of the sheriff's vehicles. It was not until she emerged from her car that she spotted the first sheriff, laying face upward on the ground. With a little effort she could then see the slumped body of the second man. With a sudden comprehension of the potential danger, she withdrew her weapon. She knew that she had two options – one, to take cover behind one of the other cars. The second option was to summon backup and support. She opted for the latter. The option chosen was the wrong one. As she reached for the radio in her cruiser she too heard a crack, and she too felt the impact of a bullet that would rip into her lungs.

⤛⤜

The slick-top carrying Cap and Mike crawled to a slow stop as it left the road and into the driveway. Upon passing a few cottonwoods they could see part of the carnage, rising their anxieties and fears as they evaluated the scene.

"I wouldn't get any closer," Mike cautioned.

Taking heed, Cap stopped the vehicle at the edge of the tree line, allowing a utility pole and a couple of distant pinon trees to provide cover.

"This is a real bad situation," Cap observed. "Mike, I want you to take to the road and keep the backup safe, and out of the driveway. I'm going to radio in and get SWAT support."

"Will do," Mike complied.

Reaching the road before other officers arrived, he halted them before they could proceed. Eyeing the immediate surroundings, and spotting someone on the porch in a neighboring yard, Mike then barked his orders.

"Trimmer, I want you to get to that house, and get that old guy out of harm's way. Bring him here so we may question him. Stay low below the adobe wall, and out of the sight line from that doublewide." Seeing the several sheriff cars responding from both counties, he continued with fast and emphatic orders. "Perry. Valadez. You two take a couple of sheriffs and check out around the perimeter. Make sure no one comes or goes out of that house. And make damn sure you use all the cover you can get. This fucker appears to have a deadly aim, so for God's sake, no heroes."

Bringing his directives to a temporary conclusion, Mike glanced back towards Captain Guiterrez, and he was not pleased at his superior's movements.

"Cap, for Christ's sake. Get yourself better cover," he shouted before sneaking his way back to his boss and the car.

"No! You stay there!" Cap sharply replied back into Mike's direction. "It's much too risky."

Mike obeyed and crouched low beside a cottonwood. His heart began to race as he watched Cap move closer to the front of the cruiser. Mike began to rise. Cap's glance back commanded him otherwise.

"Stay where you are, Mike. That's an order. I think I saw Officer Mendle move. I'm going to try to reach her and give her aide."

"Don't do that," Mike countermanded. "It's not safe."

Cap clearly heard Mike's protest. He also clearly saw the need of one of his people, an officer down and one who may be clutching on a thin thread of life. To him, no options were available. As a captain he had to exercise his duty by the book. As a human with a free mind and a compassionate soul, he could do no less than to render assistance.

He again heard Mike's passionate plea imploring him to remain concealed and safe on the right side of the cruiser, a position he crawled to after making a call for additional support.

He's commanding orders at me as a good leader should, ran through Cap's mind. *When we get back I must thank him for it. For now, I have more important things to think about.*

Without any further deliberation, Cap hunched himself into a low but moveable crouch. He had managed to grab the first aid kit from his car, and he secured it tightly under his arm. He did not remove his weapon from its holster. Cap knew that it would be useless to him if he did not know where the assailant hid, probably out of range. With one empty hand he would have less to interfere with his mobility to dart from one location to the next.

His own heart heavily pounding, Cap took one more deep breath before he made his move. The flow of new air into his lungs gave him freshly charged energy, quieting the trepidation trapped inside of him. With another inhale he made his run. Seconds later, after reaching his destination, he collapsed himself over his wounded comrade. Keeping low, he felt for life signs. There were none. No breathing, no pulse. Lifting the female officer's eyelid with his thumb confirmed to him that he had made the attempt in vain.

"God! I'm sorry," he half cried as he gently caressed the young officer's temple.

Feeling pity for the contorted body that lay beneath him, Cap made the effort to move the lifeless body into a less agonizing position. It was an effort that may go against procedures, but it was an effort of one caring individual for another. It was an effort he should not have done.

Raising his body for the angle to position hers, Cap heard a crack. A tenth of a second later he felt the pain. He fell paralyzed atop of the body of his slain officer. He blinked his eyes several times before he realized the seriousness of his wound.

Visions danced before him. He saw Margarette's face aglow with all the happiness she had given him. Teresa's and Charlene's laughter echoed in his ears, and he had regrets that he would not be able to attend their school play. Men and women in uniform marched to the cadence of discipline and honor, and it filled him with pride.

With a smile on his face Captain Eduardo 'Cap" Guiterrez closed his eyes. His sleep became long and peaceful.

Mike's head sank in anger and in rage. The scene he witnessed convoluted his emotions. Relying upon his training, he struggled to refocus for the job that lay ahead. Once done, he snapped back into the mode of a police officer.

"You guys stay back. I don't want anyone out in the open." Mike snapped his command with crisp authority as he neared his men. "When SWAT gets here they'll take over. They're equipped for it."

A look over to the next driveway revealed Patrolman Trimmer and the elderly man hurrying to the road.

"Are you the one who called in the complaint?" Mike asked.

"Yes, sir."

"Please, can you tell us anything? Do you know who the shooter is?"

"I don't know him. He doesn't live here. He came here about an hour ago, and I could tell by how mad he was there was going to be trouble."

"Did you hear him say anything?"

"He was shouting for Eddie."

"Eddie lives there?"

"Yes. He's not home. His girlfriend was home."

"Do you know if anyone else is in the house?"

"Yes. Eddie's younger brother, about fifteen. I don't know his name."

"Anyone else?"

"The other woman."

"What other woman?"

"The woman who came with him. She's a big woman. Maybe five foot six, but big. Big body. Young."

"What made you call us?" Mike calmly asked the questions while at the same time regaining his own composure to help the old man feel more at ease.

"There was noise and arguing. Then I heard what I think was a shot. After that, things became quiet. That's when I called you."

Mike thanked the man, and he then made his way over to the SWAT force that had just arrived. He fully explained the scenario and concluded it by saying, "Jim, it's your game now. I want you to get that bastard out of there. Alive, if possible. Do whatever you feel necessary, you're in charge of that operation."

Lead by Sergeant Jim Torres, the SWAT team took over. Seven well-protected and well-armed men surrounded the perimeter of the doublewide, all keeping in radio contact with their leader.

The sergeant tried to make contact with the sniper through his bullhorn. A bullet, ricocheting off of the adobe wall the sergeant chose for cover, greeted the contact. A moment passed before another attempted contact was made. The reply was the same.

"That does it," Sergeant Torres decided. "Rodriguez. Dell. Use the gas."

Responding to the radio command, the two SWAT officers, positioned at opposite ends of the house, launched their tear gas grenades through the windows. An immediate plume of smoke became visible.

A second lapsed, then ten. Darker smoke, indicating a fire had ignited, mixed with the gas. Another ten seconds lapsed, but before more time could be ticked off, the front door burst inward. A figure of a man appeared. A rapid fire of shots from his weapon was then heard. A volley of shots from law enforcement answered them. The figure spun and swerved. He did not fully go down, trying with all of his remaining power to again return the fire. He never succeeded as the constant barrage of bullets stopped him dead before his body fully touched the ground.

Smoke from the tear gas, the expanding house fire, and of firepower ascended skyward, while the rancor of their smell lingered on. Movement froze to that of a snapshot as each involved witness assessed the finality of the moment. Soon a woman's pleading voice could be heard.

"Help! Please…help me!"

As they watched, the SWAT men could make out a figure crawling to the opening of the door, first a hand, then a head, then a second hand thrusting forward to secure anchor on the lip of the porch steps. Taking in the overall situation, and coupling it with the information provided by the elderly neighbor, Sergeant Torres made his conclusions. The scene was now under control. He signaled for two of his men to attend to the woman, but allowing for unforeseen predicaments, the men were to approach with the utter most caution while their brothers in arms provided the necessary cover.

Minutes later the incident came to a close. The house fire was being extinguished. Medical and rescue were allowed to proceed, but their job was limited. A body count of three civilians, one of which included the assailant, and four law enforcement officers comprised of the total dead. A sharp blue sky could not brighten the dark gloom of the enactment performed only minutes before.

As the new lead officer, Mike Shannon took full charge. His objectives were twofold: one, to accumulate every bit of data and evidence possible, and two, to distract the grief and lurid spirits boiling within the emotions of his colleagues. Using the combination of state and local agencies, he assigned tasks for the senior officers and their men to follow. His own task was to set up a command post where the flow of information would be centralized, and where the top brass from the state police and sheriff's department could assemble. The expected army from the various media organizations was also taken into consideration.

A large SWAT vehicle was established as the center of command. A flurry of activity crescendoed to furious heights, and as expected, the state police chief and two of his deputies were on the scene, along with reporters from the print, radio, and television media. Representatives of two national cable news organizations also made their presence known.

Taking a momentary break to clear his mind and to refocus, and to temporarily be alone in the command post center, Mike sank back deep into the seat he occupied. Fighting his own inner desires to let loose, he choked off all urges to let himself weep. For relief from the mounting burdens the mid-day horror put upon him, his men, and the public, he allowed himself to be distracted by what he reckoned could be applied to quantum physics. He did not know much about the subject, but what seemed to be a matter of only a few minutes actually turned out to be the passing of two hours.

I wonder if this is what they call time travel, was the last amusing thought he allowed himself before returning to the full scope of his responsibilities. A lot more remained to be done.

"Mike. Are you okay?" was the question of concern expressed by John Ebner, State Police Chief.

"About as well as can be expected," Mike replied with a solemn air replacing his normally jovial tone.

"You and your men have been through a lot. The police world in this state has suffered some horrific losses, especially the loss of Captain Guiterrez."

It was at that point, with that reminder, tears finally welled within Lieutenant Mike Shannon's eyes.

Allowing for the soul stirring moment to pass, Chief Ebner waited in silence before telling him of his decisions.

"I've directed Major Archuletta to assume command here. Major Wilson will handle the information flow to the media."

"Yes, sir," Mike quietly replied.

"Mike, given the tragic and sympathetic circumstances, you have done an extraordinary job here. You and some of those guys out there have experienced a lot, and I want you to step back a little. It won't be easy for Archuletta either, but he should have a clearer head without the same burdens."

"I hear what you're saying, sir. I'll be all right."

"I know you will, Mike," the chief replied as he placed his hand gently on his lieutenant's shoulder. "I'm not dismissing you from any of your authority. You will be second to the major on this. It's just that I want you to step back and breathe a bit. Your ordeal has been too great."

Mike acquiesced to his police chief. He did have a question.

"Has any of the families been notified?"

"Not yet. We're preparing for that right now. I've instructed Major Wilson not to release any numbers on the body count, and definitely not any names. Not until we've notified their families."

"If you don't mind sir, I'd prefer to tell Cap's wife."

"Are you sure?"

"Yes, sir, I am. Our families know each other very well, and I think it would be best to hear it from me."

"I'll have the chaplain accompany you, if you don't mind."

"I don't mind," Mike softly replied.

"Good. We will finish gathering information here, and you can start pouring over it in the morning."

"That's fine, sir."

Mike gave his superior a salute, and then embarked upon his next arduous ordeal.

A rookie highway patrolman drove Mike back to Santa Fe. From the back seat Mike gazed at the back of the young cop's head with its neat crew cut. Looking more like he should be in high school, Mike wondered if the young man could fully comprehend the impact of the events that took place. Not only the senseless loss of lives of fallen comrades, and the horrifying image that the media was bound to display, but also the pain and agony that will be put upon the surviving family members and their friends. He, himself, was embarking upon a mission where he would further relive that pain. He prayed to God that the young officer would never have to experience anything else like it.

Mike pressed the automatic dial on his cell phone. The first call he made was to his wife.

"Mike, hi. There's a rumor going around that there was some kind of shootout in Espanola. Anything serious?"

"Yes, very serious," Mike stoically replied.

Teri heard the strain in her husband's voice, something she could not recall ever hearing before. "Tell me, sweetheart. Are you all right?"

"I'm all right, hon." Mike could hear a sigh of relief at the other end. "It's Cap…"

"Yes?"

A prolonged pause followed. "He's dead."

There was a silence, followed by an exasperating exhale.

"Margarette. What about her? Does she know yet?"

"No. I'm on my way to her office now. The chaplain is going to meet me outside. I was wondering…"

"I'll be there, too. We'll be waiting for you."

As he said goodbye he wondered how she knew what he was going to ask. It did not matter. He welcomed the support she was going to lend, not only to Margarette, but to Mike as well.

Tired. Exhausted. Mike arrived at the front entrance of the building that housed the Commission of Statewide Insurance, a state agency run by a private company, and the office of Margarette Guiterrez. As promised, Teri and the department' chaplain, Captain Raymond Soto, waited outside for him. Taking his lead, the two followed Mike into the building to carry out their dreaded undertaking.

Within a few minutes they watched an ebullient Margarette Guiterrez striding down the corridor to greet her unexpected guests. As expected, she did receive the promotion and the joy of her prize was written on her face, a face that slowly began to change as she saw the chaplain, and the somber expressions on their faces. She was a cop's wife, a veteran of knowing the method of delivering tragic news. She looked for positive signs, but as Teri approached her with an extended comforting arm, Margarette knew the visit was one that every spouse of every cop had feared. It was not a nightmare, but a dreaded reality.

"Nooo…nooo!" Her utterance grew into a wail. "No. Not Eduardo! No!"

Concerned co-workers appeared at their office doorways, while her top aide rushed to her side, assisting Teri with her consoling embrace. The chaplain also reached out to give his support. Only Mike stood in place, feeling helpless. He was there to deliver the grievous news, and he realized that he had done so without uttering a single word.

An hour later he was at home. A time to rest, to shower, and to try to rinse away the image of watching a friend die and of not having the ability to save the fallen hero. Forcing himself to down a sandwich, Mike readied himself to return to the office. Major Archuletta would be there, as well as his fellow officers and the work that lie ahead.

The data was mounting, and some of the revealed information, still under wraps from the media until it could be confirmed, turned out to be a shocker that would have affects upon the community.

"We have identified the remains of the sniper, and of the girl who survived from the house," Major Archuletta briefed Mike. "His name is Jesus Baca. He's from a small village called Guzman, up in the central part of Rio Arriba."

"What set him off?" Mike asked.

"According to the female survivor who was with him, Baca was irate with a guy named Eddie Real. It seems that the guy made some disparaging comments that Jesus and his brother, Emilio, were some kind of kooks who wanted to set up their own type of government."

"Hmmph!" Mike uttered in disgust. "It's nothing new for some of the people living up there."

"It so happens that Eddie Real was not home, but his kid brother, Martin, and Eddie's girlfriend, Jeanne Castro, were. It seems that Jesus Baca barged his way in, and at the same time Martin went for his rifle. They struggled, and Jesus took the weapon away from the kid."

"That's when he shot him?"

"No, not then. Jesus goes to the cabinet and pours himself a whiskey. Supposedly, Jesus was a bit drunk when he got there. He starts teasing the kid, calling him a punk, a sissy. The kid starts to argue back, and retaliates with his own insult by calling Jesus a drunken idiot. That seemed to have snapped something inside Jesus. He points the rifle at Martin, curses at him, squeezes the trigger and hits him squarely in the chest. After that, when the sheriff's department arrived, Jesus tried to keep Jeanne Castro quiet by keeping his hand over her mouth. Somehow she broke free, and Jesus kills her with one shot just as she opened the door. From there on…well, it was just a free-for-all sniping massacre."

"God!" Mike said, shaking his head. "Whoever said it was right, he was a God-damned kook."

"We got a judge to give us a search warrant. Cordova and his men are heading up to Guzman now with it."

"Good. They had best bring whatever they collect to this office."

"They will. I've given Cordova orders to bring it directly to the evidence room."

Wanting to learn as much information as possible, Mike asked his follow-up question, "Who was the girl, and where is she now?"

"She's at the hospital under tight security. She got some severe cuts and burns as a result of the tear gas exploding. At most, she'll be there overnight. Then we intend to get her held as a material witness until we have a complete picture."

"Her name?"

"You're not going to believe this, and the press is going to love it. She is identified as one Yolanda Aragon."

"Who the hell is…."

When mentally adding up all of the pieces, the familiarity of her name coupled with Major Archuletta's dramatic approach in naming her, Mike realized the sum of the answer. "You mean to tell me…she's the daughter of JoJo…"

"Yep! She's the daughter of our would-be mayor. I think that the papers are going to have a field day with this when they find out about her tomorrow."

"Shit! As far as I'm concerned, they can find out about it now."

"Nah. The press is ready to go to bed. It's too late to write about it tonight. The morning paper will be paying tribute to those who died today. Let's not screw it up with a story covering Joseph Aragon and his daughter hogging the fine print. His son has already made things a little tough on him. One more day and that bastard will be wishing he was born an eunuch."

27

Late afternoon brought frustrating news to Joseph Aragon. Unaware of the massacre north of Santa Fe, he could not understand the limited information provided to him by the state policeman who knocked upon his door. The facts given to him were vague, incomplete of the certainty as to whether his daughter was a victim or a suspect. It was only evident that she was in the hospital, in protective custody, and in need of an attorney. Uncertainty racked his brain as the election was but days away. Whatever this episode involving Yolanda turned out to be, it tormented him to the brink of rage.

Mary-Elizabeth Aragon's timing turned out to be a perfect vent for his rage. A full day of working the neighborhoods, of attending political rallies, and of performing civic functions for the buffing of her husband's image, was rewarded with a verbal tirade as she walked through the door.

"They've done it. They've gone and botched things up."

Caught off guard by the beginning of the invective outburst, Mary-Elizabeth could only be baffled by the pending barrage of words.

"Who?"

"That stupid bitch daughter of yours. She's going to destroy us. I should let the friggin' bitch rot. Screw her and her sister. Let 'em both rot."

"I don't...I don't know what you're ranting about."

"You're fucking daughter, Yolanda."

Defensively, Mary-Elizabeth shot back. "She's your daughter, too. Stop cursing at her, and tell me what she did."

The sharpness of his wife's voice snapped him from the incoherence of his rage. Controlling his fume, JoJo did manage to reply in a manner with an appearance of calm.

"The police have her in protective custody. They claim it has something to do with some shooting in Sombrio."

"My God! What did she do?"

"I don't know yet. The cop said she's in the hospital with burns and cuts. He said she's under protective custody and may become a material witness, but he couldn't say if she was involved with the shooting or just there when it happened. I tried, but he wouldn't give any more information."

"What about Evonne?"

Confused, JoJo looked at his wife with a blank expression. "I don't know what you mean."

"When I came in you were cursing at both of them. What did Evonne do?"

Forgetting what he said just moments before, he hesitantly replied, "Nothing. Nothing that I know of."

"Then why are you cussing her if she didn't do nothing?"

JoJo had no answer. He chalked it up to the many previous times he lashed out at them, usually as a result of trouble Evonne led her older sister into. His subconscious thought said that it would be no different now.

"If Evonne's done nothing, then leave her out of this," Mary-Elizabeth commanded. "The important thing now is to help Yolanda. Did you contact our attorney yet?"

"No. I haven't had time to."

"Well then, do it now. We've got to know what the hell is going on."

JoJo thought for a moment before he agreed. "We gotta get her released as soon as possible," he said as he made his way to the phone.

"Now you're being more rational," Mary-Elizabeth told him. "We want to get her home here as quickly as possible."

"That's true," he said as he stood otherwise motionless over the phone. "Damn! This is very bad timing for me. If she'd done something wrong, it can hurt me in the elections."

"Screw the election. Just make that damn phone call."

Copies of fax reports lay atop Sam Dawes' desk. They were printed accounts confirming what he had already heard over the phone from numerous sources, and in total, they did not give a clear enough picture of the events that took place during the past three hours. All he knew was that four cops, to include Captain Guiterrez, and two civilians were slain by a supposedly crazed gunman who in turn was gunned down. Sam was also aware that there was one civilian survivor, a Yolanda Aragon. It was unclear in any reports if she was a possible victim, an accomplice, or just a witness. Based upon his conversation with State Police Chief Ebner, he assumed he would soon have to draw up the paperwork requesting a judge to hold the woman as a material witness. Confirmation of her involvement would be determined later by the police, and after they had time to sort out all of the facts. He doubted that the burden of their losses would slow down the process. If anything, they would expedite it.

Sam did not put any significance to the name of Yolanda Aragon. He lived in New Mexico way too long to not know that there were probably a hundred other women with the same name in his jurisdiction. Whoever she was, it remained certain that his office would have to handle whatever charges brought against her. Since she was in the hospital for an overnight observation, the final determination of possible charges would not be known until the next day.

What was also not yet determined was the complete motive behind Jesus Baca's actions, just preliminary reports. Obviously, no charges could be filed against a dead man, but if there was some kind of conspiracy as one computer report suggested, then the matter would be wide open. His office would soon have its hands full.

It was better to just sit back and wait, to first let the police do their job. Sam's responsibilities were unclear without enough detailed information, so he decided to remain in his office making him immediately available for when services from his office were needed. In the meantime, he ordered a meal to be delivered, worked on some lesser files, and reviewed the facts from the faxes and email reports, all the while waiting for conclusive police reports.

While he mourned the loss of life for all of the officers who died, it reached beyond the normal loss of life. On a personal side, his heart bled for Captain Guiterrez and his family. There was also a strong sympathy for Mike Shannon. Sam knew both men, one only slightly over dinner and a few meetings, and the other as a close personal friend. He had deep respect for the man he knew but briefly – his professionalism and his viewpoints on crime and of morality. For that, even with the limited acquaintance, he would miss him. He knew Mike much better and he knew him to be resilient, that he would bounce back from the turmoil. Whether there would be a change in the man, Sam did not know. Given time, he doubted that his bubbly friend would change much. A bit more grave perhaps, but knowing the essence of the man, he doubted Mike's character would ever become different.

Reflections on his own life entered his mind. There had been flux in it, especially where Francesca was concerned. A huge boulder had cascaded down on the road of their relationship. Getting around the obstacle would still leave a question mark as to where the road might lead, he simply did not know. For now, he decided to push it aside and worry about the matter at hand.

***

The dead may not have been people they knew, but those within the Santa Fe Police Department felt they suffered a loss of some of their own. In a sense, as comrades who shared the everyday dangers of their jobs, they did. The gray atmosphere slowed down each person's duty, bringing it to a virtual standstill. It may have been the shock of sudden news, or it may have been a reminder of how tenuous life can be while performing the duties of a cop. It may have been a combination of both, but in either event, the jolt carried an impact that brought tears into the eyes of several.

Francesca was not immune. Compassionate tears streamed from her eyes upon learning of the deaths, especially that of the captain. She knew Cap only briefly, meeting him in his office when she first joined the department and sitting down at the same dinner table with him and his wife for Mike's Italian banquet. It was an evening where she came to know his honest, and the sincerity in which he gave a conviction of his thoughts. Combined, they gave her a profound respect for the man. Little did she perceive that the evening would be a prelude to the events in the weeks to come.

Cognizant of the fact that she was not up to the chores of going through the various case files, reading details which blurred as visions of mayhem kept playing in her mind, Francesca decided to seal them for the day. They would be reopened once her senses became cleared. Peering around at her fellow violent crimes officers, she guessed they too were on the edge of doing the same.

Taking things into her own hands, she visited her boss's office. "Captain, I don't mean to be pushy, but I think we should have our people close shop for the day. Unless something urgent arises, let them work on mundane things."

Captain Tessa weighed her suggestion and looked up. "You know, it's the best idea yet. We'd like to keep them from the morbidity of what took place, but we don't want them screwing up important files because they can't concentrate."

"I agree, sir."

"Why don't you go out there and give them the shit list to work on. If things get done, fine. If not, no big deal. At least it'll keep their minds occupied."

"Very good, I'll do that. Besides, there's only a little over an hour left to the shift."

She turned to leave, but was stopped by the call of her name.

"Francesca, one minute please. How are you holding up under the stress of today's ordeal?"

"I guess about as well as can be expected. I've gone through this a few times while with the APD, but I never knew any of the victims. This is a little different. I didn't know Captain Guiterrez all that well, but I did know him, and I had a good respect for him."

Tessa sighed, acknowledging with his agreement. "I've known Cap off and on for about ten years. A good family man, a damned good cop. A good man." Taking a long glance at Francesca, Tessa asked his question. "How would you feel about joining me and a few others and be part of the honor contingent representing the SFPD at his funeral?"

A tear ebbed in her eye as she replied. "I'd be honored."

"This is horrible! Shocking! This kind of monstrosity should never happen." The indignation was clearly expressed by Ruben Gonzales as he lit a panatela. "The families of those poor officers…what they must be going through."

Tommy Trujillo gave a resigned sigh that told his boss they shared the same view. He had seen expressions like this before from Gonzales, but usually the air of mockery attached itself to the emotion. Ruben Gonzales' emotion of grief seemed genuine however, and Tommy wondered if it were possible that the actor within the politician had truly been touched by the tragedy in Sombrio.

"Stuff like this only brings unwanted attention to us. This attracts people from the news media and big shots from law enforcement who'll be watching us. We do not want that."

Tommy began to grasp the emotional display, and upon doing so he realized that it did not alter his boss's true concerns.

"What do we know about the Jesus Baca character?" Gonzales asked, wanting to get to the bottom of the sudden tragic event.

"He's a nobody from Guzman. A drunk who got in and out of a lot of brawls."

Gonzales took some comfort in knowing that the assailant was not a local to the immediate Espanola area, but he could see that his trusted aide had something more to tell him. Something more disturbing.

"Okay, Tommy. By the look on your face, I can tell this is not the worst of it."

"No, I'm afraid it isn't."

Tommy Trujillo's tone was disquieting. Gonzales could see he was trying to ease his way into revealing the additional bad news.

"So, please, come out with it. Let's hear about the rest of the woes."

"Jesus Baca is the brother of an Emilio Baca who's been working for the Aragon campaign." Tommy watched Ruben Gonzales' eyes widen, but he expected the last tidbit of information to make his eyes explode. "We haven't confirmed it yet, but we believe the girl who survived is Joseph Aragon's daughter."

"What!"

"According to my sources at the sheriff's department, the Aragon girls and the Bacas have been hanging out a lot together. That's how the brothers got involved with the campaign."

A stream of exhaled white smoke ascended upwards along with Gonzales' only comment. "Whew."

"The state police are trying to keep a lid on releasing her name until they can determine her involvement, and that she definitely is his girl."

"There is too much coincidence for her not to be," Gonzales said. "Once it is confirmed, the press is going to have one God-damned field day."

"This probably knocks the hell out of Aragon's chances of becoming mayor."

"To a degree, yes," Gonzales conceded as he drew in on his cigar. "How much depends upon her involvement with the slaughter. If she was part of it, Aragon is finished. If she comes out looking like a victim, he might loose some votes, but I don't think it would be enough to see him being defeated."

"What about Emilio Baca?"

"Now that could be even more of a problem. It depends upon how much the investigators reveal to the press, and the connections they make. If they see Emilio Baca as just a casual supporter, it won't affect the election as much as finding out he is actively involved."

"The press is bound to find out sooner or later."

"That's true. However, the election is now less than a week away. The later they find out about all of the details the better. If it takes them a few days to fit all of the pieces to the puzzle, it will be too late to make any difference."

"What do we do now?"

Gently rolling his cigar between his fingertips, Gonzales answered. "First, we take care of our own problems. I would like you to prepare a statement that we'll release to the public, telling them how horrible this all is. I want you to also get me the list of family members so that I can give them my personal condolences."

"I'll get right to it," Tommy said, giving his obedient assurance. "What do we do about the situation?"

Drawing softly on the cigar, New Mexico Senator Ruben Gonzales thought for a moment before deciding. "I think we will wait and see," he replied, releasing the harsh smoke from his lungs. "We'll just wait and see."

Another seven hours remained before the newspapers hit the streets, deeply informing the readers of the dreadful details of the day before. It would not be complete since the investigation team deliberately withheld some specific information pending clarification. Yet, the entire northern section of the state became fully aware of the losses. The electronic media played their part, but word of mouth carried its way on the waves of information that flowed over hills and mountains, and through the valleys of the counties.

The dart games were finished and Alex retired to his favorite seat at the bar to sip a fresh bottle of cold brew. Gregg soon joined him.

"It sure ain't the same without Mike and Sam here," Gregg began.

"What am I, a shadow on the wall?" Alex lightly jabbed. "I'm here, so that should be your bright spot."

"By the way, where were they tonight?' Gregg asked with his usual innocence.

Alex exchanged a dubious look with him before answering, slightly chiding his friend. "Where the hell have you been? Haven't you heard about the shooting north of here?"

"A little. I heard a couple of cops were killed in Espanola, but…"

"There were four killed," Alex cut in. "Two of them state cops, and one of them was Mike's boss."

"Oh, God!" Gregg exclaimed. "What about Mike, he okay?"

"As far as I know, yes. But I can sure as hell imagine what he's going through."

"Jeez!" Dennis lamented. He was another dart player who was sitting nearby, listening in on the conversation. "Those damn guns. I think they should take them all away."

"Come on now," Gregg responded defensively. "I own a couple of them. You don't see me shootin' at cops."

"Maybe you don't, Gregg, but too many nuts will shoot at anybody for no reason whatsoever."

"I'm with Gregg on this," Alex spoke up. "The main problem is keeping them out of the hands of the nutcases. Don't make the responsible people pay for the actions of a few lunatics. Besides, where do you draw the line without abridging other constitutional rights? Big Brother government agencies are already controlling a lot of our freedoms."

Not wanting to be totally put down by the opinion, the dart player did argue. "Guns are dangerous."

"So is crossing the street," Alex gave a flippant reply before leveling his next comment. "So are knives. So are many government rules and regulations, but only a few people are demanding that we get rid of them." He waited a second to see if there would be a response. "This is a gun state, and sixty percent of the people have them for hunting while others for defense. This is especially true in the rural areas where they have only one or two cops who may be responding to calls ten or twenty miles away. For those people, a gun might be their only protection."

"That may be true, but…"

Gregg defiantly cut him off. "All I can say is, if I don't give anybody any trouble they got no right to try and take my guns away."

They sat in silence for a moment before Dennis posed another question to Alex.

"You say the constitution protects people who have guns, but there are people who don't agree that's true. Who do we believe?"

Alex shrugged his shoulder before he answered. "Hey, I'm not Sam. I'm not a lawyer, thank God. In effect, the Second Amendment says, '...for the security of a free state, the right of the people to keep and bear arms shall not be infringed.' Our founding fathers incorporated this clause so as to allow people a means to protect themselves not only from crooks and invading forces, but also from governmental tyranny. It was a carryover from the British Rule's imposition of trying to denying guns to the colonists. Nowadays, to protect themselves from rebellion against any government directives, the fed agencies want to see that consideration ignored"

"So that means that they can't take guns away from people, right?" Gregg asked.

Again Alex shrugged. "Except for convicted felons and the mentally ill, I would think not.

"First, the High Courts have to consider why this amendment was written. Back then, England's King George wanted the colonists stripped of their arms. When the Second Amendment was provided for, it was intended that the people be able to protect themselves from those that would mean to bring them harm. That would include the ruling government.

"However, that being said, I think the determining factor may circle around the word 'infringe'. If there are laws banning or regulating guns, I would think that is an infringement. That would include licensing."

"New York City has some of the toughest gun laws for a long time, so it must be legal," the player opined.

"Not necessarily," Alex replied.

"What do you mean? If the laws weren't legal they'd a gotten rid of them."

"As I said, not necessarily. They've had the Sullivan Gun Control Laws on the books for more than several decades. In fact, if you remember Bernard Getz when he shot a few thugs on the subway, the jury found him not guilty for defending himself. He still served about a year because he used a gun that was unlicensed. Only cities like Washington D.C.'s and Chicago laws have been challenged and overturned by the Supreme Court. Despite that, those cities are finding ways to get around the court's decision."

"Why hasn't the New York City been challenged?" Gregg asked.

"Two reasons. The people who live there feel secure with the law requiring gun owners to have a permit, and no one has been wealthy enough to contest it. The second, my guess is that the die-hard liberals who are dominent there would fight tooth and nail to keep it from getting to the top court."

"You got to admit though, it works," Dennis commented.

"Who the hell are you kidding," Alex sharply contradicted. "New York, and especially Chicago, Baltimore, D.C., and L.A., are leaders in the country in crimes committed with guns. The great majority of guns used in those crimes are illegally gotten and homemade specials. They're used with or without any laws."

"Yeah, but think of how many people would be killed if they didn't have the laws."

"The counter argument would be, just think of how many people would not have been killed if the victim had a gun for protection. Criminals don't think like you or me. Most are smart enough to lay off of people they cannot read. If they cannot read whether you have a gun or not, the odds increase that they'll leave you alone. Today, the way most left-leaning municipalities go after people who own guns, the victim gun-owner often pays the higher legal price."

"I heard that the guy who did the shooting was some kind of separatist" The Dennis said. "What do we do if these people start an uprising?"

"I think it's something we'd have to contend with if and when the time arises, with or without any laws."

"You better be careful," Gregg joked. "Someone might think you're some kind of right wing extremist."

"Far from it. I detest them because they're no different from the radical left. Timothy McViegh who did not have any respect for innocent lives. I may agree with some of their complaints, but not with their tactics. Like supporters of the different Tea Parties and other conservative groups, I prefer to change things within the system. I'll change my mind only if the government uses excessive force against innocent people who are protecting their constitutional rights."

Alex made his comments, leaving the others to ponder them. After a couple of minutes Gregg asked him, "What do you think they should have done with the Espanola shooter if he had lived?"

"What do you think? Try him and put him away for four or five lifetimes."

"You mean you wouldn't want to see him executed?"

"Not unless you could guarantee that his appeals were swiftly handled. Although this might be the exception, I'm not highly in favor with the way the death penalty is meted out in this country. Prosecutors today are too intent on convicting people as opposed to determining the real truth. I think it is very likely that as many as five percent of death row inmates were wrongly convicted because of overly zealous, win at all costs, prosecutors."

"Then you are against the death penalty."

"Only to the degree that an innocent man could be executed. Life is too precious to let that happen."

"You should tell that to Sam," Gregg suggested.

"I did. He knows how I feel. Whether he agrees with me or not is something else. Besides, knowing the kind of man he is, I don't think Sam would ever be guilty of sending an innocent person to death." As a finalizing comment, Alex added, "At least I hope not."

28

Emilio had just wakened from an evening nap, and as he entered the kitchen to pour some coffee he saw Evonne sitting at the table playing a game of solitaire. In the background the CD played romantic Mexican music. The volume was low, and it did not interfere with the otherwise stillness of the house.

Motioning to the coffee being kept warm on the burner, he asked, "Do you want some?"

Evonne's shake of her head was her non-verbal answer. He did not know if she was listening or just reacting. She seemed more intent in studying the cards sprawled out on the table.

"Where's my brother and your sis?"

"Dunno. Ain't come back from town yet."

Glancing at the wall clock that showed nearly twelve, Emilio had a surge of concern. "They've been gone since this morning. It's not like him to stay in town so long without checking in with me."

"Maybe they're on their way back now, or maybe they're just screwing around. They're old enough, so we don't gotta worry about them like they were our kids. And, since our cell phones aren't working up here, we'll just have to wait till they get here and tell us."

Ignoring Evonne's apathetic attitude, Emilio went on with his say, "It's not like him. I just hope that idiot didn't get drunk and have an accident."

"You worry too much."

He did not like her disinterest, but he kept quiet. Except for times like these, ever since they met some two years before, they got along well. He had no serious interest in Evonne, and under normal circumstances he would have ditched her long ago. The circumstances were not normal. Evonne and Yolanda had leeched unto the Baca brothers, and if given the opportunity, Emilio imagined that the Aragon girls would have drained him of his ambitions as well as his blood. Jesus enjoyed their attention, and that was a good reason to keep them around. That, and a private secret that Jesus so carelessly revealed to them at the beginning of the relationship. In recent months, Joseph Aragon's political ambitions gave Emilio all the more reason to keep the girls around. They might well be this ticket to fulfilling his lifelong dream.

"He's my brother. I always worry about him," he reminded her.

"He's a little nuts, too. Maybe that should be a good reason for you to do so."

Evonne was goading him and he knew it. Every so often she tested the fires to see how far she could stoke them without getting burned, to see if he would loose his constant muzzled cool. Emilio knew she wanted to discover what kind of man he would be if he ever lost it. He refused to surrender, denying her the satisfaction. He was his own man, and he was not going to let some half-wit broad break him. Not even if she is the daughter of Joseph Aragon.

He kept his cool as he managed his comeback. "You don't seem too concerned that your sister's with him."

"She's big enough to take care of herself," Evonne said with her own sense of unemotional coolness.

Emilio was ready to chide her for her attitude when he was stopped by the sound of movement outside. He knew immediately that it was not his brother and Yolanda. The flashing lights of several police vehicles told him otherwise, and that he should be prepared.

Rushing to the window he watched as the cars rolled in, fanning the front yard, each facing his home, their headlights illuminating the house. Emilio's first impulse was to run to his cabinet and seize one of the loaded rifles. A second sense rescinded the urge, and it instead compelled him to walk outside to meet the police head on and unarmed. Like a scared child, Evonne followed behind him with his every move.

Raising his hands in the air in a surrender mode to show that he bore no weapons, he approached to the edge of his porch and shouted, "What's going on? What are you doing here?"

Three searchlights focused their beams upon him.

"This is Lieutenant John Cordova, New Mexico State Police. Please stand where you are. Do not move," came the announcement from over the bullhorn.

Freezing as instructed, Emilio and Evonne conceded that efforts to move on their part would be futile.

"What's going on?" Emilio demanded.

"Are there any other people inside your house?" Lieutenant Cordova persisted with his routine.

"No. No one. What is happening?"

Emilio's questions met no verbal replies. He was instead able to see six uniforms, two of them Rio Arriba County sheriffs, spread out and encircled the front of the house with their weapons drawn. As he watched, three more police vehicles approached the driveway from the road. The dark night prevented him from distinguishing what agency they represented, but he knew they were there for additional backup. He still did not know the seriousness of their visit.

Lieutenant Cordova issued new instructions. "I want you and the woman to step five paces forward, and three paces away from each other."

Hesitantly, Emilio and Evonne complied, maintaining the distance they were ordered to keep.

"Keep your hands high in the air and drop to your knees."

When they knelt they were ordered to lock their fingers behind their heads.

They continued to comply with all of the demands. Soon, four police officers came forward, two for each subject. Their distances spread out as they approached. As one kept his weapon trained, the other patted down their selected subject. Satisfied that both were clean of any concealed weapons, the officers backed off but still kept their weapons focused. Emilio was surprised that neither he nor Evonne were handcuffed.

"Please identify yourself," Lieutenant Cordova commanded as he stepped forward.

"I am Emilio Baca. I live here. This is my friend, Evonne Aragon.. Emilio managed to answer calmly, but his head was still reeling with confusion. Becoming verbally defiant, he spoke, "Tell me. I demand to know what's going on."

"You and Ms. Aragon may rise off of your knees. We have a search warrant, signed by Judge Nikki Mascarenas at ten-fifty this evening, authorizing us to search your home."

"You still haven't told me what this is about," Emilio's tone became more defiant and demanding.

"You are the brother of one Jesus Baca?"

"Yes, I am. What's he done?"

Despite the dislike he developed for Emilio, Lieutenant Cordova wanted to be humane about the way he delivered the news. He took a moment before he gave his reply. "I am sorry to tell you that your brother is dead. He was killed early this afternoon in a shootout with police. Before that, he shot six people to death." He could see Emilio's jaw slacken, and his eyes widen in disbelief. With a glance at the woman he could see a shocked expression on an otherwise stony face.

"Is your sister one Yolanda Aragon?" Cordova asked Evonne.

"Yes," was the cold and blunt reply.

The lieutenant found it curious that she did not ask about the welfare of her sister. He went on to volunteer the information. "You may be glad to know she was not seriously injured. Still, she's in the hospital in Santa Fe. We now have her under protective custody."

He was again surprised to see no expression of relief or any other form of emotion from the woman. He turned his focus back to Emilio in time to see tears well in the man's eyes as his body began to tremble.

"I am surprised that you were not aware," he said to Emilio. "The incident's been broadcast all evening over the television and radio."

"We…we don't watch television. We don't listen much to the radio." Tears were now streaming down his face. "How…how did it happen?"

As Lieutenant Cordova explained in detail about the massacre, his fellow state officers began their intensive search. The deputy sheriffs remained outside to provide backup should the need arise. It did not.

Leaving the two under the watchful eyes of the deputy sheriffs, the lieutenant joined the search being conducted on the inside. One bedroom was neat except for a made bed that looked as though someone had slept atop of the covers. Drawers were pulled out, with its contents emptied out onto the floor. The closet, with only two winter coats, two pair of dress slacks and five shirts occupying it, was checked for any loose paneling that could be loose and capable of concealing valuables or weapons. None were found.

The guns in the living room gun case, all neatly polished and oiled, were inventoried and confiscated, as were four handguns, four hunting knives and a filleting knife. A receipt was written up to act as a claim for the house's occupant. After a thorough check of the kitchen, living room, and a third bedroom, anything that was not of interest to the police was left in tact.

It was the second bedroom that drew the most attention, the room belonging to the former Jesus Baca. All of the items, clothes, shoes, knives, empty shell casings, pictures and wall hangings were inventoried, packaged and carted out of the room. Among the items that interested the lieutenant were newspaper clippings that dated back several years, and a prayer missal with a folded note in it which read, 'Jesus, A token of our deed, Your Friend, Yolanda.' Cordova found it interesting that a man who had just killed six people could once have been religious. As with all other items, this too was placed on the inventory list and placed with all other articles destined for an evidence check at headquarters in Santa Fe.

The outside storage shed contained nothing more than a lawn mower and various truck parts. The Baca's second truck sat beside it. In all, the Baca property was sparse of possessions, with most of the items for evidence coming from the gun rack, and from the bedroom belonging to Jesus. The search and seizure took less than two hours.

"These are receipts for what we are taking with us," Lieutenant Cordova said as he handed Emilio the slips of paper. "With the exception of the three marijuana joints we found, the rest of your possessions will be returned to you if and when they clear our investigation."

Sorrow and anger co-mixed within Emilio. "You got no right taking things."

"I beg your pardon, sir. The search warrant gives us that right."

"You cops kill someone, and then you get the right to take his property. It's…"

"Excuse me, sir," Lieutenant Cordova cut him short. "Your brother killed six people in cold blood. Four of those killed were police officers."

"You kill him and then you come here and spit on his home. That's why we consider people like you to be pigs."

"You can rant if you want, that's your business. I know you feel bad about your loss, but that doesn't help the families of the people your brother killed. Now, we do not have anything on you, or on Ms. Aragon, so we'll leave you. Our office will be in touch with you if we have any questions. If not then, then it will be when we release your brother's body."

"Fuck you. One day, all you police will pay for this."

The lieutenant chose to ignore the comment as he walked back to his cruiser. One by one, the sheriff and state police cars left the property, with Cordova's vehicle picking up the rear. Emilio and Evonne were again alone in a now emptied house.

Minutes passed before either spoke, both preoccupied with their own burdened thoughts. Emilio's was one of loss. Evonne's was one of self-concern.

"I gotta go home and see what my folks are going to do about Yolanda."

Emilio did not say a word, in part because his personal fog kept him from hearing.

"We must get her free as soon as possible," Evonne continued, aware that she was not getting through. "At the very least, she needs an attorney to tell her to keep her trap shut and say nothing."

"Uh?"

"You ain't heard a frigging word I said. We need for my sister to keep her mouth shut, before she says something she shouldn't."

"Why?" Emilio asked, slowly registering that he was being spoken to.

"Why! That's a Goddamn stupid question. If she starts talkin', there's no tellin' when she'll stop. She'll probably blab about our little secrets, then we are all screwed."

More and more Emilio began to comprehend Evonne's concern. He bobbed his head in approval, but he kept what he was thinking to himself. He was perfectly willing to let the younger daughter of the man he admired take control.

"After I finish here, I'm gonna take my sister's car and go home. Whatever you decide to do is your business, but for now we gotta keep a distance from each other for a while."

A silent look at Evonne told her that he understood. It did not tell her his inner most thoughts.

So, that bitch doesn't need me anymore. She's leaving me to fend for myself. Fine. Screw her. I'm of no more use to her or her father, so the hell with it, let her go. I got more important things to worry about right now.

29

Sleep came at two o'clock in the morning. Five hours later Mike sat behind his desk going over the flood of accumulated data.

"Good morning," Major Archuletta greeted his lieutenant. "Did you get enough rest?"

"Good morning, sir," Mike exchanged the pleasantry. "Right now there's too much adrenaline flowing to get much rest. I couldn't get it even if I wanted to."

The major then cued Mike in on his decision. "I discussed it with the chief, and we decided that for the time being I'm going to assume Captain Guiterrez's responsibilities plus a few of yours. We don't want to disrupt the current command structure. You'll take over this case until completion, and we've decided to bring Cordova down here temporarily to assist you. As the senior officer, you're in charge."

"Very good, Major." Mike accepted the responsibility without any protest, and without any satisfaction. Bringing things to a solid close would be his tribute to his fallen captain and friend.

"Cordova should be in here about nine. He knows about the decision, so when he gets in you two can get right to work." The major started to leave, but stopped to make one final comment. "You are a good man, Mike...one of our best. The chief and I thanked God you were not injured. So remember what I told you, if you start feeling drained I want you to go home and rest."

Mike appreciated the praise, but it did nothing to fill the hollowness within. He had witnessed death several times in the past, his years as a cop exposing to him too much of it. Even the death of a family member or a friend did not leave as much of a void. The only thing he could figure, something he would adopt as an explanation was that he, himself, was on hand as direct witness. He watched as Cap was struck by a single gunshot, and except for the cover of a tree and the precautions he took, Mike reasoned that he could have met the same fate.

After studying the data and the statements of witnesses of the previous day's nightmare, Mike went downstairs to evidence lockup. The collected evidence was sorted into two separate groups: One from the actual scene, and the other a collection from the Baca home. Spent shell casings and the death weapon itself were prominent items from the scene, all of which could only retell a story Mike knew all too well. Not a single piece could alter that story in the slightest. Perhaps the second group could at least provide insight as to the thinking of a man who showed a total disregard for life.

Piece by piece he arranged the evidence taken from the Baca residence in straight rows on three tables. Five rifles, four handguns, and an assortment of hunting knives were the first to be laid out. Next were the personal affects that included newspaper clippings and a prayer missal.

Scanning the firearms, Mike wondered why anyone needed so many weapons. He never hunted, so he conceded that the different powerful rifles might be needed to bring down various large game. The rifles were too powerful for rabbit or birds, so the game had to be large, something like the deer and elk that were bountiful in the mountains of the northern part of New Mexico. He could only guess at the need for the handguns.

He picked up the prayer book, flipped the pages and found Yolanda's note to Jesus. Nothing was inscribed on the inside of the cover that could have identified to whom the book actually belonged to.

The note was a strange one that left Mike at a complete loss. He made a mental note of it, storing it as something to be explored later. Mike closed the book and studied the black embossed cover. He had no idea as to what the initials stood for. Definitely not Jesus Baca, or anyone within Yolanda Aragon's immediate family. It left Mike to conclude that the prayer book once belonged to another party. Who, he did not know. The question became another note to be recorded for further exploration.

The next things he looked at were the newspaper clippings, and his eyes focused on the headlines that caused his mind to pay a special attention. There were six, and the top two covered the slaying of Karen Daughtrey and Georgina Becaud. He scanned them before picking up the other four. The oldest went back a bit over seven years.

BODY OF SLAIN TOURIST FOUND NEAR ARROYO

It covered the story of a young woman, a Sandra Baber, who was strangled and stabbed, her body found in an arroyo that passed the southeast end of a shopping mall. Robbery was ruled out since no money or other valuables were taken, and her car was found within the mall's parking lot.

The second article, dated some two years later, read:

WOMAN'S BODY FOUND ON CONSTRUCTION SITE

Twenty-four year old Jeanne Miller was murdered, and her body was found behind the motel she stayed at, a new construction site that would be home to some retail stores. Her body was battered, and strangulation was the cause of death. Again, robbery was not a motive.

Twenty-seven months later:

BODY FOUND ON ROADSIDE IN LONE BUTTE

Eighteen months later:

WOMAN FOUND STRANGLED NEAR CIRCLE DRIVE

The deaths of the last two women were similar to the others, and the motives for each were never established.

Christ! These are some of the unsolved cases Madrid is working on, was one of Mike's immediate thoughts. *Why the hell would a guy like him save such clippings?*

Mike left the evidence room with two nagging questions. The first might be satisfied with a phone call. After pulling a file, reviewing its contents, he pushed the keys connecting him with the rectory.

"Father Gomez? This is Lieutenant Mike Shannon, New Mexico State Police."

"Lieutenant Shannon. My, God, how are you my son?"

"Fine, father." Mike knew where the priest's conversation was going to lead, and out of courtesy he let the reverend continue.

"I read all about the tragedy in the morning papers. I pray you are holding up well."

"I am, father. Thank you."

"Thank God for that. Please, tell me, how may I be of help to you?"

"I've been going over Monsignor Serrano's file, and I have one or two questions."

"By all means. I'm just amazed that you have time to work on that now."

"It's something that has just come up," Mike explained. "After going over the list of personal affects belonging to the monsignor, I noticed there was no prayer book on the list. Wouldn't it be normal for a priest to carry one with him when issuing the Last Rites?"

"Why, yes. It would. I guess it was something we overlooked. Then again, Monsignor Serrano had three of four of them."

"I see. Please, tell me something else father. Would it be normal for a priest to have his initials imprinted on the front cover?"

"Normally, no. However, we did have a few copies made that way. It was a token gift a few of his fellow priests decided to give him in honor of the many little favors he used to do for us."

The answer was one Mike wanted to hear. After thanking the priest, he hung up the phone and contemplated his next phone call. Within five minutes he was on the line with Detective Sergeant Francesca Madrid.

"Mike!" Francesca said with a startled tone. "My God! How are you doing?"

"All things considered, I guess I'm lucky to be alive." Mike bit his lip in punishment, believing that his comment seemed too blatantly callous. Even if events are horrifying, it's not uncommon for some cops to be flippant, especially for one who usually tried to bring the bright side to things. If they did not, many would be spending more time sitting in a therapist's office instead of at their own desk.

"Mike, before you say anything, please let me express my deepest condolences. Everyone here is in grief, especially those who knew Cap."

"Thank you, Fran. We really appreciate that." Not wanting to dote any more on the deaths of his comrades, Mike quickly broached his subject. "Let me ask you, how soon can you come over. I have some things we should look over together. I think we may have a break or two coming our way."

"Sure. What is it about?"

"We'll talk about it when you get here. You might be pleased."

"Okay. Give me about twenty minutes."

Francesca found Mike in his office talking with Lieutenant Cordova who had just come in. She knocked and entered. "Am I disturbing anything?"

"No, Detective, you're not. Come on in." Mike rose to greet her, and to make an introduction. Once done, they each settled into their chairs.

"Last night John brought back some evidence confiscated at the Baca residence in Guzman," Mike began. "Some of it included newspaper clippings on a few murdered girls. I had a chance to look at them earlier, and that is why I called you." He went on to elucidate his findings. "It can all be circumstantial, but the cop in me doubts it. I think we both may have something to go on."

An appreciative smile broke on Francesca's face. "God, I hope so." She then turned her attention to Cordova. "Lieutenant, did either the brother or Evonne Aragon show any strange behavior? Did he protest about the search?"

"Surprisingly, very little. I don't think he expected us to find anything out of the ordinary. Besides, he was in shock over his brother's death. As far as behavior, he was a bit hostile and she was coldly silent. She didn't even ask about her sister."

"You said he was hostile," Mike interrupted. "What did he do?"

"Just words. It's obvious that he doesn't like cops, and before we left he said the police will pay for this."

"Oh! Did he indicate how?" Francesca asked.

"No, he didn't," Cordova said before he explained. "Up in those areas law enforcement usually gets along very well with the people. However, there are a few who resent any type of law enforcement. I chalked it up to him being one of them."

Mike concurred by nodding his understanding. "The sick part is, his brother enacted that resentment."

"What do you recommend we do next?" Francesca asked.

"Start drilling the girls," Mike said with decisive authority, "starting with the one we have in custody. Then bring in the brother to see what he knows."

"Good! You have any objections of my being there?" Francesca asked, almost certain of the answer.

"By all means," Mike replied. "Those clippings cover murders you're handling…maybe others. The Yolanda girl is in protective custody, and probably will be for at least another day before her lawyer springs her. Let's question her at the detention center, and pick up her sister and question her here."

"To keep them from communicating with each other," Francesca said as a matter of fact.

"I'll give Sam a call. As DA, he should be there."

Mike noticed a peculiar look on Francesca's face at the mention of Sam's name. As a friend he wanted to ask her why, but decided to wait until the meeting concluded.

"Should I bring in Emilio Baca," Lieutenant Cordova asked.

Mike thought for a moment before making his decision. "Nah. We got nothing on him. Let's wait until we've spoken to the girls. Then we can haul his ass in, if need be."

The meeting drew to a close, and despite the heaviness of the past day's slaughter, there was a slight air of buoyancy shared between them. A little flicker of light might begin to glow at the other end of a troubling tunnel.

After Lieutenant Cordova left, Mike abruptly asked, "Fran, is something wrong between you and Sam?"

Francesca was caught off guard by the question. She could only muster a shrug as a reply.

"I don't mean to stick my nose in where it doesn't belong, and I haven't seen Sam for over a week now. Till then, he showed signs of being a happy little puppy, and I don't want to stick my foot in my mouth when I see him later."

"It's just a lover's spat," Francesca tried deflecting the comment by evading the true issue.

"Then why the troubled look? We all have lover's spats. It's what keeps relationships from getting boring."

Francesca fought hard to keep a normal composure, but the tear that ebbed in her eye betrayed her.

"Oh-oh! I hope I didn't say something wrong. I was just trying to be a friend."

"No, that's okay," Francesca replied as she wiped away her tear. "You've been though a lot for me to burden you with my problems."

"Forget about that," Mike gently told her. "If a friend has problems, I'll try to help regardless of what else is going on. So speak up, it might help."

Francesca looked up at Mike with her saddened eyes. "That's very thoughtful of you, Mike. It's just…it's just that while digging around I found out that Sam was once involved with Julie Fletcher."

"With…" Recalling that the Fletcher case was still classified as one of the unsolved ones, Mike immediately added, "He never mentioned her to you?"

"No, he didn't." Grasping for her words, she went on, "When I found out I began to…well, I began to…"

"You began to suspect that Sam had something to do with it," Mike said, finishing her sentence for her.

"It's just…that I…"

"Forget about that, Fran. We all know who the real perp is. Your detective work should have told you as much."

"It's just that I had to find out about it on my own. He never told me about the relationship until I uncovered it. He had his chances to tell me, but he didn't."

"So, now you think he may have been responsible in some way."

"I know what you're saying, but that's not all of it," Francesca started forcing herself to speak.

"Okay. What else did you find out?" he asked, coaxing her to tell him.

Francesca told Mike about the rest of her discovery as it pertained to the Georgina Becaud case. Mike listened, paying attention to her every word.

"Wow," Mike shook his head. "You do realize this is all very circumstantial, don't you? Even if he did speak to her that night, I don't think there is any way to connect him."

"I know," she admitted. "I was actually hoping that when your man arrested Officer Flores we had our suspect, but it was not to be. Now, if the evidence you have is any indication, I know that I may have screwed up big time."

"That's right, Fran. You may have," Mike critically agreed. "I really hope the clippings are a clue that leads somewhere. It'll not only solve a couple of homicides, but it might also clear your way of thinking about Sam."

"I really hope you're right," Francesca meekly replied.

"Have you given any thought of how you'll square things with him?"

"I have, but I have not been able to come up with any solutions," Francesca answered.

"I don't envy you on that one." Mike studied the female detective whose eyes were cast downwards. A slightly more fatherly approach came to mind. "Fran, I've never been in such a situation, so it may be easier for me to speak. You let your suspicions as a cop interfere with your love life. I can't tell you that it should not have, but your mistake was being too quick to confront Sam with it."

"You're probably right," she admitted.

"Sam is a very private guy, and from what I know he did love the girl. That's probably why he never told you. The damn thing is, you confronted him a couple of day's ago. Today we have a lead that might very well take us into a totally different direction."

"I know. My timing stinks," Francesca said as her eyes focused away.

"That's right, it does. But you had no way of knowing," Mike said, using it as an excuse. "The thing is, there wasn't enough to confront Sam. Maybe I'm wrong, but maybe it was the deceived woman in you that made you do it."

This time her eyes gave their attention to him. "You think so?"

"I don't know," Mike shrugged. "I'm no expert on women. But, when you found out he was once serious about Julie Fletcher I think the woman in you, and not the objective detective, took over."

Humbly, she replied, "You may be right."

"The important thing is what you're going to be able to do about it? That's a tough one. It's something you have to figure out by yourself, but if you need a sounding board I'll be all ears."

"Thank you," she sheepishly said as she rose to leave. "I really appreciate you taking the time to listen, especially in light of what's happened?"

"Think nothing of it, Fran. As I said before, regardless of the circumstances, if a friend needs me I'll be there. In the meantime, I'll be in touch with you in about an hour, once I'm able to coordinate the interview with the girls, and can arrange for Sam to be there."

Francesca departed leaving Mike alone with his duties, and his thoughts. It has been one hell of a couple of days. He reached for the phone to arrange for the interrogation room at the detention center. By the end of the morning he expected having a very detailed discussion with Yolanda Aragon. With a little luck, he would have another with Evonne shortly thereafter. After that, well just maybe, he'll have one with the grieving brother of the deceased killer.

30

"We must know how this happened," Joseph Aragon railed into his youngest daughter. "Getting involved with crazy people like that doesn't help our image."

"Shit! You should be more worried about Yolanda," Evonne shot back. "To top it off, you didn't complain when they were working on your campaign."

"That guy worried me. I didn't trust him. You ask your mother, she'll tell you."

"Bull! You'd take help wherever you get it. What you should be worried about is Yolanda being in jail."

"Christ! She could've gotten killed yesterday, and you're worried about her being in jail." JoJo tried to dismiss Evonne with a wave of his hand, knowing it was futile. "She's in protective custody, not under arrest. She was a victim, so they don't have anything to charge her with."

"Cut the crap, pops. You know as well as I do that if they want to, the cops will try to pin something on her. She should have a lawyer."

"She's got one. My guy's going over there this afternoon to try and get her out today," JoJo advised.

"Too late! He should be there now."

"What do ya' mean, too late? She ain't going anywhere, and a couple of more hours ain't gonna make much difference."

Evonne was frustrated with her father's reply. Hoping a calmer approach might get through to him, she warned him of what could happen. "Look! Yolanda hasn't done nothing, but if you give the cops a chance they'll find a way to implicate her. Next, they'll be accusing her of pulling the trigger."

What Yolanda said made sense to him. JoJo had as much distrust of the police as she did, and it caused him to do a little rethinking. "All right, I'll give the lawyer a call. Maybe he can get there earlier."

The doorbell rang before Evonne could reply, drawing an annoyance from both. "Who the hell can that be?" JoJo grumbled as he went to the door.

Evonne followed closely behind him, with apprehension dominating her curiosity.

"Aragon residence?" A seasoned state police officer addressed him. A younger officer stood in the background.

"I'm Mr. Aragon. What can I do for you?"

"We are looking for your daughter, Evonne Aragon."

"She's right here…"

Evonne's poke in his back was not quick enough to keep her identity from being revealed.

"Ms. Aragon, we've been asked to escort you to our office. Our superiors want to talk with you."

"What is this about?" both Aragons demanded.

"Sorry, but I really don't know."

Evonne wanted to protest, but it was JoJo who stopped her. He accepted the fact that any evasiveness would not look good later on if a formal summons were to be issued. "You'd better go with them."

"Hell! What can I tell them? I wasn't there."

"I know, so you shouldn't have to worry."

"Hell, then I'm not telling them nothin' without a lawyer."

"You don't need a damned lawyer. They probably just want to ask you some routine questions."

"I don't trust them, pop. They always find ways of twisting things. I want an attorney present."

Relenting, JoJo gave in to her. "Okay. I'll call him now. Let him decide which is the best way to handle this is."

Grabbing a couple of her personal items, Evonne departed with the police officers. As she was leaving, she turned her head over her shoulder and repeated her demand. "Remember. Call the lawyer, and do it now!"

$$\approx$$

An hour earlier, shortly before noon, three people sat in a small conference room, awaiting their subject. When Yolanda Aragon was brought in, it was Mike who took the lead.

"Miss Aragon, my name is Lieutenant Mike Shannon with the New Mexico State Police. Please, be seated. Make yourself comfortable." Mike's first goal was to make the girl relax, to make her feel at ease and to establish some trust. "Are you doing okay, Miss Aragon? Is there something we can get for you? Coffee? A Pepsi perhaps?"

"No…thank you." Yolanda was leery of all police, but she took to the gentle fashion in which the officer approached. She began to feel that perhaps he had some idea of the ordeal she had been through.

"So that you know everybody, this is Detective Sergeant Francesca Madrid, and this gentleman is our district attorney, Samuel Dawes." Before he made the introductions, Mike withdrew a small tape recorder and switched it on. "I hope you don't mind this, but we would like to get as much on tape as possible, in case we forget something."

Yolanda looked at him, feeling a bit unsure, but made no objection to having her words recorded. "No…I don't mind."

"Thank you," Mike said before he continued. "Now, before we begin with any of the harder questions, let me ask you…how are you feeling?" Indicating to the bandages on her arms and a small cast on her left hand, "Did you receive any major injuries yesterday?"

"The doctor said I had a mild concussion," Yolanda freely admitted. "Got some bruises and some cuts, too. My arm…my back."

"Well, I'm very sorry to hear that. Considering what you've been through, you're very fortunate. Did the doctor take care of them? The wounds, I mean."

"Yes," she replied as she touched a bandage on her arm.

"And, they are nothing serious?"

"No."

"Is there any other physical problems you might have?"

"No. Just trouble sleeping."

"Oh? You mean the doctor didn't give you a tranquilizer or anything?"

"He did. It's just…well…you know."

"Yeah, I think I do. Are you feeling well enough to talk with us?"

"I…I think so."

"Good. Now if you start feeling ill or something, let us know. There's a pitcher of water on the table here, so feel free to help yourself at any time."

Yolanda's nod said, "I will."

"Now…in your own words," Mike said softly, like a priest coaxing a confession from a child, "please tell us what you remember about what happened yesterday. Start from the very beginning, from when you and Jesus left his home yesterday morning."

Yolanda showed a little apprehension and fright, and she stuttered as she began to speak. "I…I…er…I mean we…"

"Take your time, Miss Aragon. It is more important to try and tell us what you remember. You don't have to rush."

"Yes…well…when we left to go into Espanola Jesus seemed to be still very angry," she began.

"You mean he was angry earlier?" Mike asked, wanting clarification.

"Yes, since the day before yesterday. He became angry when he found out that this guy, Eddie Real, was thrash mouthing him."

"I see. So then he planned to confront Eddie Real?"

"I guess so. But, I didn't know it at the time. To be honest with you, I didn't know where we were going until we got to this guy's house. When we got there Eddie wasn't home, just his brother and some woman…Eddie's girlfriend, I think." Yolanda went on to account for every detail she could remember. She concluded her summary by reliving the trauma of the tear gas and her escape from inside the house, to her being taken into custody.

The telling of her story lasted over a half an hour, with a few interruptions by Mike who, from time to time, sought clarification of certain details. When she finished Mike sat back, stretched, and sympathetically said, "Wow. You sure as hell went through a lot." Then, with a little nice consideration, he added, "I'll tell you what. Let's take a bit of a recess. It'll give you a chance to relax for a little bit."

Mike and the two observers stepped out of the conference room and entered a smaller office. When he left he took the tape recorder with him.

"If you ask me, she was caught by surprise by what happened," Mike announced.

"I agree," Sam said. "In my opinion she had no idea as to what was about to happen."

"Likewise, I agree," Francesca said, offering her opinion. "I think she is innocent of any involvement. She could have easily become a murder victim herself."

"Let's not tell her yet," Mike advised. "I'd like to keep her guessing as to whether we believe her story or not. It might help with the next round of questioning, the real reason we want to talk to her."

They again gathered into the conference room, Yolanda was still sitting where they had left her. This time Mike brought a can of Pepsi with him.

"This is for you. You've been here for a while, so I figured you can use a little refreshment." After he placed the can in front of her, Mike again pulled out the tape recorder, this time with a fresh tape.

At the other end of the room, Francesca and Sam exchanged glances, acknowledging Mike's motive for the little gift. The soda would not only help to once again establish trust, but it might eventually make her feel uncomfortable with a need to go to the bathroom.

Before beginning the second round, Mike and Sam also exchanged glances. Mike knew he had to take caution in the way he posed his questions. Although the high court ruled that police could question suspects without an attorney present, no one wanted a possible booking to be nullified due to a technicality because of coercive questioning.

"Yolanda," Mike began, using a warmer familiar approach. "Can you please tell me, what was your relationship with Jesus Baca?"

"We were friends," Yolanda volunteered.

"Just friends. I see. So then there wasn't anything more between you, like boyfriend and girlfriend, or anything like that?"

"No, we were just friends. Him and his brother helped my dad with his campaign."

"Oh, that's right," Mike expressed with a false surprise. "It's your dad who's running for mayor. How do you think he'll do in the race?"

"Okay, I guess," Yolanda answered with uncertainty, not sure if the question was going to lead anywhere.

"He probably will, but I don't know what's tougher, actually being mayor or running for the job. Either way, there're a lot of hassles."

Yolanda shrugged, not knowing what the correct answer was.

"What did the Baca boys do to help out your dad?"

"The four of us, them, me and my sister, we hung posters and handed out fliers. Emilio did a lot of talking to try and get people to vote for my dad."

"Was he good at it?"

"I think so. People seemed to like him."

"Umm, umm. What about Jesus? Did he greet people?"

"No. He wasn't good at anything like that."

"I see. Why do you think that was? Was it because he was too volatile?"

"I'm not sure," Yolanda replied to a question that made her feel uncomfortable, like one might feel when saying something ill against a dead man. "Jesus…he had a…bad temper. Many times he had to be calmed down. Emilio was the only one who could really do that."

"Tell me, Yolanda. Did he ever loose his tempter with you…treat you bad in any way?"

"No, never. He was always nice to me."

"So he never treated you badly. Maybe because you had a fondness for each other, right?"

"Maybe."

"Did you two ever get romantically involved?" Mike began to push the envelope that would ultimately lead him to where he wanted to go.

"We thought about it, but we decided to just be friends. We really liked each other."

"So, you once in a while gave each other gifts."

"Sometimes." Yolanda felt relaxed enough to talk freely in what was beginning to feel like an exchange of conversation as opposed to questioning.

"You gave each other trinkets and stuff like that?"

"Well, yes, a couple of times. Mostly it was things like candy, or beer, or sometimes something like a magazine. You know, little things."

"Yeah, I think I do. Something like a prayer book, or something like that." Mike made the statement casually, and he saw an alarmed response in Yolanda's eyes. "As a matter of fact, we found the one you gave him. I must admit, being a religious man myself, it was a very thoughtful gift to give someone."

Francesca and Sam, as observers could see a tension rising with Yolanda's subtle movements: a look away, a scratching of her arm, and a shift in her sitting position. They both wondered how Mike would pursue it. They found out as he eased the interview into another direction. Hopefully, it was a ploy that was being used to set up a return.

"I'll tell you," Mike said, confiding in Yolanda as though she were his friend. "I was really surprised by how little we confiscated from the Baca house. Usually, when we use a search warrant we come back with a heck of a lot more. Most of what we collected belonged to Jesus." Seeing that Yolanda was not giving any response, he continued. "We brought back the prayer book, his rifles and a few handguns, different types of knives, some of his clothes. But, the strangest things we brought back were some newspaper clippings. They were about murdered women. Six of them, in fact. I just can't figure out why someone like him would want to save something like that."

Yolanda's uneasiness worsened as she almost inaudibly replied, "I don't know." She took a deep drink of her Pepsi in an effort to regain some calmness, but the three people present could see a rise in her agitation.

"You don't know? Jeez! It's too bad you don't, because we'd really like to gain some insight as to what made Jesus tick." Mike's tempo increased not allowing Yolanda to fully think or respond. "You see we have a very deep concern about that. We cannot figure out why someone like him would want to save newspaper articles on the deaths of several different women. It creates a suspicion that in some way he might have been involved."

Yolanda trembled. She again began to drink, but her visibly shaking hand caused her to spill the soda as it reached her mouth. Watching the drink stream down her cheek, Mike signaled to Francesca for a tissue. It was also his way of letting the detective to join in on the questioning.

Stepping forward, she handed Yolanda a few tissues. As she did so she spoke.

"The lieutenant is correct, it does create a cloud over the man. If you can tell us anything you know about him, it would help us enormously."

"I…I don't know nothing…." Yolanda quietly responded as she tried to avoid eye contact. Tears began to ebb from hers.

Seeing this, Francesca stepped to the other side of the table and sat down opposite Mike, sandwiching Yolanda in between. Leaning forward to directly face the upset woman, Francesca spoke in a mildly comforting voice. "Your tears are saying that you know something. Please, tell us. What is it that you know?"

"I don't know anything. I…I…"

"Then why are you so upset? Why the tears? You know something, so please tell us."

Still shaking, Yolanda tried to deflect the question. "I…don't. I…"

"You apparently do. You must realize that not telling us could possibly implicate you for not cooperating in a police investigation. You can go to jail for that."

The dam overflowed as tears began to heavily stream down Yolanda Aragon's face.

"Please tell us, Yolanda. We must know."

Sobbing through her tears, Yolanda broke down. "They killed her."

Francesca and Mike exchanged quick victorious glances. Not letting the full impact of the revelation take hold, Francesca demanded, "Who?"

"That woman…a few years ago."

Not sure of which victim was being mentioned, Francesca blurted out a name. "Who? Sandra Baber?"

"I don't know her name," Yolanda answered through her tears.

"How do you know this?" Detective Madrid's questions were becoming rapid fire quick.

"They told me."

"They? Who are they?"

"I mean Jesus told me. He said he and Emilio killed the woman."

A pause settled as Francesca and Mike exchanged another elated glance. A breakthrough had been made.

"Thank you, Ms. Aragon," Francesca said with a softening tone. "That is the kind of help we need. Now, if you please, tell us what you know. Don't be afraid of saying too much. Every detail might be important even if it seems trivial to you, so tell us everything."

Yolanda fumbled with her tissues as she dried her face from the wetness of her tears. She took an extra moment to gain strength in her voice.

"One night…several months ago…we were sitting around getting stoned on beer and weed," she began as she fixed her gaze on the Pepsi can before her. "Emilio kinda fell asleep where he was sitting, so me and Evonne and Jesus just sat around tellin' stories."

"You mean your sister was there," Francesca said as a matter of fact as she exchanged another glance with Mike.

"Yes…she was just there, like me," Yolanda said with a bit of consternation.

"Don't worry about it," Francesca quickly replied in an effort to minimize her own comments. "What we really want to know is what Jesus had to say. I assume that's when he told you about what he did."

"Well…yes. We was now tellin' our little secrets when he says, 'I got one'. So we asked him to tell us, and he does."

"What did he tell you?" Francesca easily asked in an effort to prod her along.

"Well, he starts telling us what him and Emilio did." Yolanda paused, unsure of how to continue.

"Please, Yolanda, I don't mean to make this too difficult for you. It would help if you relate everything he told you. Just as much as you can remember. From the beginning."

"I'll try." Yolanda paused long enough to review her memory before she continued. "We begged him to tell us about his secret, so he did. He said one night Emilio and him were in Santa Fe, just hangin'. He says they were both getting bored, but it was Emilio who was bummed out. He was pissed about all the tourists in town, and the way they acted as though they owned it. It was warm…"

"You mean it was summer, then?" Francesca asked.

"Yeah. July or August, maybe."

It confirmed to Francesca that the time correlated with the time of the year in which Sandra Baber was killed. "I'm sorry. Please go on."

"Well…anyway…he says Emilio was pissed…you see he always hated the people who come here and taking advantage of the people who live here. Emilio…well…he is always so very cool when you see him, but inside…inside he's got a passionate hate for these people. Anyway, that's when he says to Jesus, 'I'd like to kill one of these assholes. Maybe they'll then go away'. Jesus laughed and then said, 'why don't we?' Emilio then looks at him with a smile and says, 'you know bro, I've been holding it in too long… maybe we should'." She paused to sip her Pepsi.

"Then what?" Francesca verbally pushed her.

"Jesus says they then go down to the southwest mall and start scouting around. It was getting late, and the mall was closin', but Emilio and Jesus start walkin' around the outside. They were on the backside of the mall, there was only one car there, and it was dark. Emilio sees the car's got outa state plates on it."

"Did he tell you from where?"

"I don't know. I think he said Washington or Oregon, or somethin' like that. I really don't remember."

Sandra Baber was from Virginia, the opposite coast from where Yolanda's unsure recollection was telling them. "That's not very important. Please, go on and tell us the rest of what Jesus said."

Yolanda finished the contents of her soda before continuing. "Jesus says they then got their own truck and parked close to the car. He says they slumped down in the seats and looked for someone to come. About ten minutes later he says they saw this woman coming toward the car.

Nobody else was around and it was dark, so they waited until she turns her back to unlock the door. That's when Emilio goes up around her and grabs her from behind, putting one hand on her mouth and the other on her throat. He starts choking her as she struggles. Jesus says he sees she's tryin' to fight back, so he brings his knife with him from the truck and he stabs her. She dies right there. Then suddenly it starts raining and they don't know what to do with her, so they see the arroyo and they throw the dead woman into it."

Francesca sat back and mentally reviewed the Baber file. No blood was found in or around the car, however she realized that the rain must have washed it away.

"What was your reaction when he told you the story?"

"I figured it was just a story to make us feel scared. He liked doing things like that. Later, when Evonne and I was alone, she says she remembers reading about it."

"Did you have any reaction then?"

"I don't know how I felt. I figured it was none of my business."

More glances were exchanged between Francesca, Mike, and Sam. A moment passed before Francesca asked her next question. "We're still bothered by something. You told us about Jesus and Emilio killing one woman. But, the clippings from the newspapers covered six different murders. Tell me, what do you know about them?"

"Jesus says there were more, but he never told us about them."

"Why not?"

"Emilio…he was sleeping, but wakes up before Jesus could tell us more. Jesus tells Emilio what he told us. Emilio gets mad and tells him to shut up. He was so mad, I thought he was gonna bust Jesus one."

"But, you said a moment ago that you thought Jesus was just trying to scare you. Didn't Emilio getting mad at him tell you to think otherwise?"

"Not really," Yolanda answered to cover her possible mistake. "Jesus often pissed off Emilio, so I figure he was doin' it again. I didn't think much of it."

"You told no one about this?"

"No…we told no one."

Francesca studied the girl before her, and then she made eye contact. "Ms. Aragon, I'm sure you realize this is very serious. You can serve some very serious time in prison if you deliberately concealed information like this."

As before, Yolanda began to tremble. The look on her face said she had some secrets that she was desperately trying to hide.

"We'd like to know everything you know about this and other murders," Francesca persisted.

Finally, Yolanda totally broke down, her eyes tearing, her body shaking, and her movements gave the suggestion of a stray animal trying to elude the net. "I...I don't know nothing. I...I want to have a lawyer."

"You can..." Francesca tried to speak.

Through her tears, Yolanda again made her demand, "I said I want to have a lawyer."

"Okay, Miss Aragon. You will have one," Sam spoke up, breaking his long silence. "You don't have to tell us any more about what you know regarding those murders until you have counsel," he told her, sounding as though he was there to protect her. In reality, as the district attorney and as an officer of the court, he was there for her just as much as he was there to find justice for the victims. To him, it was not a conflict. It was a duty he had to uphold in the name of justice. He also did not want to take a chance that either interrogator would breach the line, dismissing the useful information they had already skillfully gathered.

Mike turned off the tape recorder and buzzed the intercom to signal security that the session had come to a close. While he waited he had a couple of more casual questions, but he inserted a fresh tape into the recorder.

"Do you know a Cornelius Toohey?"

This time her eyes went into a stare, but her reply was, "No...I don't."

"Oh, well," Mike shrugged. "One last question. Did you know Father John Carrol Serrano?"

Her whole demeanor changed again, fear and apprehension taking hold anew. She nervously repeated, "I...I want to see my lawyer."

"So you shall," Mike told her. "We'll be back a little later on to continue our discussion."

A guard arrived and escorted her from the room. The three investigators remained silent, letting their glances converse for them.

"We got a real live one here," Mike broke the silence. "Not only does she solve one murder case for us, but she may have the answers for a few others."

"At the very least, we now have grounds to hold her," Sam said, injecting his viewpoint. "She's no longer just a material witness."

"What's our next move?" Francesca asked, hoping that Mike and Sam were on her wavelength.

The two men looked at each other, but Sam was content to let Mike speak for both of them.

"Our next move is to have a nice little talk with her sister," Mike said, confirming what the other two had in mind.

❧

Pacing in a different conference room two miles up the road, Evonne Aragon was angry for having to wait for nearly two hours. If no one came to her soon, she was determined to walk out and leave. It turned out to be wishful thinking on her part. Three minutes later her interview began. Mike introduced himself, Francesca, and Sam, and asked Evonne to take a seat. Unlike with Yolanda, he took a harder tone forcing the Aragon sister to heed his command. His overall tactic was going to be different. At his cue, he had Francesca turn on a second tape recorder to record the pending proceedings.

"I don't know why you want to talk to me," Evonne snapped, almost defensively. "I did nothing. I wasn't even there."

"We know you weren't," Mike replied as he stood before her. As he did, Francesca placed the already recording tape recorder on the table, and the same introductions were made. "We just got back from having a nice little conversation with your sister."

"So?"

"So we had a good chat about several things, including a couple of other murders." Mike waited for her reaction before he would talk about specifics. Stoicism hid any anxiety she may have had.

"I don't know what you're talkin' about," Evonne curtly replied.

"Oh? To begin with, she first told us about the woman Jesus and his brother killed."

Evonne's jaw slackened before she spoke. "I still don't know what the hell you're talking about. I don't know of any murders those two guys did."

"That's interesting, because that's not the way we understand it. Yolanda told us the whole story of how the four of you got stoned, of how Emilio fell asleep, and then of how Jesus bragged about killing a woman in a mall parking lot. But, that's just the small part of it."

"I....er..." Flustered, Evonne was at a loss for words, and Mike was not about to let her find them.

"We also talked about other murdered women. And, about Father Serrano. Here, let me play just a small part of what she told us, this way you won't think I'm trying to trick you."

Trickery was what he had in mind as he displayed his own tape recorder and set it on play. Yolanda's telling of the killing of a woman at the mall was all he intended to let her hear. It was enough.

"That bitch!" Evonne exploded. "That God damn bitch! I knew she wouldn't keep her mouth shut!" She started to rise, but Mike's looming presence kept her pinned in her chair. His position was just right to look down on her, and to twist a knot a little tighter.

"It seems you two have some very serious problems which could put you both away for a very long time."

Furious, Evonne could only think of the betrayal by her sister. "That bitch! She's trying to pin it all on me."

"She doesn't have to," Mike coaxed her without telling her how to save herself. In her fog of rage, Evonne snapped at the bait.

"You're damned friggin' right, she doesn't have to. It was her and Jesus who were responsible."

"Responsible for what? Tell us."

"She got turned on by that story Jesus told us. She wanted to know what it felt like to kill someone. Jesus…he didn't like priests, so he dreams up this plan to do one in. That really turned her on." Evonne started to go into more detail, but she abruptly stopped.

"So, what happened?" Mike asked.

"I don't know. I wasn't there."

"What about Georgina Becaud and Karen Daughtrey?"

"Who?"

"The two other women who were murdered over the last couple of months."

"I don't know nothin' about them," Evonne answered quickly with a defensive edge. "Yolanda and Jesus didn't talk about what they did to do them in."

"So, you are telling us that you had nothing to do with any of the slayings?"

"No, I did not…have anything to do with the slayings, that is." Suddenly realizing that she already spoke too much, Evonne once again became defiant. "I'm not telling you anything more. Not without a lawyer."

Mike gazed down on her, letting her feel the discomfort of his stare. "That is your right, and so it shall be. Meanwhile, we are going to have to detain you until your attorney comes."

Before Evonne was taken away to be put in holding, Francesca had a nagging question.

"Tell me if you will, Ms. Aragon. Do you speak any French?"

The question baffled Evonne for a moment. Not seeing any harm in giving an answer, she gave one. "I don't know what that's gotta do with anything, but yeah. I speak some French. Emilio taught me how to speak a little of it."

It was now established that two of her suspects spoke French. "Thank you," was Francesca's satisfied reply as she clicked off the tape recorder.

Sam waited until Evonne was taken from the room before he spoke, anticipating the next step. "Between your tapes and the video behind that mirror, I think we have a lot to go on. I guess it's time we go back and question Yolanda again."

"You got that right, boss," Mike enthusiastically agreed. "But first, we're gonna have ourselves a sandwich. This crap is making me hungry."

Before taking off for lunch and then to the detention center, Mike picked up his messages. One in particular pleased him, and as they left the headquarters building he passed the information on to Francesca and Sam. It made their lunch that more enjoyable.

Yolanda, together with her attorney, was waiting for them. After a few legal formalities, the session began. Mike produced the tape recorder, but this time he set it on play.

"I think you should hear this," Sam told Yolanda and her attorney.

An array of emotions danced upon Yolanda's face as she listened to her sister's voice on the tape, and all of the emotions were distressful. Tears and body shakes played their part. When the tape reached its end, the dismayed attorney put his hand on her now limp shoulder.

Mike continued to add to the woes. "You've heard the recording and what your sister had to say, but that is not all. That purple stole I mentioned earlier…well, we have it in evidence, and before I left my office I had a message confirming that the only female print we have on it belongs to you."

"We better stop now. We would like a few minutes alone together," Yolanda's attorney cut in and informed the others.

"We understand," Sam spoke for all. "I think you should also remember that we now have your client's thumb print on an important piece of evidence, a stole that once belonged to the late Father Serrano. As Lieutenant Shannon just told you, this was confirmed to us about an hour ago." Allowing for the attorney to absorb the information, Sam paused before he left the two alone. "Just flash us on the intercom when you are ready." With that they left the room leaving the attorney and his client for their private consultation.

Forty-five minutes later they were summoned back into the room.

"What kind of an arrangements can we make?" the attorney asked.

"That depends," Sam replied. "I'm sure we can avoid the death penalty." It was a bit of a grandstanding move on his part, mainly to impact Yolanda Aragon.

Accepting Sam's challenge, the lawyer responded. "We both know there's no death penalty but, my client has advised me that she is willing to give you her full cooperation, so surely you can do better than what you've mentioned."

"We both know that is not possible unless we know the full scope of what she is going to give us. However, you have my word that based upon what she tells us, I will give it much consideration."

They spent the next fifteen minutes negotiating the terms for her cooperation. All others, including Yolanda who was listening to the bargaining regarding her fate, remained quiet. When they finished, Mike installed a fresh tape to record phase one of Yolanda Aragon's actual confession. After recording the date, the time, the location and the names of those present, he began.

"Miss Aragon, do you freely admit to your involvement with the deaths of Father John Carrol Serrano, with a Miss Georgina Becaud, and with a Miss Karen Daughtrey?"

"Yes…I do."

He instructed her to speak louder before asking her to repeat the reply. Once done, he started with the Father Serrano case.

"In your own words, please give us a complete account of what had happened on the night Father Serrano was murdered. We do know, based upon forensics and evidence, that he died in late November or early December. Can you provide us with a date?"

"Not exactly…I don't remember. It was definitely the last day or two in November."

"I see. Was it the same night he was called from the rectory and lured to the Waldo exit off of I-25?"

"Yes."

"That would then make it the evening of November 29. Please continue. Tell us what you did."

"Evonne…she and me made up this plan. She called the priest and pretended she was a policewoman trying to help a dying man. I was to wait outside the rectory, and I was to call her on the cell phone when he left. I was in my father's old car and waited. When he left I called Evonne and followed him. It was a very bad night. There was ice…and snow. Evonne wanted me to keep in touch, because she was afraid he might not make it. But, he did."

"So, did you follow him from the rectory all the way to the Waldo exit?"

"Yes."

"What happened when he got there?"

"He got off the highway at the exit, but I didn't drive down behind him. I stayed in the off-ramp and watched. I saw him go under the overpass, and I got out of my dad's car and walked. I made sure he couldn't see me. Evonne had our car parked on the other side of the highway, but she hid behind some trees near the overpass. I managed to get down and join her. By this time the priest went over to where Evonne left our car. When he did that, Evonne sneaked over and crouched behind his, but first she locked it to make it hard for him to get in. When he came back to get into his car, that's when Evonne attacked him. He screamed. He pleaded for her to stop, but she didn't."

"Tell me," Mike asked. "Why do you think Evonne decided to do this?"

"Evonne always had a a mean streak in her, and once in a while she would tell me that some day she would like to do someone in. I don't know why, but she just did."

She paused, giving Mike an opening to ask, "While she was bashing the priest, tell me…what did you do?"

"I just stood there…I watched. I was scared, but there was nothin' I could do. After he died, Evonne and me dragged him and put him in the field. It was snowing, so we were not worried about hiding his body. We read where the police found his car but could not find him, so I guess the snow kept his body covered until some state workers accidentally found it."

"You had his prayer book and his stole. How did those items come into your possession?"

"There were two cars parked in the church lot, so I wasn't sure which was his. He left his car unlocked, so I looked into his glove compartment. I saw his registration and the book. It looked very nice, so I took it."

"As a prize?"

"I don't know…it's just that it seemed that I should take it."

"And the stole?"

"When the father went to his car he slipped…on ice maybe. When he did, it fell out of his pocket. I picked it up before I followed him."

"I see. Please tell us, what was your motive to murder Father Serrano?"

"Evonne's."

"We don't understand."

"Ever since that night Jesus told us about what him and Emilio did, Evonne got turned on. Like I said before, she said she always wanted to do something like that…for the thrill of it. Then one day she hears about the priest and how he dissed my dad. He says my dad is not a good leader, that all my dad wants to do is divide people by pretending he's interested in them. This pissed Evonne off. She says the priest doesn't know what my father really wants, and that the priest is just a lover of Anglos and rich people. That's when we sat down and talked about what we'd do."

"And you. How did you feel about this?"

"I was afraid. It's not like something you do every day."

"But, you went along with it."

"Excuse me, Lieutenant, but you're mis…"

"I'm sorry," Mike said with a wave of his hand, stopping the attorney from completing his say. "I'll rephrase it. Did you cooperate with your sister?"

She reflected for a moment. "Yes. Evonne's always a lot smarter than me. She always knows what to do, and she was right about the priest. He really didn't care about the problems our people have."

Mike stretched back and gazed at Yolanda Aragon. He determined that she was convinced in her own attitude about the priest.

"And, the women?" Mike switched. "Your sister says that you and Jesus killed two women."

"That's not true."

"Oh?" There was a long drawn out pause as everyone waited for Yolanda to shed complete light and reveal the exact truth.

"Me and Evonne did."

Mike paused and looked at both Francesca and Sam. Admitting to her involvement told them Yolanda was not going to hide any information. "Please explain," Mike continued.

"After we killed the priest, Evonne was on…she was on a high – a rush. She said it made her feel powerful. Nobody would ever find out what we done. She said she could do it again, only this time to some tourist. Those who show no respect for us and what we believe in, our culture. Do what Emilio and Jesus did. Then one night, we're sittin' in a restaurant, and we see this young woman walk in. We first saw her through the window from where we were sitting. We saw she had outa' state plates. She walks in carrying a drawing pad with her, and she seems self-absorbed. We watch her sit down in a booth, and Evonne gets up, tells me to stay where our table was, and she goes over and sits in a booth across from the woman. The woman starts drawing and Evonne sees her doin' it. So she starts to rap with her. A couple of minutes later she sits at the woman's table and later, when the woman leaves, Evonne comes back and sits with me."

"Then what happens?"

"Evonne shows me a key card for where the woman was staying at. Then she gets up and walks outside. A few minutes later she comes back in again. She tells me that the woman is spending the night in the motel across the street from the restaurant, and that she watched what room the woman went in."

"You mean the woman gave her a key to her room?"

"No. You see when Evonne sat rappin' with her she found where the woman was staying. Evonne sat in the same seat with the woman, only the woman's bag was in between. It was open, and Evonne could see two plastic keys in it. When the woman wasn't lookin', Evonne took one."

"Uh-ha. What happened from when Evonne came back and joined you again at the table?"

"Evonne tells me what we're gonna do. We waited an hour or two until we saw the light go out in the woman's room. Then we waited another half-hour to give her a chance to fall asleep. While we were waiting I got really scared. There was a police car in the next lot with his flashers on. I think he was giving some guy a ticket. Evonne tells me not to worry, and we climb the steps up to the room. She uses the card key and unlocks the door. Then she sneaks in. I'm waiting outside to see that no one's coming. Then I hear noise inside the room, so I go in and I see Evonne on top of her. She had a pillow over her face. Then she takes away the pillow and chokes her. I watched, but I did nothing. Evonne is big and strong. She didn't need my help."

Mike stole a glance into Francesca's direction. A nod of her head confirmed the mode in which Georgina Becaud had been murdered.

"What about Karen Daughtrey? How did you kill her?"

"We followed her up from The Plaza in our car. We followed her up Hyde Park Road toward the ski basin for about ten miles. We see her pull into a hot bath place, so we check in ourselves. We thought we might'a lost her, but when we checked the ladies bath we find her. So we wait until she's finished and we leave when she leaves, and follow her up the road a coupla' more miles. We see her pull over, so we pass her and a little ways up we take a U-turn, and we park maybe a hundred feet away. This time Evonne tells me to stay in the car and beep if I see someone who might be coming. I don't know how long I waited, but when Evonne comes back she's smiling and says,'I did it'. Later, I read about it in the papers."

"So, from what you've told me, you didn't actually kill anyone yourself."

"No, I didn't. Evonne did."

"But, were you there when she killed these people?"

"Yes."

Mike veered his questioning. "We now know what happened to the priest, to Georgina Becaud, and to Karen Daughtrey. You told us that

Jesus confided in you about killing Sandra Baber. There are three other dead women, so what do you know about them?"

Looking up at Mike, she replied, "Nothing."

He sensed truthfulness in the response. That, plus the fact those murders appeared to have happened before Jesus ever told them about the first killing of Sandra Baber. Also, the fact that she was cooperating seemed to verify that she had no reason to lie now.

"In other words, you're saying you had nothing to do with their deaths?"

"Yes...sir."

"What about the Baca brothers? They never told you about their involvement?"

"No. When Emilio got mad at Jesus, Jesus never spoke about the others. He just became happy when we, mostly Evonne, told him about what we did. That's why he musta' saved the newspaper stories. We kinda thought that they musta' killed other people, but Jesus is loyal to his brother and he never told us about them?"

"What about Emilio? Did he know what you did?"

"I don't think so 'cause he never spoke about it. We told Jesus that it was our secret, and he really liked us, so we knew he'd never tell."

The next hour was spent cleaning up questions, seeking clarification, and finalizing a deal with Yolanda Aragon's attorney. Later on in the day formal charges would be filed against her. Based upon the taped confession, formal charge would also be filed against Evonne Aragon.

"So, neither Emilio nor Jesus Baca had anything to do with those murders," Francesca flatly stated when they were finished with Yolanda.

"Not with the ones she confessed to, anyway," Mike replied.

"That still leaves Emilio Baca. What do we do about him?"

Mike looked at Sam and said, "I think we get ourselves a warrant and have my boys bring him in. If anything, we at least have a chance to nail him for the Sandra Baber murder."

"I'm concerned about hear-say evidence," Sam advised.

"It might become hear-say evidence, but we'll worry about that later. The newspaper clippings and a couple of other little things should be enough. In the meantime, let's hear what Ms. Evonne Aragon has to say for herself after she hears her sister's confession."

It was seven-thirty that evening when the three of them called it quits for the day. Evonne, with another attorney present, listened to the tape and refused to answer any questions. Nobody cared, for Sam had what he wanted, and he quietly vowed to go after her with a legal vengeance. He was certain he would not get it, but this was one case that craved for the calling of the maximum penalty. A deal was made for Yolanda, and he would honor it. She did not kill anyone, yet she was a follower and an abettor, and because of it, she too was a murderer. She could have prevented the crimes, but she did not. If it were not for a legal deal, there would have been two maximum penalties on his agenda. Depending upon the apprehension and charging of Emilio Baca, a second maximum penalty might still be in the offing. Whether or not the jurors would hand out such a penalty was questionable. Still, he had to try.

It was Mike's voice that brought Sam back from his deeper thoughts. "I have only one regret. The newspapers won't get this scoop until tomorrow. That gives JoJo one more day before they shove their stories up his ass."

Sam and Francesca walked quietly away from the state police building towards their cars.

"Sam, wait," she halted him as he started into the direction of his car.

Heeding her voice, he froze in his steps, still facing away from her.

"Sam, we've had a long but rewarding day. We've finally been able to bring to a close a few of the files."

"Yes, it has been a rewarding day," Sam said as he turned to face Francesca. "It seems that we both learned one heck of a lot."

She did not know if it was intended or not, but Sam's choice of words and the delivery had a stabbing effect, cutting through her tangled emotions. Looking into his eyes in an effort to control his attention, she then uttered words she chiseled out to say since the first confessions were made hours earlier. "Sam, I am sorry."

Sam returned her gaze, but she could not read his expression. Nor did he say anything.

"I did something wrong and I hurt you. I'm very sorry." This time she broke the gaze and looked downwards to conceal her shame.

"Thank you," Sam softly replied.

"I read things into the facts, and I didn't allow myself to…to…"

Sam could tell that she was struggling for the proper words, so he decided to help her. "The word is 'trust', Francesca. Regretfully, you did not trust me enough to look beyond the circumstances."

She returned her eyes to his face, and they spoke what her voice was saying. "You're right, Sam. I broke that trust. For that, I'm very truly sorry."

An early spring wind blew, and droplets of rain began to fall. They stood there assimilating the moisture as it hit their clothing. The tiny raindrops that hit her face served to make her teardrops loom larger.

"What now?" she asked, uncertain of what the future held.

"I don't know, Fran. I truly don't know."

Each went to their cars, and each drove home alone. Only the images of the day's proceedings kept them company. It had been a very rewarding day, and the files would soon be laid to rest. The victims of these crimes would soon find peace. Still, the dominating image that Francesca and Sam carried with them was the face of the other, and the damaged love they shared between them.

31

It was early that same morning when Ruben Gonzales collapsed. He had just inhaled deeply from his first cigar of the day when the dizziness set in. The ever-present Tommy Trujillo immediately called the paramedics, but by the time they arrived Ruben Gonzales managed to revive on his own. Despite the urging of Tommy and the EMT's, Gonzales complained that he had too many things he had to attend to, so he refused to go to the hospital.

"I'll set up an appointment later through my doctor. What I'd like for you to do, Tommy, is to call my daughter. If she is not too busy, I'd like to see her here sometime this afternoon."

A widower, Ruben Gonzales had two daughters, one a disappointment, and the other his pride and joy. Elena, his older daughter, was his disappointment, but she granted him a favor by following her husband and settled in San Diego. She did not like the politics, and she despised the stranglehold it held over its people. Her father was the political leader, and she disdained him for it. That, and the fact that he earned much of his wealth by catering to those she deemed loathsome.

Maria Gonzales-Fuentes, his youngest, was his delight. She had three children, and she headed the local chapter of a social services program. Moreover, she followed in her father's footsteps and over the last few months, after deep and prudent consideration by her father, became next in line to take charge. Ruben had always groomed her for it, but he was also very cautious as to whether or not his followers would take to a woman leading them. Over time she proved herself, and now he made his decision, a decision that would alter both of their lives.

"You know what happened earlier," Ruben Gonzales, the father, began.

"Yes, dad. You should have called me immediately. I shouldn't have found out from a neighbor calling to see how you were." Maria's tone was harsh and scolding, like that of a daughter being kept in the dark.

"I know, and I'm sorry. I had my reasons."

Seeing that it was to be a family discussion between a father and his daughter, Tommy thought it best to take his leave. "I'll be outside on the porch should have need for me."

"No, Tommy, I want you to stay," his boss stopped him. "What I am going to say to my daughter, I want you to hear." Returning his attention to Maria, Ruben spoke. "I have been thinking about this for some time. My illness this morning made my decision for me. I am now ready to retire, and to pass on my power. Normally, it would be passed on to the oldest child, but we both know that is not possible. You, Maria, have proven to be the most deserving and you have made me proud. Over the next three to four months Tommy and I are going to prepare you to take my place. There will be an election for the state senate this November, and you are going to succeed me. There are many young turks out there salivating for this day, but do not worry about winning for I can guarantee you will."

"Thank you, father," Maria humbly replied.

"I am not finished. With my help, Tommy here will teach you everything about our enterprises. You already have some experience, and you've done well. It will be our job to ease you into the role, and to give you the polish you'll need to be as good as I'm sure you will be at it."

Having finished with his decisive announcement, Ruben Gonzales stretched out his beckoning arms, welcoming is daughter to entwine herself in them. Except for a single tear, Maria proudly and strongly united with her father in the embrace.

"When shall we begin?" Maria anxiously awaited the answer she wanted to hear.

"We begin right now," Ruben told her. "The first decision we must make concerns Joseph Aragon."

"Daddy, you know how I feel about that fool. He's a real idioto." She used the Spanish word to derisively rank him.

"Yes, I do. However, never let your feelings interfere with the usefulness some idiots may bring to you," Ruben schooled her. "If someone can help you, you sometimes have to look past that person's overall stupidity."

"I know dad, and I accept it. As I see it, Aragon is washed up. His daughter and that bloodbath in Sombrio was the first nail in his coffin. Now I understand his other daughter has been brought in for some kind of questioning."

"That's what I've heard," the father smiled. "It seems like we have the same source of information. I have a strong feeling things are going to get worse for him." Taking a pause, Ruben then posed his next question to his daughter. "I am curious. What do you think we should do?"

"What I am about to say goes beyond how I feel about him. In my opinion, the man is now a bomb with a clock that is ready to go boom. I think we should dump him, dad. I think we should dump him before he contaminates us with the problems that man's now got."

Ruben studied his daughter and smiled. "You make a very fine student. I happen to agree, Joseph Aragon can wind up hurting us. We have got to cut the chain we've put around him. I now doubt if he will win the mayor's election, but if he does it must not appear that we helped to put him there. I think Tommy should prepare a press release condemning his daughter's involvement with the shooting, even if she's innocent."

"I think it is definitely the correct thing to do," Maria agreed.

"You see that, my dear," Ruben proudly spoke. "Already you are thinking like me. I'm just sorry that I did not bring you into this a lot sooner. Someday, you are going to be as good, if not better, than you father."

"Thank you, daddy," was the happy reply from his daughter, Maria Gonzales-Fuentes, the future state senator from Rio Arriba County.

Not long after his daughter left his home, Ruben and Tommy returned their attention to immediate political matters. More information came in informing him of the additional murder charges linking to the Aragon sisters and the Baca brothers. Ruben could see a new light shine, giving him the chance to seize upon another opportunity.

"In some ways, all of this may become a blessing in disguise," he advised his assistant.

"Oh, in what way?" Tommy asked with curiosity.

"With the Baca boys supposedly being responsible for some homicides, and with their separatist leanings, Antonio Mondragon's support is damaged. It'll be even more so if they indict JoJo's two daughters."

"I see what you mean, Mondragon will be less of a threat to us politically."

"That is correct," Ruben replied with a lack of full satisfaction inflected in his voice. "And yet, the man remains a threat, especially now that I'm ready to step aside. If I know him, he will more than likely try to take advantage of Maria's newness and inexperience."

Tommy could read the road to where this was going. "What do you think we should do about him?"

"I'm not entirely certain," Ruben replied evasively, but allowing Tommy to pick up on the drift. "Aside from his form of irritating politics, Antonio has one other constant fault. He likes to drink a lot. Oh, if only we could make all that disappear, it would really be nice."

Although there were no directions or orders, Tommy knew that a blessing was given. As he had so faithfully done in the past, he would do what he knew had to be done soon into the future.

The bombshell hit Joseph and Mary-Elizabeth Aragon, and it fulminated with the impact of a nuclear blast. The echoes shouted across the city and the state with a reverberating concussion, shaking the Aragons and all of their ardent supporters. The news broke on the late evening television broadcasts as a special report, causing the Aragon home phone lines to erupt with non-ending inquiries from the news media and concerned allies to the campaign. Unable to use their cell and regular lines, they resorted to keeping in touch with the defense attorneys by using a seldom used private cell-line Mary-Elizabeth previously established for family emergencies.

Sitting alone in his darkened den, despondent over the course of humiliation fate bestowed upon him, JoJo wiped the silent tears from his now reddened eyes. His only comfort was the half-emptied third drink of scotch.

"Sulking around here, getting drunk and feeling sorry for yourself ain't gonna make the problems go away," Mary-Elizabeth chided her husband.

"I'm not felling sorry for myself," JoJo protested. "It's just that I don't know what to do."

"What to do! Hell, JoJo! There ain't nothing we can really do. It's up to the attorneys now."

"But how? How can such a thing happen?"

"How the hell am I supposed to answer that?" she shot back. "They're both grown women, so they should know better. Those Bacas were just a bad influence on them."

"But, that Emilio guy. He seemed like a good kid. He was smart, and…"

"I warned you about them." Mary-Elizabeth interrupted him, and annoying him as she did. "I told you not to trust them."

"Bullshit! We both had a question mark about the dumb ass, Jesus. But you agreed with me about the potential the smart one, Emilio, had. So cut the crap."

"I tried warning you a couple of times…"

"Get off it, will ya. You did no such friggin' thing." The gauge of his temper stepped up a few degrees. Altering the course of the conversation, JoJo ranted. "Now we're fuckin' ruined. Those two bitches of yours have ruined what we wanted to do for our people. They destroyed my chance to become mayor."

"Come on, uh!" Mary-Elizabeth said, as she continued to taunt him. "There are four days left before the vote. You might still win. But, so what! Right now you couldn't lead our people into anything. You and your potential chances are screwed from here to hell. Admit it. You're now what is called a classic fuck-up."

JoJo's scotch glass went flying, deflecting off of the top of his wife's shoulder and into the stone setting of the fireplace. "Shut up! I've had enough of your mouth. Shut up, or I'll shut you up!"

With a look mixed with fear and shock, Mary-Elizabeth backed out of the room. "You bastard! You God damned friggin' bastard! You can't…"

"I said, shut up!" JoJo shouted, raising his fist as he took a step forward. "Get out of this room, or I'll let you know what this feels like."

Backing off entirely, knowing that she dared not further cross the imaginary line, Mary-Elizabeth fled the room. JoJo was alone again. Ignoring the shattered glass as he crossed by the fireplace to the bar, he fixed himself another scotch. He had problems that needed drowning. With any luck, Joseph 'JoJo' Aragon would immerse those problems, and send them to the bottom of the bottle.

32

Francesca's phone rang at seven in the morning on Saturday, disrupting any chance she had of sleeping in late, and denying her the opportunity of restoring the energy lost during the draining week that just ended. Her mindset was not ready for a new homicide.

"Did I wake you?" Mike Shannon was at the other end.

"Not really," Francesca fibbed. "I was about ready to get up anyway."

"Good. How would you like to take a trip with me up north a ways?"

Clueless, she asked, "What's up?"

"We're going to track down Emilio Baca a few miles east of Tierra Amarilla, just before we reach Hopewell Lake. He skipped his house before our guys got there. After questioning a few people, we've determined that he's gone to his cabin in the high country."

"Sure, I'd be glad to," Francesca enthusiastically replied.

"I figured since he's your prime suspect, you'd like to be with us when we pick him up. Once he's collared and we bring him back to Santa Fe, he'll be in your custody."

"Thanks, Mike. How soon are we going?"

"Well, I'll give you a chance to wake up a bit. I'll pick you up in about an hour. We'll grab some coffee at McDonalds before the drive."

The smell of fresh spring sweetened the air, and budding new flowers colored the view. Spots of old snow could be seen from the highway, from Conjilon on north. The warming temperatures would soon melt away the reminders of an unusually harsh winter. Occasional glimpses of deer and elk, meandering through the blanketing forest along US-84, is usually a special treat to someone whose time is spent mainly in the city.

Mike kept to about five miles above the speed limit on the two-lane winding road, passing daydream drivers only under the best of circumstances. The drive from Santa Fe to Tierra Amarilla took an hour and forty minutes. Once there, he met up with Sergeant Jim Torres and members of his SWAT unit outside the once besieged county courthouse. After reviewing their plans, the four vehicles left in tandem with Sergeant Torres' four by four taking the lead. Twenty minutes later they eased along the roadway, and along the edge of the old Baca property. Not knowing the complete layout of the land, Mike and the SWAT team commander emerged from their vehicles to observe the overall terrain, each slowly walking along the roadway to assess the view.

"There's the driveway," Torres pointed out. "It's a bit muddy with an incline. It'll be better if we let our heavy duty four by fours take the lead."

Mike agreed, and they returned to reunite with the rest of the team.

The cautious drive up the driveway was not as bad as it first appeared, winding for a quarter of a mile until a clearing emerged before them. Stopping to again assess how the land flowed, Mike and Torres walked catlike up the road until it leveled out. Trying to use as much cover as the trees and bushes would afford them, they visually surveyed the land and spotted an old log home some three hundred feet away, resting atop a small hill.

"This must be the place," Mike said.

"Yeah," Torres answered as his eyes studied the cabin and the surrounding area. "He's got a drive-around driveway. That's good. Most of it's obscured by firs. That's also good should we need cover. But first, I want our people to equip themselves with heavy arms and whatever else we may need."

Back together as a team, the men readied their rifles and shotguns. All members, including Francesca and Mike, donned bulletproof vests. The always dangerous escapade was now fully under way.

The vigilance of keeping a watchful eye paid off for Emilio. Eyes ever glued to any activity outside the cabin, he spotted the police uniforms of two cops at the edge of a tree line. His first impulse of confronting them was quickly dismissed when he saw one dressed in what appeared to be combat fatigues. Obviously, more of the pigs in camouflage colors were in hiding. He had a suspicion as to the reason why; The Aragon sisters more than likely revealed Jesus' secret just to save their own skin.

Quickly pulling on his snow boots and insulated jacket, he grabbed his already prepared backpack, and the rifle he kept in the cabin. After a glance around the inside to search for something else he might need, Emilio headed through the back door and into the snow-covered woods.

They spotted a pick up truck, unintentionally concealed between a tree line and the berm that slopped downward from the front of the cabin. Pausing, they judged the situation, searching for signs of activity, or of unforeseen dangers. Through his binoculars, Sergeant Torres watched for human movement at the windows. There was none, just the movement of sparrows fighting for territory in which to build a new nest. Except for a gust of spring's chilly wind, all else was still.

Directing his men with hand signs, the SWAT sergeant pointed to two of his men and motioned for them to move forward and establish a concealed position some seventy-five feet closer to the cabin. Once there, with rifles high and sighted, they surveyed the breath of the cabin for potential dangers. Satisfied that it was relatively safe, the signal was given for the others to join them. A leapfrog of the routine was continued until no further secured positions could be established, leaving only a hundred feet between them and their ultimate objective. Storming the cabin was the last course of action, making the one hundred feet give seem like an illusion of a thousand yards of open land suitable for target practice.

Flanking six SWAT team members out, Sergeant Torres kept his eyes attentively attached to the cabin. Feeling the timing was right, that the danger was at a minimum, he gave the voice command over the headset for them to move forward. Without hesitation, they stormed the cabin, each keeping a steady cross-scope to find unexpected perils. There were none, and within fifteen seconds two team members were at the cabin door, while the others covered them from their assumed positions. One man turned the knob to find it unlocked. He slowly pushed the door forward an inch to keep it from closing shut, and his partner waited until it was accomplished. At his signal, the four others burst through the door in military fashion, rapidly pointing their weapons crisscross around the interior, all the while barking orders to anyone who might be there. Within a minute from the onset of the assault it was over. The cabin was empty. While the others checked the interior for unseen hazards, the team leader gave his sergeant the all clear from the doorway.

Satisfied that the situation was secure, Sergeant Torres led his lieutenant and the detective into the cabin. Eyeing the surroundings, the three awaited a report.

"The cabin is empty, sir," the team leader addressed his superior. "However, the coffee pot is still relatively hot."

"That means he must have seen us coming," Sergeant Torres reasoned. "Have your men give me a complete check around the exterior."

Not waiting for any report, he along with Mike and Francesca went to the narrow back door. Immediately visible to them was the blanket of white leading to the base of the rising mountain, a half of a mile to the north. The snow was pockmarked by deer and elk hoof-prints, and a jagged line created by a man's legs. There were also large patches of land not covered with snow, and where the footprints came to an end.

"Looks like we don't have to guess where he is heading," Mike stated the obvious.

"No, sir, we don't." Once again studying the terrain before him, the sergeant made his decision. "My guess is he's heading straight up. The mountain base juts up over the west, and it'll make it hard to scale around the boulders. If you notice, there's a pasture to the east. He wants to avoid that so he can't be easily seen. He probably is going straight till he reaches the mountain base, and then he's going to follow it east to take advantage of some tree cover."

"Any suggestions?" Mike asked.

"Yes, sir. I'm going to flank our men out, seventy-five feet apart. Two men to the west, and the rest of us to the east. The squad leader and I are going to follow his footprints as far as we can. We should be able to determine his ultimate direction by doing that. I don't think he has too much of a jump on us."

"Can we follow behind you?" Francesca asked, eager to join the trek.

"I'd recommend against it," Sergeant Torres replied. "One, you and the lieutenant don't have the proper footwear for the snow. It might get deep in some spots."

"And two," Mike continued, "we'll have to keep post back here, in case we have to set up a more elaborate radio communications. Hopefully we won't need it, but I might have to summons additional support." Making certain the sergeant and the rest of the SWAT team could be protected, he then asked Torres, "What is the range of your radios in an area like this?"

"It'll be pretty good, unless we start winding around the mountain base," Sergeant Torres informed him.

"Okay, then. Here's the deal," Mike began with a summary of his orders. "We're not entirely prepared for this, so don't go beyond voice range on the radio to this cabin. Secondly, if within thirty minutes you don't find him then turn back. We'll call in for reinforcement, and for a couple of trackers and a chopper that's properly equipped."

"Agreed," the SWAT leader answered.

Watching the team set off on their search, Mike silently wished them luck. The next task was for him and Francesca to search the cabin for evidence that could be used against Emilio Baca.

⋰⋰⋰

The lay of the land leveled, and the snow blanket dissipated. Unlike the rise that accumulated drifts served to it by the wind, the snow atop the level ground had mostly melted. Throughout the woods could be found fallen trees hit by bolts of lightning, rotting and eaten away by ravenous termites. It was still cold, and the termites were still dormant, but hollow trunks provided unseen shelter.

Sheltered by a heap of broken tree limbs, Emilio peered out from his hiding place in the hollow opening of a trunk. He watched as two fully armed state cops wearing battle armor pass about forty feet away in either direction. He could not be sure, but he thought there might be six or even ten hunters in police uniforms searching for him. He conceded that he was in no position to challenge them, and laying out of sight until they were well past him was his best alternative.

❦

The flat dry land stretched for about three hundred feet before the next rise that was covered by more blankets of snow. Torres and his men halted at the line, and looked for fresh footprints. They found none.

The sergeant radioed his halt of progress to Mike, then he turned to his squad leader. "What do you think?"

"I'll bet on going east."

"I think you're right. Slant all of the men out to cover the dry land, and we'll take it east." After all of the men were made clear on the instructions, they resumed their forward search.

❦

The timing was right with no cops in sight, so Emilio used the cover of the woods to make his move. Confident that the hunters were off to the east, Emilio planned his next path. Pushing away the tree limbs that provided camouflage covering the hull of the trunk, he eased himself out, kept his body low, and started off to his new destination, a destination opposite of his pursuers.

❦

"The men won't be back for at least another half hour," Mike advised Francesca. "I'm going down to the vehicles and bring up some communications equipment, and also some batteries in case we might need them."

"Do you need any help?" Francesca volunteered.

"Nah. You check things out around here. I'm leaving my radio with you in case they check in. I'll be back here in just a few minutes."

"Fine."

Alone in the cabin, she continued her check of the interior only to find nothing of importance that could be used in court. The furniture, the kitchen equipment, the extra clothing were sparse, and the walls were bare of any adornments. The old dry-wood floors were cover with tattered rugs scattered about. She tried to draw a psychological profile of Emilio Baca and came to the determination that he, and his deceased brother, were men of little means and were content with it. Everything in the cabin was based upon basic needs and simplicity. Then again, she figured that this might be the very way of existence for most people living in this part of the state. They did not have much, and accumulating possessions was less likely then those living in and around the city areas. Jobs and income had to be at the absolute minimum. It was their land that kept them going; that gave them pride and a sense of security. Beyond that, little else seemed to matter.

Francesca continued to peruse the room and make her deductions when the back door opened. Having her back turned and thinking it was Mike, she started to say, "That was quick." She quickly stopped with the realization that something was wrong. Mike left through the front, the cold air entering came through the rear.

"Who are you?"

She heard a shaky voice snapping at her as she turned to face the hallow hole of a rifle pointed at her. She could see the questioner was as surprised as she was.

Momentarily baffled, Francesca raised her hands at the sight of the weapon, before asking, "Are you Emilio Baca?"

"I asked you who you are. I thought all the cops were out there searching. You with them?"

Trying to keep her calm, and trying not to say anything to provoke sudden action from him, she responded. "We only want to ask you some questions."

"Cut the bull, lady! You don't bring a cop's army along just to ask me questions."

Thinking fast to find answers, she replied, "They left me behind just in case you might come back." Her thoughts quickly turned to Mike. He could be coming through the door at any time, and she tried to come up with a way to warn him.

Looking at her open bulletproof vest, Emilio made his own deductions. "That's crap, too." Then, adding his own protest of innocence, he said, "You know damn well I didn't have anything to do with those killings in Sombrio."

That was her opportunity to create a delaying conversation, "We know you didn't. We only want to ask questions that might help us to understand why the shootings occurred."

Emilio eyed her for a moment, studying her. Something did not seem right.

"You're lying, lady. I don't believe a fucking word you're saying. So, cut the crap! For one thing, you're in civvies. Those guys out there are in combat fatigues.'

"That's because I'm only here to ask you a few questions."

Emilio did not like her answers, and irritation was setting in. He kept his finger nervously positioned at the trigger of the rifle, ready to squeeze should his target make an improper move.

"Get your hands higher and fall on your knees."

"There's no need for that. I just want..."

"Shut up, and drop to the floor before I drop you from here," he ordered as he watched her comply. He could not figure it out, but something was wrong with her appearance. Before he could think further about it, she interrupted him.

"Please, Mr. Baca. All we want to do is to ask you a few questions."

"I said shut up! I'm the one who's gonna ask questions."

Emilio's thinking process sped. His first thought was what he would do with the woman on her knees before him. It brought flashbacks of a couple of nights earlier, and the anguish of having to go through such a procedure of following the orders commanded to him by the cops when they invaded his Guzman home. He hoped to make her feel the same humiliation. His second thought was how to treat her. He decided that he did not want to harm her for she might be a useful hostage.

"Like I said, I didn't have nothing to do with those killings. I don't know what Yolanda told you, but…"

He stopped himself as it suddenly became very clear to him that he might be saying too much. Yolanda did not implicate him with his brother's actions, but she did talk. She must have. She must have told the police the little secret she knew about him.

"Damn!" was his one word conclusion.

"Mr. Baca…"

"Shit! You people wanna…"

The front door opened in mid-sentence.

"Mike watch out!"

Simultaneous to Francesca's shout Emilio swerved and fired a single shot at the door's direction.

For Mike, his years of training paid off. His reflexes caused him to fall off to the side, causing him to curse as he dove down upon the radio he carried in his arms. As he fell, he could hear both the rifle crack and the twang of the bullet as it hit, leaving a hole where his head had been on his side of the wooden door.

With her own reflexes, Francesca rolled to her right while her right hand reached for the service revolver inside her open flap jacket. Responding like a trapped cat, clawing out against its attacker, Emilio recoiled and fired another shot at the empty spot where Francesca had been. Now several feet off to his right, Francesca rapidly fired three shots without taking aim. Two of them pierced Emilio, one in his stomach and the other in his chest. As his rifle flew airborne from his hands, his body spun from the impact of the bullets.

Eternal seconds of stillness passed as the world flew past for three different individuals. For two of them, the world would again slow down to a normal breathing pace. For the third, it raced faster and faster, even in his breath, as it reenacted the days and nights he once lived. Flashes of his youth, of being with family, with his brother, of being on his land, and of wanting to be a savior to his people, all played out before him. Oddly for Emilio, appearing before him was the extended bit of play that took place only a minute or two earlier, when he ordered the woman cop to her knees. He never thought about the weapon she concealed inside her chest protector. Emilio grimaced, not out of pain but out of overlooking the glaring obvious. He stared at the dimming ceiling, wondering why he felt so cold. There was no pain. Just coldness. For the last time Jesus' face came before him. With a childlike affection, it stayed with him until there was no more light to show his brother's face.

⸙

The rifle shots echoed through the trees and spread out though the woods, freezing the SWAT team where they stood. Sergeant Torres signaled his men to turn around, and while doing so he got on his radio to Mike. Long minutes passed before he got a response.

"Bring your men back in," was Mike's command. "Our suspect is down on the floor here in the cabin. Your men don't have to come in with weapons ready. The guy's dead."

Turning to Francesca, he motioned to where he came in, and said, "Thanks."

"Wha…" Francesca replied feebly as she felt a drain ache through her body.

"You saved my life. Are you all right?"

"Yes…yes. It's just that I feel so…so exhausted."

"That's unusual. Usually the adrenaline gets people pumped up," Mike said as he helped her to her feet.

"Maybe that's it."

"What's that?"

"I think I burned up every bit of that adrenaline."

Mike grinned and wrapped his arm around her shoulder, escorting her to the steps on the porch so she could get some fresh air. "That's possible. At least you still have a chance to burn some in the future."

He did not have to say it, but Francesca knew Mike was referring to the lifeless corpse on the floor behind them. There was more work to do. She had to start wording up her report, Mike had to call in for a morgue pickup, and Sergeant Torres had the task of doing a wrap up of the scene, and then ready their arms and equipment back into their vehicles. But there was no rush, and each could proceed at a leisurely pace. Mike and Francesca needed their minutes of being alone, and to share in silence the fateful moments soon to be stored into the past.

33

The Monday morning newspapers gave more details of the previous week's events, delving into the motives of the psychological makeup of the Baca brothers, and of Evonne and Yolanda Aragon. A second page article covering the capture of Emilio questioned the circumstances of his death, probing the official police accounts, hinting that an investigation was warranted to review the police activities at the scene.

"It seems like we can't win," Mike said to Francesca as they ate breakfast at a local restaurant frequented by those in blue. "We take two suspects into custody, but the papers harp on the one we killed because he tried to kill us."

"I guess you can call it media justice," Francesca replied, still feeling unsettled from her first experience of being in a fatal predicament. "I think what bothers me most is the lack of coverage of the families of the victims. Finally, they have the opportunity to see justice being done for their dead loved ones."

"The papers will eventually cover them," Mike told her. "They'll do it once this settles down. That'll give the press a chance to bring it all back to life, and sell more papers."

"Then they're just being vultures," was Francesca's hardened response.

"Maybe so, but unfortunately it's the way the world works." Pointing to another column in the local paper, Mike spoke with a happier note. "At least JoJo Aragon is suffering from this."

317

"As well he should. He raised two daughters who turn out to be murderers, and he uses his political career to divide people. A man like that doesn't deserve to be a dog catcher, let alone mayor."

"He won't be. At least not this go-round." Mike informed her, educating Francesca to Santa Fe politics. "There will still be enough supporters to give him a good showing, but not what he needs to win. Not this time around."

"Oh?"

"The memory of the voters in this town is short lived. Many people will remember this, but regretfully many will forgive and forget. And, the way this city is growing with bleeding hearts, he'll find a way to gain a fresh group of supporters. Those are the ones who'll vote for him four years from now, when he decides to run again for mayor. That'll give him plenty of time to heal the wounds, and to work on gaining sympathy. This guy's a pro at it."

"I'm not politically hip, but how can they support a man like him."

"Welcome to the real world, detective. Santa Fe and Northern New Mexico are not your every day America. That's one of the many reasons why they call this place The City Different."

"I still don't understand," Francesca confessed.

"It's not easy to make simple, but I'll try. There is a loyalty factor. People here get behind one of their own. All that needs to be done is to tell people how bad they're being treated, and they'll think you're a savior. Fortunately, some of those attitudes are changing, but it'll be quite a while before it is significantly reflected.

"Then there's the factor where a lot of people relocate to here. Most of them are young and idealistic, which is fine in its own right, but they are not very well informed. They believe what they hear about how the people here are being suppressed.

"It's true, many of the people are suppressed, but mostly by their own business and political leaders. It's a matter of profiting by paying slave wages, and of keeping political power by keeping people down enough so they don't go anywhere. All the while they'll keep blaming those evils on the outsiders. They've been doing this for centuries, beginning with the Indians. The problem is widened when the newcomers don't go out and look for themselves. Instead, they listen only to the stories told to them by the people they hang out with, mostly those who sit around drinking beer all day while never trying to pull themselves up by their own bootstraps."

"It sounds almost absurd," a frustrated Francesca replied. "Surely, people must have a mind of their own."

"Now, you're the one who's being idealistic," Mike admonished her with a grin. "Many of these newcomers don't. They are attracted by the beautiful mountains, and the arts, and by the multitude of different types of people touring in and around The Plaza."

"Are all so naïve?"

"No. Obviously," Mike replied. "The ones I mentioned are the most visible. There are many people from the Midwest, and other places, who are captured mostly by the beauty of this place. Once they learn more of the people who are native, they then decide if Santa Fe is all they dreamed it would be. It takes usually a year or two."

"Then what?"

"Then they accept the city for what it is, and they get along well."

"And, if they don't?"

"Then they live here miserably ever after, or they pack up and leave."

Francesca drank her coffee and thought about what Mike told her. "And you. Why did you stay?"

"Me?" Mike said with a boyish grin. "I love it here. I've been here for more than twenty-five years, and I've loved every moment of it. I've had the good fortune of meeting the right people, and of meeting my wife. Her ancestry goes back many generations in Santa Fe, but I love her because she managed to look past all of the hang-ups and became her own person. The same could be said for Cap and his family."

The mention of Cap's name caused both of them to subconsciously pause for a second. It was Francesca who continued the discourse.

"You know, all my years of growing up and living in Albuquerque, I've heard stories about Santa Fe."

"Most of them not good ones, I assume," Mike cynically stated, aware of the ridicule Albuquerqueans often have about the state's capital, while at the same time they ignored the similar traits that they possess.

"Most of them weren't," Francesca answered. "A lot of it had to do with attitudes. Mostly, with service and getting things done right."

"Some of it's true. Then again, it's a problem throughout most of the country. It's just more prevalent here. We have too many contractors or service companies who make promises they don't keep. They just don't deliver. Often the job is not finished until months after it's scheduled to be, often workers quitting before the job's only half done. I can't tell you how many times a service guy comes hours after the scheduled appointment, if he shows up at all."

"How do you get around that?"

"Simple. You've got to realize that there are still a few good people who stick to their word and do a good job. When you find them you don't forget them."

"That's understandable. It's a matter of keeping a customer because you've earned it. I'd like to think that I'll keep my job because I've earned the right to keep it. The way you've earned the right to keep yours."

"Gee, thanks," Mike modestly replied. "After seeing the way you've handled yourself, I don't think you'll have to worry. The fact that I'm here talking to you gives testimony to it."

Humbled by Mike's praise, Francesca finished with the French toast on her plate. She took a moment to screw up the courage to ask her next question.

"Mike, I'm curious. Do you talk to Teri about your work?"

"Yes," Mike replied without giving it much thought. "We often talk to each other about our work."

"That's not what I really meant. I mean, did you tell her of how close that bullet was?"

Mike looked at her with an expression that suggested she asked the wrong question. "No, that's something you don't discuss with your wife. Not if you love her. It might make you feel like some sort of hero inside, but for her it becomes a nightmare. She will be reminded of how there might be a day when you don't come home. It's bad enough Teri has to see what Margarette is going through, so I don't have to fill her in. Besides, I'd have to tell her that I have you to thank for my head still being on my shoulders."

"No...I..." Francesca started to blush in response to the teasing compliment.

"No...I...what? Don't be ashamed, you saved my butt. Take pride in it, it's something good you did. Remember this, you may one day be in the same type of predicament. So keep the positive side of what you did. God forbid, you may someday have to do it again."

"Thanks," she said softly.

"I think I know why you asked me the question," Mike delved. "You haven't talked to anyone about the close call you had, or what you had to do. Right?"

"No, I haven't. It's a strange feeling, something of a conundrum. I admit, I'm still shook up, and I feel I might have to talk to someone so I can get it off of my chest. However, if I do I'm afraid it might sound like I'm boasting."

"Don't worry, you won't be. What about Sam, have you talked to him, yet? He already knows what went down by reading our reports."

"I did," she replied evasively. "When I turned mine in."

"That's not the same," Mike mildly scolded her. "Look, aside from what you told me, I'm not sure of what's going on between you two. To an extent, it's none of my business. However, you two have shared something together. I'm sure Sam would like to listen."

"I don't know."

"Give it a try."

"It's a little more complicated than that. Since the last conversation you and I had, the only time I've spoken to Sam was strictly business."

Mike sat back and motioned the waitress for the check. "I'm not sure what to tell you without sticking my nose in too deeply, but it seems to me you two have to get together and talk things out."

Francesca appreciated Mike's good intentions, and she told him so. "You're not being nosy, and I appreciate that you were responsible for Sam and I getting together. We have some problems to work out, problems that I've been responsible for. We're going to have to find the time to sit down and talk."

Dismayed that his two friends were having romantic complications, Mike could only sigh. "I hear what you're saying." Pulling out his wallet and removing money to cover the morning meals, he brought the meeting to a close. "Well, there is still a lot that needs to be done at the office. See you tomorrow?"

Knowing what he referred to, Francesca gave her solemn reply. "There will be a lot of us from the department at the services for Cap. A number of us will be taking part in the funeral procession."

"Thanks. I know I'll be speaking for the top by saying that we'll be glad to see you there."

They left the restaurant, each going to their own office, and each with their own agenda to tend to. In their own individual ways, each was grateful that the nightmares of the past several days would soon fall deeply behind them.

34

The sun shined brightly, warming the gentle breeze that wrapped the many mourners. A rustle of tree leafs played in harmony with restrained sobs, and the priest reciting a prayer of farewell. Eulogies were eloquently spoken, but none could truly replace the encomium whispered in the hearts that knew him. A sea of tears flowed from the meek and the strong, all knowing that their pictured memories would last their lifetime.

Taps chillingly blared, sounding the final salute, and the American flag was smartly folded in the traditional triangular fashion. The presentation was made to his loving wife, and New Mexico State Police Captain Eduardo 'Cap' Guieterrez was laid to rest.

Led by Chief Ebner of the State Police, the rest of the top brass, and by Lieutenant Mike Shannon, an earlier procession from the chapel to the cemetery was viewed by many, each paying silent tribute. Only a few actually knew him, yet each felt a special fondness for a man who had made the ultimate sacrifice. The division of politics, of religion and social orders, and of racial, ethnic and cultural demands all took a step aside to pay homage. If the now departed captain could witness the tribute he would be pleased with the momentary unity of all people. It would make his forward journey a peaceful one.

As the Captain's second in command, and as a hero who survived the massacre, Lieutenant Shannon was bestowed the honor to eulogize for the department, and to lead the honor guard. His thoughts were with the captain and his family, and they were with the family of his own. His inner prayer was that his family, as well as the families of his brothers and sisters in uniform, would not have to bear the burden of witnessing the same ceremony for their loved ones. Recalling the burial rites of a day earlier for the officers slain during the carnage, he realized that his prayer was already too late. Looking toward to tomorrow, it might still be heard.

In the privacy of his own mind he thought about Cap's years on the force. They were good ones, and only a few short years were left before the captain was eligible to retire. Mike thought about the good he did, and the good he was yet to do. It saddened him even more to think that an uncaring bullet, fired by an uncaring human, could end all that.

His mind took time to focus on his own career. It, too, had been a good one. Modesty, however, kept him from doting on the contributions he had made while serving on the force. They may not have been equal to the captain's, but they were of great value to the force, and to the people with whom he served. The value was great enough to allow him to rise to the position he now held.

Of greater concern was the affect his being a state police officer had on his family. There were the early years when his assignments took him to different corners of the state, causing Teri and their child to be alone for days at a time without a father. There were extended periods when he had the duty of serving in Santa Fe, but with each promotion, first to sergeant and then to lieutenant, a new move to a different part of the state was necessary until a local vacancy had opened. Fortunately, his last promotion resulted in a move that lasted only four months. For the last two years he was happy to serve at home, and with his captain.

They were difficult years, but not trying. The foundation of love within the family saw to that. Still, Mike regretted the hardships Teri had essentially raising their son alone, and he lamented the loss of the many months of not fully serving his role as a father. He was eligible to take the exam for elevation to captain, but he had doubts if he would do so – not if it meant being apart from those that he loved. He denied them enough, and it was time for him to give less consideration to his career and to give more to what was dearest to him. His family.

While watching the final steps of the tribute to Captain Eduardo 'Cap' Guieterrez, Lieutenant Mike Shannon set the mental priorities of what the future would bring.

35

Alex Dombrowski rose at the usual six a.m., showered, shaved, dressed, and prepared his breakfast. While waiting for the water to boil for his morning tea, he stepped outside to pick up the morning newspaper dropped off by the carrier. True to his daily routine, he read the news while eating the morning meal.

Three articles dominated the front pages, each covering a different subject, but each was hinged together by recent events. The dominant headline pronounced the winner of the mayoral election.

DURAN WINS MAYOR'S RACE

WINS WITH 40% OF VOTES

ARAGON SECOND WITH 34%

The headline and the article brought him pleasure. While he conceded that he did not know much about the man he voted for, Alex took delight in knowing his vote was one of many against the despicable likes of Joseph Aragon. He felt that perhaps now the city could slowly get back to normal. Within time the new mayor would help to repair the gapping holes, holes that ripped into the relationship of the city's people by the caustic derisiveness of the one time leading candidate. Usually A-political when it came to local politics, he took satisfaction in knowing his vote helped to defeat the man he had a verbal confrontation with only a couple of weeks before.

The second article he glanced at was the arraignment of the would-be mayor's two daughters for the murders of two women and a priest. He knew a little something about the cases from his conversations with Mike. The suspicion had always been that the priest was the victim of a thrill-kill, however it was not until the cases were solved was it realized that at least two of the women were victims for the same reason. It made him think about the kind of mayor Aragon would have been should he have won. If not apprehended, Alex wondered if the Aragon girls might have felt their father's power, encouraging them to commit more evil. He could only guess, and he was glad that it would not be something he would ever get to know.

His eyes turned to the third article that touched him, as it did others throughout the state.

HUNDREDS BID FAREWELL TO A FALLEN HERO

Alex never met the slain police captain, but he knew of him. Aside from reading an occasional article printed about the man, or of a case his division was working on, a good deal was revealed about him during conversations at Ray's Pub. Sam, and especially Mike, often praised the man's character and his dedication to the department, to his people, and to people in general. From this, Alex developed a respect for the man, and regretted not ever having met him in person. He could only conclude that Cap's death would now leave a void, not only in the state police department but in the community as well.

He scanned a fourth article written on page three of the newspaper. It covered the death of an obscure politician who led various separatist movements within the state. The five-paragraph article did not reveal too much about the man except that he was killed when he lost control of his car, crashing through a guardrail and tumbling down the side of a mountain in Northern New Mexico. Alcohol was believed to be the cause.

Having a light workday planned, he leisurely moved about tending household chores. Taking a break from that, he went out to his yard to water the grass and flowers. It was then that he decided to check upon his friend and neighbor, Eloi.

The morning was quieting down as the neighborhood children were off to school, and the traffic of cars racing to work decreased. Eloi was usually up and about at this time, often taking his daily walk through the mobile home park and the surrounding area. Today it seemed too quiet, so Alex decided to pay him a visit and to check on the elder's well being. As he walked into the old man's driveway he picked up the newspaper and, except for when Eloi was down with the flu, it was something he was seldom used to seeing.

After knocking and waiting on the porch a couple of minutes, an uncomfortable feeling overcame him. This was not the first time he had to wait for the slow moving elder to respond to his call, but still, it did not feel right.

Deciding that he waited long enough, Alex took it on his own to try the door handle. It was unlocked, so he took a step inside as he called out Eloi's name. There was no reply. Stepping fully into the room, which was the home's kitchen, he again called out Eloi's name.

A deeper concern emerged as he moved further into the house, and he listened to the disturbing silence. He repeated the call of his name until he reached the living room. That is when he realized that there would never be a response. He looked down at the frail old man, his body slumped in his favorite lounge chair, and his glasses dangling from one ear. An untouched supper was seen on a dinner tray beside the chair. A tear then welled within his eyes. Alex knew that he would never again sit and talk with the kind and venerable man. The converstions would remain in his memory, as well as the man himself. It caused him to realize that the present had now faded into the past, but the future, with fresh faces and new ideas, remained before him.

With a nod, a jesture, and a silent prayer, he said good-bye.

36

For several nights, solitary footsteps could be heard pacing the floors in houses that stood in different parts of the city. They were listened to by the ones who made them.

The anxiety and trauma caused by the recent mayhem were slowly receding to the recesses of the past. Still, as they faded away from the minds of two people, they left a scar that reminded them of what the future could bring. The two people had to look past the tragedies that may or may not come tomorrow. They had to accept that ominous days could still lie ahead, but that those days should not prohibit them from living their lives. It should not prevent them from finding happiness, and from not forsaking their love. Kismet would always play a teasing role, but it was for the actors to pull the strings.

As he sank deeply into the sofa, his lonely thoughts occupying his mind, it was Sam who realized that he must make the move. He slipped on his spring jacket, walked through the door and entered the star filled night. The stars were friendly, and they uplifted his spirits, giving him a newfound hope. Within twenty minutes he would convert that hope into the words he intended to speak to the woman he loved.

It was a few minutes past ten in the evening when the doorbell rang. Setting aside the novel in which she tried to loose herself, Francesca rose with a feeling that she knew who the visitor would be. It might have been attributed to a woman's intuition, or maybe it was merely deductive reasoning, but whatever the reason, she welcomed it.

"Hi," Sam greeted her, his eyes revealing that he came calling with a determined purpose.

"Hi." Francesca returned his greeting, her heart beating faster at the sight of him. Her feelings told her the reason why he was there.

"May I come in? We've got to talk."

"Yes," she replied as she stepped aside and watched him enter. She noticed that the confident air he usually displayed around her was mixed with a touch of uncertain awkwardness.

"Coffee?" Francesca inquired, delaying matters with her hospitable offer.

"Yes, please."

Sam sat himself on the sofa while Francesca clicked on the flame under the coffee she brewed when she came home. She liked the aroma of the old-fashioned percolated mix. She used that, and the task of laying out cookies, to distract her thoughts, all the while delaying the chat she and Sam were to have.

Francesca drilled herself, asking what he will say. How will she respond? They were the questions gnawing at her. Finally, she told herself to shut up and listen to what he had to tell her. It then dawned on her that his visit might be for professional reasons. *God! I hope not.*

"I've brought some cookies, but if you're hungry I can fix a snack" she offered as she placed down the tray.

"No, thank you. I just ate a couple of hours ago."

A long period of silence lapsed. He tried to figure out what he wanted to say, and she tried to correctly guess what she wanted to hear.

"I'd like to apologize," Sam began. Somehow, an apology was not what Francesca expected. "I was a little too hard on you the other night when we left Mike's office, and I'm sorry."

"I'm not sure that an apology from you is necessary," Francesca told him after she had a chance to regroup her own thoughts. "I was the one who let this whole thing get out of hand."

"Actually, the events of the last few days got me thinking about things, a reevaluation of them. The Baca take-down up in Tierra Amarilla, and Cap's funeral...those things are very sobering."

"I haven't seen the final reports yet, but..."

"Please, Fran, let me continue," Sam gently stopped her. "It's not the reports I'm here to talk about. Sam took a sip of his hot coffee, using that moment to assemble his next comment. "Cap's funeral affected me deeply yesterday, and that's what got me really thinking."

"I'm sure it got a lot of us thinking," Francesca commented. She then winced inside for having interrupted him.

"Yes, no question about it. But, only a few of us shared the same kind of thoughts."

"What's that?" she asked, genuinely curious.

"There were some of us, and I'm sure I wasn't the only one, who were not seeing Cap's remains being interred. Instead, we were seeing our loved ones."

Neither said a word for a somber moment. Each let the impact of Sam's comment sink in to stir their emotions.

"What I am saying," Sam finally continued, "is that I don't know what I would've done should anything have happened to you."

Turning sideway so that Sam could not immediately see how his words touched her, Francesca picked a spot in the room to focus her attention. Her confused mind tried to form a reply, but she was unable.

"Sam, I...I..."

Her stirred emotions choked her uncertain words, and her tearful eyes closed tightly.

"Sssh..." Sam whispered softly as his hand tenderly caressed hers. "It's been hell for me for the last several days. It got me to rethink about things that are most important to me, and you, Francesca, are at the very top of them."

Her glistening eyes met his, and her arms welcomed his embrace.

"Oh, Sam, I'm so sorry. I broke my trust in you, and I thought I lost you."

Tenderly stroking her hair with his fingers, he tried to comfort her.

"Trust works two ways," he spoke. "I came to realize that I also broke the trust. I should have told you about my involvement with Julie Fletcher, about what she meant to me. I should have been open with you and told you why I was a regular customer at that restaurant. Mostly, it was the one place where she and I never went to together. But fate once in a while plays strange tricks, and it played one here."

"No, Sam. You don't have to explain anymore. I understand."

"It's just that I don't want to keep things hidden. I want to be open with you."

"That will take the two of us."

"Maybe so, but we must find a way to work things out and put all this behind us. I truly want to. I don't want to loose you, because Fran…I love you."

Sliding their arms to each other's waist, they faced each other so that their lips could meet. Soon after, their arms were again entwined, this time to display the love each had to give, and for the other to receive in welcoming bliss.

Time did go on, and the wounds were healed. A slight scar remained, but neither ever tried to take notice of it. A district attorney and a cop, two different lives that shared a similar judicial path, soon united to find a path that would lead them into their lifetime of personal happiness. Reconstructing from the ruins caused by distrust, they built a home from the mosaics of love.

37

Seven months faded into the past, and another winter was knocking on the doors of Santa Fe. An uncertain storm approached from the northwest and across the region's four corners. Yet, the forecast called for a tamer winter. Unlike the previous year, this one held promise of moderate snows, and unlike the previous year, there was a promise of very little discontent. But the season was young, and no one could forecast what really lay in store.

Only two figures could be seen in the corner of the bar where dart players usually sat. To the dismay of the diehard players, and to Ray's Pub, there was a diminishing interest in the sport. As regular players found new pastimes, there was no one to replace them, leaving an undeniable portent of the future.

"There's no sense in even trying to put another league together," off duty Captain Mike Shannon conceded. "Nobody has enough interest anymore."

"Too bad," Alex Dombrowski agreed. "It's a shame to watch it die, but sixteen years was a pretty good run in this town."

"Yeah. I guess I'll take up golf again."

"You can always play darts up in Los Alamos or down in Albuquerque."

"Nah…too far to drive. What about you?"

"Me…? Alex thought for a moment before he decided to spring the news. "For me it won't matter. I won't be here."

"What! How come?" Mike was taken by surprise. "Where the hell are you going?"

"I'm not sure yet. Maybe Phoenix. Maybe Las Vegas, or Reno. I haven't decided where yet."

"What about your business?" Mike asked.

"I already have a buyer. We signed the contract last week. He'll take over on January first, and I'll hang on for another month to introduce him to my clients. After that, I'm gone."

"Then what? Do you know what you're going to do when you get to wherever you're going?"

"Nope. I'll worry about that when I get there," Alex's air was casual, showing little concern about the future.

"Jeez!" Mike shook his head, still rocked by the sudden news. "So, why the big move?"

"I'm tired, Mike. I'm tired of a lot of things here."

The earnest reply prompted Mike to pursue with another question, "Like what?"

"I'm tired of the unsettling politics. I'm tired of the pretension...of the social mindset. I'm tired of the people. Basically, I'm tired of living with arrogant stupidity, and the people who are proud of their stupidity."

"Gee, thanks," Mike answered, pretending to be offended.

"Present company excluded, of course."

"Too late. You've already insulted me," Mike said, playing with him. Adjusting to the suddenness of Alex's announcement, he opined his view. "You know, old buddy, you will run into those problems no matter where you go. You'll still have to face them. Either that, or take off again."

Alex smiled at his friend's concern. "That's very true. But, at least they'll be new problems."

Mike returned the smile to quip. "That's one way of looking at it. Still, if and when the time comes to face them in the next place, what are you gonna do? Move to Alaska?"

"I guess I'll have to worry about it then. Maybe I'll take off, and maybe I'll confront them."

"Well, maybe I'm dumb, but I don't understand your logic. You could always confront those problems here."

"Not really," Alex confessed. "I originally come from the theater world, and when I first came here I was enamored by the arts in Santa Fe. I saw a great potential, and thought it might be an excellent way to expand myself. At first, things were great when I got excellent reviews for the roles I played. The money wasn't great, but I was happy. After a while, I became disillusioned. More dilettantes moved in, and the quality of theater moved down. I voiced my displeasure, and I soon found the opportunities disappear."

"You could have upped and left then."

"That was my Catch-22," Alex replied. "I suddenly found myself almost broke. I didn't have enough money to leave, even if I wanted to. Fortunately, at the time I had a part time job doing pest control, but the pay was low and I couldn't even meet my day-to-day living expenses. That's when I decided to go into business for myself. The business did very well, and suddenly I was in a position where I just could not walk away from it."

"You're walking away from it now," Mike said.

"Yep. I had to make the decision of sticking around, making good money but being discontent, or split. I chose the latter."

"Good luck to you, pal," Mike wished him, uncertain if he agreed with his friend's decision. "One thing I don't understand is, why you came here in the first place to do theater work. Why not stay in New York?"

"Hell, I would need four or five million bucks in my back pocket if I wanted to keep living back there. A million wouldn't cut it."

"Yeah, I hear ya'."

They poured a couple of fresh beers, and savored the cold tingle as they drank. A moment or two of serene silence passed before Alex inquired of Mike's new position.

"So, how do you like being captain?"

At the urging of his boss, State Police Chief Ebner, Mike reconsidered about taking the captain's test and passed. He also got to stay in Santa Fe, taking over the vacancy left by his captain's death.

"Let's see, how can I put it? Since taking over the division there is more work and responsibilities, but on the other hand, it's true what they say. Rank has its privileges."

Alex sensed a lack of enthusiasm from Mike in talking about his two-month old promotion. He attributed it to the circumstances under which the position became open a few months before. Abandoning his curiosity about Mike's present rank, he inquired about the future.

"So, tell me. Any chance of you someday becoming chief of police?"

Mike grinned as he gave his reply. "Someday, maybe. However, I don't expect to be on the force long enough for that to happen."

"What do you mean?"

"Like you, pal, I've made some decisions. I'm giving it another eighteen months. Then I'll be maxed out on my pension, and I'll be calling it quits."

It was Alex's turn to be shocked. "Man! Here I thought you'd be a cop for life. What made you come up with that decision?"

"Honestly, a couple of reasons. Mainly, it's because I want to spend more time with my wife and my boy. He'll be off to college soon, but I want him to know that I'll be there for him."

"When did this come about?" Alex pried.

"I started thinking about it a few months ago. Cap's death got me thinking, and I concluded that I don't want Teri to go through what his wife did. I got a couple of things being stoked on the fire, so when I retire I'll switch. It'll keep me busy, but at least my wife won't have to worry whether I'll make it home safely or not."

"So, that'll be the end of your police career."

"Not exactly," Mike informed him. "I'll still have the ties. As you know, I'm a good friend with our current mayor, so if he's still around when I retire, and if the slot opens, I'll put my name in to become city police chief. However, that's still a way into the future, and like what you said, I'll worry about it then."

"Damn, I guess we're both full of surprises tonight," Alex mused.

"Yeah, but I'm the one who's sticking around. I'm not up and leaving like some guy I know," was Mike's bantering reply.

They sat for another hour together, sharing beers and mutual ribbing. As always, the ribbing was taken as it was intended – good-natured needling of one friend to another. Mike was a master at it, and Alex was content to leave it that way. It was the one thing they had in common, coming from the streets of Brooklyn. People from other cities in other states might not be accustomed to it when hearing it for the first time. They might at first be caught off guard, not knowing how to interpret the 'ragging' as it was called in Brooklyn. Once they got to know the source they too understood and welcomed it. For Alex, within a few months, it would come to an end.

The dart league soon folded. Ray's Pub is now gone. Mike, Sam, and Alex did get together from time to time, but that too eventually changed. The people who hung out solving all of the world's problems at a homey bar soon moved into different directions. Mike and Sam kept tightly in touch, and Alex went elsewhere to find new discoveries.

EPILOGUE

Life in The City Different goes on. People continue to relocate to the ancient city, while others move on. Despite the flux, there will always be those who are native. Be it one generation or be it twenty, they are the ones who will truly make the city tick. No matter what each has to offer, the ones who have just moved in, or the affluent that live in Santa Fe for only part of each year, will only lend their influence. They will never really be able to contribute a significant change. Only those who were born to the area assume that right. Be it for the good or for the bad – be it for the benefit of a selected few or for the community as a whole - it is only the local natives who will really decide.

Some people come to The Santa Fe and they are captured by the beauty of the mountains, by the charm of the culture and the arts, and by the quiescence of the atmosphere. Some come to Santa Fe and fall in love with its people. There is much to fall in love with.

Some people come to the place called The City Different, they rest for a while, and then they move on.

www.ingramcontent.com/pod-product-compliance
Lightning Source LLC
Chambersburg PA
CBHW052108030426
42335CB00025B/2885